Impro

'*Impro* is the most dynamic, funny, wise, practical and provocative book on theatre craft that I have ever read' (James Roose-Evans).

Keith Johnstone's involvement with the theatre began when George Devine and Tony Richardson, artistic directors of the Royal Court Theatre, commissioned a play from him. This was in 1956. A few years later he was himself Associate Artistic Director, working as a play-reader and director, in particular helping to run the Writers' Group. The improvisatory techniques and exercises evolved there to foster spontaneity and narrative skills were developed further in the actors' studio, then in demonstrations to schools and colleges and ultimately in the founding of a company of performers, called The Theatre Machine.

Divided into four sections, 'Status', 'Spontaneity', 'Narrative Skills' and 'Masks and Trance', arranged more or less in the order a group might approach them, the book sets out the specific techniques and exercises which Johnstone has himself found most useful and most stimulating. The result is both an ideas book and a fascinating exploration of the nature of spontaneous creativity.

'The book's incredible achievement is its success in making improvisation re-live on the page . . . Get Mr Johnstone's fascinating manual and I promise you that if you open at the first page and begin to read you will not put it down until the final page.' (*Yorkshire Post*)

'He suggests a hundred practical techniques for encouraging spontaneity and originality by catching the subconscious unawares. But what makes the book such fun is the teacher's wit. Here is an inexhaustible supply of zany suggestions for unfreezing the petrified imagination.' (*Daily Telegraph*)

The front co . . . *se, an*
improvised . . . *Moose*
Theatre Com . . .

Other books in this series

Clive Barker
THEATRE GAMES

Peter Barkworth
THE COMPLETE ABOUT ACTING

Jean Benedetti
STANISLAVSKI: AN INTRODUCTION

Annika Bluhm
THE METHUEN AUDITION BOOK FOR MEN
THE METHUEN AUDITION BOOK FOR WOMEN

Peter Brook
THE SHIFTING POINT

Tony Coult and Baz Kershaw
ENGINEERS OF THE IMAGINATION
The Welfare State Handbook

Jerzy Grotowski
TOWARDS A POOR THEATRE

John Hodgson and Ernest Richards
IMPROVISATION

Constantin Stanislavski
AN ACTOR PREPARES
AN ACTOR'S HANDBOOK
BUILDING A CHARACTER
CREATING A ROLE
MY LIFE IN ART
STANISLAVSKI'S LEGACY

IMPRO
Improvisation and the Theatre

KEITH JOHNSTONE

With an Introduction by
IRVING WARDLE

METHUEN DRAMA

First published in paperback in 1981 by Eyre Methuen Ltd
Reprinted 1982, 1983, 1985, 1987

Reprinted in 1989 by Methuen Drama,
Michelin House, 81 Fulham Road, London SW3 6RB
Reprinted 1990, 1991

Published in the USA by Theatre Arts Books,
A division of Routledge, Chapman and Hall Inc,
29 West 35th Street, New York, NY 10001

Originally published in hardback
by Faber and Faber Ltd in 1979
Corrected for this edition by the author
ISBN 0 413 46430 X

Printed in England by Clays Ltd, St Ives plc

AN 338
7192
ENT

Contents

INTRODUCTION 9

NOTES ON MYSELF 13

STATUS 33

SPONTANEITY 75

NARRATIVE SKILLS 109

MASKS AND TRANCE 143

APPENDIX 206

Introduction

If teachers were honoured in the British theatre along-side directors, designers, and playwrights, Keith Johnstone would be as familiar a name as are those of John Dexter, Jocelyn Herbert, Edward Bond and the other young talents who were drawn to the great lodestone of the Royal Court Theatre in the late 1950s. As head of the Court's script department, Johnstone played a crucial part in the development of the 'writers' theatre', but to the general public he was known only as the author of occasional and less than triumphant Court plays like *Brixham Regatta* and *Performing Giant*. As he recounts in this book, he started as a writer who lost the ability to write, and then ran into the same melancholy impasse again when he turned to directing.

What follows is the story of his escape.

I first met Johnstone shortly after he had joined the Court as a 10s-a-script play-reader, and he struck me then as a revolutionary idealist looking around for a guillotine. He saw corruption everywhere. John Arden, a fellow play-reader at that time, recalls him as 'George Devine's subsidised extremist, or Keeper of the King's Conscience'. The Court then set up its Writers' Group and Actors' Studio, run by Johnstone and William Gaskill, and attended by Arden, Ann Jellicoe and other writers of the Court's first wave. This was the turning point. 'Keith', Gaskill says, 'started to teach his own particular style of improvisation, much of it based on fairy stories, word associations, free associations, intuitive responses, and later he taught mask work as well. All his work has been to encourage the rediscovery of the imaginative response in the adult; the refinding of the power of the child's creativity. Blake is his prophet and Edward Bond his pupil.'

Johnstone's all-important first move was to banish aimless discussion and transform the meetings to enactment sessions; it was what happened that mattered, not what anybody said about it. 'It is hard now to remember how fresh this idea was in 1958,' Ann Jellicoe says, 'but it chimed in with my own way of thinking.' Other members were Arnold Wesker, Wole Soyinka, and David Cregan as well as

Bond who now acknowledges Johnstone as a 'catalyst who made our experience malleable by ourselves'. As an example, he cites an exercise in blindness which he later incorporated in his play *Lear*; and one can pile up examples from Arden, Jellicoe, and Wesker of episodes or whole plays deriving from the group's work. For Cregan, Johnstone 'knew how to unlock Dionysus': which came to the same thing as learning how to unlock himself.

From such examples one can form some idea of the special place that teaching occupied in Devine's Royal Court; and how, in Johnstone's case, it was the means by which he liberated himself in the act of liberating others. He now hands over his hard-won bunch of keys to the general reader. This book is the fruit of twenty years' patient and original work; a wise, practical, and hilariously funny guide to imaginative survival. For anyone of the 'artist type' who has shared the author's experience of seeing his gift apparently curl up and die, it is essential reading.

One of Johnstone's plays is about an impotent old recluse, the master of a desolate castle, who has had the foresight to stock his deep-freeze with sperm. There is a power-cut and one of the sperm escapes into a goldfish bowl and then into the moat where it grows to giant size and proceeds to a whale of a life on the high seas.

That, in a nut-shell, is the Johnstone doctrine. You are not imaginatively impotent until you are dead; you are only frozen up. Switch off the no-saying intellect and welcome the unconscious as a friend: it will lead you to places you never dreamed of, and produce results more 'original' than anything you could achieve by aiming at originality.

Open the book at any of the exercises and you will see how the unconscious delivers the goods. Here are a group of hippopotamuses knitting pullovers from barbed wire, and a patient suffering from woodworm who infects the doctor's furniture. There are poems transcribed from thin air, masked actors magicked back to childhood, Victorian melodrama played in extempore verse. At the point where rational narrative would come to a stop, Johnstone's stories carry on cheerfully into the unknown. If a desperate schoolmaster kills himself he will find a plenary session of the school governors awaiting him at the pearly gates. Or if our hero is swallowed by a monster, he will change into a heroic turd and soldier on to fresh adventures.

I have seen none of this material in performance, either by students or by Johnstone's Theatre Machine company; and one of the book's achievements is its success in making improvisations re-live on the page. Like all great advocates of the unconscious, Johnstone is a sturdy rationalist. He brings a keen intellect, nourished on anthropology and psychology, to the task of demolishing intellectualism in the theatre. And where no technical vocabulary exists, he develops his own down-to-earth shorthand to give a simple name to the indescribable. In rediscovering the imaginative world of childhood, he has re-examined the structural elements that bind that world together. What is a story? What makes people laugh? What relationships hold an audience's interest, and why? How does an improviser think up what comes next? Is conflict dramatically necessary? (The answer is No.)

To these and other fundamental questions the book returns unexpected and invariably useful answers. Answers that extend theatre into the transactions of everyday life. One's first impulse on reading about these actors' games is to go and try them out on the kids, or to have a go yourself. Like this.

> From anthills in the north
> I come with wand in hand
> to slay all people there
> that I could understand.
> At last one heap was left
> Untamed by all my foes
> until I caught the bees
> and dealt them mighty blows.

That was a nonstop poem written in fifty seconds flat. It may not be much, but it is more than I have ever got from any other text-book on the imagination. The difference is that Johnstone's analysis is not concerned with results, but with showing you how to do it; and his work ranks as a pioneer contribution to the exceedingly sparse literature of comic theory from which comic practitioners really have something to learn. It certainly has more to offer than Meredith, Bergson, or Freud, to whom the suicidal hero of Heathcote Williams's *Hancock's Last Half Hour* turns in his time of need; dipping hopefully into *Jokes and their Connection with the Unconscious*, and then dropping the book with the despairing cry, 'How would he do second house at the Glasgow Empire?' If Hancock had picked up this book, there might have been a happy ending.

IRVING WARDLE

Notes on Myself

As I grew up, everything started getting grey and dull. I could still remember the amazing intensity of the world I'd lived in as a child, but I thought the dulling of perception was an inevitable consequence of age—just as the lens of the eye is bound gradually to dim. I didn't understand that clarity is in the mind.

I've since found tricks that can make the world blaze up again in about fifteen seconds, and the effects last for hours. For example, if I have a group of students who are feeling fairly safe and comfortable with each other, I get them to pace about the room shouting out the wrong name for everything that their eyes light on. Maybe there's time to shout out ten wrong names before I stop them. Then I ask whether other people look larger or smaller—almost everyone sees people as different sizes, mostly as smaller. 'Do the outlines look sharper or more blurred?' I ask, and everyone agrees that the outlines are many times sharper. 'What about the colours?' Everyone agrees there's far more colour, and that the colours are more intense. Often the size and shape of the room will seem to have changed, too. The students are amazed that such a strong transformation can be effected by such primitive means—and especially that the effects last so long. I tell them that they only have to think about the exercise for the effects to appear again.

My own rediscovery of the visionary world took longer. At a time when I seemed to have lost all my talents as a creative artist I was driven to investigate my mental images. I started with the hypnagogic ones—the pictures that appear to many people at the threshold of sleep. They interest me because they didn't appear in any predictable sequence; I was interested in their *spontaneity*.

It's not easy to observe hypnagogic images, because once you see one and think 'There!' you wake up a little and the image disappears. You have to *attend* to the images without verbalising about them, so I learned to 'hold the mind still' like a hunter waiting in a forest.

One afternoon I was lying on my bed and investigating the effects of anxiety on the musculature (how do you spend your afternoons?). I was relaxing myself and conjuring up horrific images. I had recalled an eye operation I'd had under local anaesthetic, when suddenly I thought of *attending* to my mental images just as I had to the hypnagogic ones. The effect was astounding. They had all sorts of detail that I hadn't known about, and that I certainly hadn't *chosen* to be there. The surgeons' faces were distorted, their masks were thrusting out as if there were snouts beneath them! The effect was so interesting that I persisted. I thought of a house, and *attended* to the image and saw the doors and windows bricked in, but the chimney still smoking (a symbol for my inhibited state at the time?). I thought of another house and saw a terrifying figure in the doorway. I looked in the windows and saw strange rooms in amazing detail.

When you ask people to think of an image, their eyes often move in a particular direction, often up and to the side. I was placing my mental images upwards and to the right—that's the space in which I 'thought' of them. When I *attended* to them they moved into the 'front' of my mind. Obviously, at some time in my childhood my mental images had frightened me, and I'd displaced them, I'd trained myself not to look at them. When I had an image I knew what was there, so I didn't need to look at it—that's how I deluded myself that my creativity was under my own control.

After a lot of practice at *attending* to the images I conjured up, I belatedly thought of *attending* to the reality around me. Then the deadness and greyness immediately sloughed off—yet I'd thought I'd never move through a visionary world again, that I'd lost it. In my case it was largely my interest in art that had destroyed any life in the world around me. I'd learned perspective, and about balance, and composition. It was as if I'd learned to redesign everything, to reshape it so that I saw what *ought* to be there, which of course is much inferior to what *is* there. The dullness was not an inevitable consequence of age, but of education.[1]

Contrariness

At about the age of nine I decided never to believe anything because it was *convenient*. I began reversing every statement to see if the opposite was also true. This is so much a habit with me that I hardly notice I'm doing it any more. As soon as you put a 'not' into an assertion, a whole range of other possibilities opens out—especially in drama, where everything is supposition anyway. When I began teaching, it was very natural for me to reverse everything my own teachers had done. I got my actors to make faces, insult each other, always to leap before they looked, to scream and shout and misbehave in all sorts of ingenious ways. It was like having a whole tradition of improvisation teaching behind me. In a normal education everything is designed to suppress spontaneity, but I wanted to develop it.

Cripples

I made a two-minute film for a TV programme. It was all in one shot, no cuts. Everyone who saw it roared with laughter. There were people rolling on the cutting-room floor, holding their sides. Once they'd recovered, they'd say 'No, no, it's very funny but we can't show *that*!'

The film showed three misshapen but gleeful cripples who were leaping about and hugging each other. The camera panned slightly to reveal that they were hiding around a corner and waiting for a normal person who was approaching. When he drew'level, the cripples leaped on him, and bashed him to pulp with long balloons. Then they helped him up, as battered and twisted as they were, and they shook hands with him, and the four of them waited for the next person.

A Psychotic Girl

I once had a close rapport with a teenager who seemed 'mad' when she was with other people, but relatively normal when she was with me. I treated her rather as I would a Mask (see Masks, page 143)—that is to say, I was gentle, and I didn't try to impose my reality on her. One thing that amazed me was her perceptiveness about other people—it was as if she was a body-language expert. She described things about them which she read from their movement and postures that I later found to be true, although this was at the beginning of a summer school and none of us had ever met before.

I'm remembering her now because of an interaction she had with a very gentle, motherly schoolteacher. I had to leave for a few minutes, so I gave the teenager my watch and said she could use it to see I was away only a very short time, and that the schoolteacher would look after her. We were in a beautiful garden (where the teenager had just seen God) and the teacher picked a flower and said: 'Look at the pretty flower, Betty.'

Betty, filled with spiritual radiance, said, 'All the flowers are beautiful.'

'Ah,' said the teacher, blocking her, 'but this flower is especially beautiful.'

Betty rolled on the ground screaming, and it took a while to calm her. Nobody seemed to notice that she was screaming 'Can't you see? Can't you see!'

In the gentlest possible way, this teacher had been very violent. She was insisting on categorising, and on selecting. Actually it is crazy to insist that one flower is especially beautiful in a whole garden of flowers, but the teacher is allowed to do this, and is not perceived by sane people as violent. Grown-ups are expected to distort the perceptions of the child in this way. Since then I've noticed such behaviour constantly, but it took the mad girl to open my eyes to it.

'Education' as a Substance

People think of good and bad teachers as engaged in the same activity, as if education was a *substance*, and that bad teachers supply a little of the substance, and good teachers supply a lot. This makes it difficult to understand that education can be a destructive process, and that bad teachers are wrecking talent, and that good and bad teachers are engaged in opposite activities. (I saw a teacher relax his students on the floor, and then test for relaxation by lifting their feet eighteen inches into the air and dropping their heels on the concrete.)

Growing Up

As I grew up I began to feel uncomfortable. I had to use conscious effort to 'stand up straight'. I thought that adults were superior to children, and that the problems that worried me would gradually correct themselves. It was very upsetting to realise that if I was going to change for the better then I'd have to do it myself.

I found I had some severe speech defects, worse than other people's (I was eventually treated at a speech hospital). I began to understand that there really was something wrong with my body, I began to see myself as *crippled in the use of myself* (just as a great violinist would play better on a cheap violin than I would on a Strad). My breathing was inhibited, my voice and posture were wrecked, something was seriously wrong with my imagination—it was becoming difficult actually to get ideas. How could this have happened when the state had spent so much money educating me?

Other people seemed to have no insight into my problems. All my teachers cared about was whether I was a *winner*. I wanted to stand like Gary Cooper, and to be confident, and to know how to send the soup back when it was cold without making the waiter feel obliged to spit in it. I'd left school with worse posture, and a worse voice, with worse movement and far less spontaneity than when I'd entered it. Could teaching have had a negative effect?

Emotion

One day, when I was eighteen, I was reading a book and I began to weep. I was astounded. I'd had no idea that literature could affect me in such a way. If I'd have wept over a poem in class the teacher would have been appalled. I realised that my school had been teaching me *not* to respond.

(In some universities students unconsciously learn to copy the physical attitudes of their professors, leaning back away from the play or film they're watching, and crossing their arms tightly, and tilting their heads back. Such postures help them to feel less 'involved', less 'subjective'. The response of untutored people is infinitely superior.)

Intelligence

I tried to resist my schooling, but I accepted the idea that my intelligence was the most important part of me. I tried to be *clever* in everything I did. The damage was greatest in areas where my interests and the school's seemed to coincide: in writing, for example (I wrote and rewrote, and lost all my fluency). I forgot that inspiration isn't intellectual, that you don't have to be perfect. In the end I was reluctant to attempt anything for fear of failure, and my first thoughts never seemed good enough. Everything had to be corrected and brought into line.

The spell broke when I was in my early twenties. I saw a performance of Dovzhenko's *Earth*, a film which is a closed book for many people, but which threw me into a state of exaltation and confusion. There is a sequence in which the hero, Vassily, walks alone in the twilight. We know he's in danger, and we have just seen him comforting his wife, who rolled her eyes like a frightened animal. There are shots of mist moving eerily on water, and silent horses stretching their necks, and corn-stooks against the dusky sky. Then, amazingly, peasants lying side by side, the men with their hands inside the women's blouses and motionless, with idiotic smiles on their faces as they stare at the twilight. Vassily, dressed in black, walks through the Chagall village, and the dust curls up in little clouds around his feet and he is dark against the moonlit road, and he is filled with the same ecstasy as the peasants. He walks and walks and the film cuts and cuts until he walks out of frame. Then the camera moves back, and we see him stop. The fact that he walks for so long, and that the image is so beautiful, linked up with my own experience of being alone in the twilight—the gap between the worlds. Then Vassily walks again, but after a short time he begins to dance, and the dance is skilled, and like an act of thanksgiving. The dust swirls around his feet, so that he's like an Indian god, like Siva—and with the man dancing alone in the clouds of dust something unlocked in me. In one moment I knew that the valuing of men by their intelligence is crazy, that the peasants watching the night sky might feel more than I feel, that the man who dances might be superior to myself—word-bound and unable to dance. From then on I noticed how warped many people of great intelligence are, and I began to value people for their actions, rather than their thoughts.

Anthony Stirling

I felt crippled, and 'unfit' for life, so I decided to become a teacher. I wanted more time to sort myself out, and I was convinced that the training college would teach me to speak clearly, and to stand naturally, and to be confident, and how to improve my teaching skills. Common sense assured me of this, but I was quite wrong. It was only by luck that I had a brilliant art teacher called Anthony Stirling, and then all my work stemmed from his example. It wasn't so much what he taught, as what he *did*. For the first time in my life I was in the hands of a great teacher.

I'll describe the first lesson he gave us, which was unforgettable and completely disorientating.

He treated us like a class of eight-year-olds, which I didn't like, but which I thought I understood—'He's letting us know what it feels like to be on the receiving end,' I thought.

He made us mix up a thick 'jammy' black paint and asked us to imagine a clown on a one wheeled bicycle who pedals through the paint, and on to our sheets of paper. 'Don't paint the clown,' he said, 'paint the mark he leaves on your paper!'

I was wanting to demonstrate my skill, because I'd always been 'good at art', and I wanted him to know that I was a worthy student. This exercise annoyed me because how could I demonstrate my skill? I could paint the clown, but who cared about the tyre-marks?

'He cycles on and off your paper,' said Stirling, 'and he does all sorts of tricks, so the lines he leaves on your paper are very interesting...'

Everyone's paper was covered with a mess of black lines—except mine, since I'd tried to be original by mixing up a blue. Stirling was scathing about my inability to mix up a black, which irritated me.

Then he asked us to put colours in all the shapes the clown had made.

'What kind of colours?'

'Any colours.'

'Yeah . . . but . . . er . . . we don't know what colours to choose.'

'Nice colours, nasty colours, whatever you like.'

We decided to humour him. When my paper was coloured I found that the blue had disappeared, so I repainted the outlines black.

'Johnstone's found the value of a strong outline,' said Stirling, which really annoyed me. I could see that everyone's paper was getting into a soggy mess, and that mine was no worse than anybody else's—but no better.

'Put patterns on all the colours,' said Stirling. The man seemed to be an idiot. Was he teasing us?

'What sort of patterns?'

'Any patterns.'

We couldn't seem to start. There were about ten of us, all strangers to each other, and in the hands of this madman.

'We don't know what to do.'

'Surely it's easy to think of patterns.'

We wanted to get it *right*. 'What sort of patterns do you want?'

'It's up to you.' He had to explain patiently to us that it really was our choice. I remember him asking us to think of our shapes as fields seen from the air if that helped, which it didn't. Somehow we finished the exercises, and wandered around looking at our daubs rather glumly, but Stirling seemed quite unperturbed. He went to a cupboard and took out armfuls of paintings and spread them around the floor, and it was the same exercise done by other students. The colours were so beautiful, and the patterns were so inventive—clearly they had been done by some advanced class. 'What a great idea,' I thought, 'making us screw up in this way, and then letting us realise that there was something that we could learn, since the advanced students were so much better!' Maybe I exaggerate when I remember how beautiful the paintings were, but I was seeing them immediately after my failure. Then I noticed that these little masterpieces were signed in very scrawly writing. 'Wait a minute,' I said, 'these are by young children!' They were all by eight-year-olds! It was just an exercise to encourage them to use the whole area of the paper, but they'd done it with such love and taste and care and sensitivity. I was speechless. Something happened to me in that moment from which I have never recovered. It was the final confirmation that my education had been a destructive process.

Stirling believed that the art was 'in' the child, and that it wasn't something to be imposed by an adult. The teacher was *not* superior to the child, and should never demonstrate, and should not impose values: 'This is good, this is bad . . .'

'But supposing a child wants to learn how to draw a tree?'

'Send him out to look at one. Let him climb one. Let him touch it.'

'But if he still can't draw one?'

'Let him model it in clay.'

The implication of Stirling's attitude was that the student should never experience failure. The teacher's skill lay in presenting experiences in such a way that the student was bound to succeed. Stirling recommended that we read the *Tao te Ching*. It seems to me now that he was practically using it as his teaching manual. Here are some extracts: '. . . The sage keeps to the deed that consists in taking no action and practises the teaching that uses no words . . . . When his task is accomplished and his work done the people all say, "It happened to us naturally" . . . . I take no action and the people are transformed of themselves; I prefer stillness and the people are rectified of themselves; I am not meddlesome and the people prosper of themselves. I am free from desire and the people of themselves become simple like the uncarved block . . . One who excels in employing others humbles himself before them. This is known as the virtue of non-contention; this is known as making use of the efforts of others . . . . To know yet to think that one does not know is best . . . . The sage does not hoard. Having bestowed all he has on others, he has yet more; having given all he has to others, he is richer still. The way of heaven benefits and does not harm; the way of the sage is bountiful and does not contend.' (Translated by C. D. Lau, Penguin, 1969.)

Being a Teacher

I chose to teach in Battersea, a working-class area that most new teachers avoided—but I'd been a postman there, and I loved the place.

My new colleagues bewildered me. 'Never tell people you're a teacher!' they said. 'If they find you're a teacher in the pub, they'll all move away!' It was true! I'd believed that teachers were respected figures, but in Battersea they were likely to be feared or hated. I liked my colleagues, but they had a colonist's attitude to the children; they referred to them as 'poor stock', and they disliked exactly those children I found most inventive. If a child is creative he's likely to be more difficult to control, but that isn't a reason for disliking him. My colleagues had a poor view of themselves: again and again I heard them say, 'Man among boys; boy among men' when describing their condition. I came to see that their unhappiness, and lack of acceptance in the community, came from a feeling that they were irrelevant, or rather that the school was something middle class being forcibly imposed on to the working-class culture. Everyone seemed to accept that if you *could* educate one of these children you'd remove him away from his parents (which is what my education had done for me). Educated people were snobs, and many parents didn't want their children alienated from them.

Like most new teachers, I was given the class no one else wanted. Mine was a mix of twenty-six 'average' eight-year-olds, and twenty 'backward' ten-year-olds whom the school had written off as *ineducable*. Some of the ten-year-olds couldn't write their names after five years of schooling. I'm sure Professor Skinner could teach even pigeons to type out their names in a couple of weeks, so I couldn't believe that these children were really dull: it was more likely that they were putting up a resistance. One astounding thing was the way cowed and dead-looking children would suddenly brighten up and look intelligent when they weren't being asked to *learn*. When they were cleaning out the fish tank, they looked fine. When writing a sentence, they looked numb and defeated.

Almost all teachers, even if they weren't very bright, got along reasonably well as schoolchildren, so presumably it's difficult for them to identify with the children who fail. My case was peculiar in that I'd apparently been exceptionally intelligent up to the age of eleven, winning all the prizes (which embarrassed me, since I thought they should be given to the dull children as compensation) and being teacher's pet, and so on. Then, spectacularly, I'd suddenly come bottom of the class—'down among the dregs', as my headmaster described it. He never forgave me. I was puzzled too, but gradually I realised that I wouldn't work for people I didn't like. Over the years my work gradually improved, but I never fulfilled my promise. When I liked a particular teacher and won a prize, the head would say: 'Johnstone is taking this prize away from the boys who deserve it!' If you've been bottom of the class for years it gives you a different perspective: I was friends with boys who were failures, and nothing would induce me to write them off as 'useless' or 'ineducable'. My 'failure' was a survival tactic, and without it I would probably never have worked my way out of the trap that my education had set for me. I would have ended up with a lot more of my consciousness blocked off from me than *now*.

I was determined that my classes shouldn't be dull, so I used to jump about and wave my arms, and generally stir things up—which is exciting, but bad for discipline. If you shove an inexperienced teacher into the toughest class, he either sinks or swims. However idealistic he is, he tends to clutch at traditional ways of enforcing discipline. My problem was to resist the pressures that would turn me into a conventional teacher. I had to establish a quite different relationship before I could hope to release the creativity that was so apparent in the children when they weren't thinking of themselves as 'being educated'.

I didn't see why Stirling's ideas shouldn't apply to all areas, and in particular to writing: literacy was clearly of great importance, and anyway writing interested me, and I wanted to infect the children with enthusiasm. I tried getting them to send secret notes to each other, and write rude comments about me, and so on, but the results were nil. One day I took my typewriter and my art books into the class, and said I'd type out anything they wanted to write about the pictures. As an afterthought, I said I'd also type out their dreams—and suddenly they were actually wanting to write. I typed out everything exactly as they wrote it, including the spelling mistakes, until they caught me. Typing out spelling mistakes was a weird idea in the early fifties (and probably now)—but it worked. The pressure to get things right was coming from the children, not the teacher. I was amazed at the intensity of feeling and outrage the children expressed, and their determination to be *correct*, because no one would have dreamt that they cared. Even the illiterates were getting their friends to spell out every word for them. I scrapped the time-table, and for a month they wrote for hours every day. I had to force them out of the classroom to take breaks. When I hear that children only have an attention span of ten minutes, or whatever, I'm amazed. Ten minutes is the attention span of *bored* children, which is what they usually are in school—hence the misbehaviour.

I was even more astounded by the quality of the things the children wrote. I'd never seen any examples of children's writing during my training; I thought it was a hoax (one of my colleagues must have smuggled a book of modern verse in!). By far the best work came from the 'ineducable' ten-year-olds. At the end of my first year the Divisional Officer refused to end my probation. He'd found my class doing arithmetic with masks over their faces—they'd made them in art class and I didn't see why they shouldn't wear them. There was a cardboard tunnel he was supposed to crawl through (because the classroom was doubling as an igloo), and an imaginary hole in the floor that he refused to walk around. I'd stuck all the art paper together and pinned it along the back wall, and when a child got bored he'd leave what he was doing and stick some more leaves on the burning forest.

My headmaster had discouraged my ambition to become a teacher: 'You're not the right type,' he said, 'not the right type at all.' Now it looked as if I was going to be rejected officially. Fortunately the school was inspected, and Her Majesty's Inspector thought that my class were doing the most interesting work. I remember one incident that struck him as amazing: the children screaming out that there were only three chickens drawn on the blackboard, while I was insisting that there were five (two were still inside the hen-house). Then the children started scribbling furiously away, writing stories about chickens, and shouting out any words they wanted spelt on the blackboard. I shouldn't think half of them had ever seen a chicken, but it delighted the Inspector. 'You realise that they're trying to throw me out,' I said, and he fixed it so that I wasn't bothered again.

Stirling's 'non-interference' worked in every area where I applied it: piano teaching for example. I worked with Marc Wilkinson, the composer (he became director of music at the National Theatre), and his tape recorder played the same sort of role that my typewriter had. He soon had a collection of tapes as surprising as the children's poems had been. I assembled a group of children by asking each teacher for the children he couldn't stand; and although everyone was amazed at such a selection method, the group proved to be very talented, and they learned with amazing speed. After twenty minutes a boy hammered out a discordant march and the rest shouted, 'It's the Japanese soldiers from the film on Saturday!' Which it was. We invented many games—like one child making sounds for water and another putting the 'fish' in it. Sometimes we got them to feel objects with their eyes shut, and got them to play what it felt like so that the others could guess. Other teachers were amazed by the enthusiasm and talent shown by these 'dull' children.

The Royal Court Theatre

In 1956 the Royal Court Theatre was commissioning plays from established novelists (Nigel Dennis, Angus Wilson), and Lindsay Anderson suggested that they should stop playing safe and commission an unknown—*me*.

I'd had very bad experiences in the theatre, but there was one play I'd liked: Beckett's *Waiting for Godot*, which seemed entirely lucid and pertinent to my own problems. I was trying to be a painter at the time, and my artist friends all agreed that Beckett must be a very young man, one of our contemporaries, since he understood our feelings so well. Because I didn't like the theatre—it seemed so much feebler than, say, the films of Kurosawa, or Keaton—I didn't at first accept the Royal Court's commission; but then I ran out of money, so I wrote a play strongly influenced by Beckett (who once wrote to me, saying that 'a stage is an area of maximum verbal presence, and maximum corporeal presence'—the word 'corporeal' really delighting me).

My play was called *Brixham Regatta*, and I remember Devine thumbing through the notices and saying that it was sex that had been intolerable to the Victorians, and that 'whatever it is now, Keith is writing about it'. I was amazed that most critics were so hostile. I'd been illustrating a theme of Blake's: 'Alas! The time will come when a man's worst enemies shall be those of his own house and family . . .' But in 1958 such a view was unacceptable. Ten years later, when I directed the play at the Mermaid, it didn't seem at all shocking: its ideas had become commonplace.

I've been often told how weird and silent I seemed to many people, but Devine was amused by my ideas (many of which came from Stirling). I'd argue that a director should never demonstrate anything to an actor, that a director should allow the actor to make his own discoveries, that the actor should think he'd done all the work himself. I objected to the idea that the director should work out the moves before the production started. I said that if an actor forgot a move that had been decided on, then the move was probably wrong. Later I argued that moves weren't important, that with only a couple of actors on a stage, why did it matter where they moved anyway? I explained that *Hamlet* in Russian can be just as impressive, so were the words really of first importance? I said that the set was no more important than the apparatus in the circus. I wasn't saying much that was new, but I didn't know that, and certainly such thoughts weren't fashionable at the time. I remember Devine going round the theatre chuckling that 'Keith thinks *King Lear* should have a happy ending!'

They were surprised that someone so inexperienced as myself should have become their best play-reader. Tony Richardson, then Devine's Associate Director, once thanked me because I was taking such a load off them. I was successful precisely because I didn't exercise my taste. I would first read plays as quickly as possible, and categorise them as pseudo-Pinter, fake-Osborne, phoney-Beckett, and so on. Any play that seemed to come from the author's own experience I'd then read attentively, and either leave it in Devine's office or, if I didn't like it, give it to someone else to read. As ninety-nine per cent of the plays submitted were just cribs from other people, the job was easy. I had expected that there'd be a very gentle gradation from awful to excellent, and that I'd be involved in a lot of heart-searching. Almost all were total failures—they couldn't have been put on in the village hall for the author's friends. It wasn't a matter of lack of *talent*, but of miseducation. The authors of the pseudo-plays assumed that writing should be based on other writing, not on life. My play had been influenced by Beckett, but at least the content had been *mine*.

Sometimes I'd read a play I liked, but that no one else would think worth directing. Devine said that if I was really convinced they were good I should direct them myself on a Sunday night. I directed Edward Bond's first play in this way, but the very first play I directed was Kon Fraser's *Eleven Plus* (which I still have a fondness for, although it hasn't prospered much). I was given advice by Ann Jellicoe—already an accomplished director—and I was successful. It really seemed that even if I couldn't write any more—and writing had become extremely laborious and unpleasant for me—at least I could earn a living as a director. Obviously, I felt I ought to study my craft, but the more I understood how things ought to be done, the more boring my productions were. Then as now, when I'm inspired, every-thing is fine, but when I try to get things right it's a disaster. In a way I was successful—I ended up as an Associate Director of the theatre —but once again my talent had left me.

When I considered the difference between myself, and other people, I thought of myself as a late developer. Most people lose their talent at puberty. I lost mine in my early twenties. I began to think of children not as immature adults, but of adults as atrophied children. But when I said this to educationalists, they became angry.

Writers' Group

George Devine had announced that the Royal Court was to be a 'writers' theatre', but the writers weren't having much say in the policies of the theatre. George thought a discussion group would correct this, and he chaired three meetings, which were so tedious that he handed the job over to William Gaskill, one of his young directors. Bill had directed my play *Brixham Regatta*, and he asked me how I would run the group. I said that if it continued as a talking-shop, then everyone would abandon it, and that we should agree to discuss nothing that could be acted out. Bill agreed, and the group immediately began to function as an improvisation group. We learned that things invented on the spur of the moment could be as good or better than the texts we laboured over. We developed very practical attitudes to the theatre. As Edward Bond said, 'The writers' group taught me that drama was about relationships, not about characters.' I've since found that my no-discussion idea wasn't original. Carl Weber, writing about Brecht, says: '. . . the actors would suggest a way of doing something, and if they started to explain, Brecht would say he wanted no discussion in rehearsal—it would have to be tried . . . .' (A pity all Brechtians don't have the master's attitude.)

My bias against discussion is something I've learned to see as very English. I've known political theatre groups in Europe which would readily cancel a rehearsal, but never a discussion. My feeling is that the best argument may be a testimony to the skill of the presenter, rather than to the excellence of the solution advocated. Also the bulk of discussion time is visibly taken up with transactions of status which have nothing to do with the problem to be solved. My attitude is like Edison's, who found a solvent for rubber by putting bits of rubber in every solution he could think of, and beat all those scientists who were approaching the problem theoretically.

The Royal Court Theatre Studio

Devine had been a student of Michel Saint-Denis, who was a nephew of the great director Jacques Copeau. Copeau had been an advocate of studio work, and George also wanted a studio. He started it with hardly any budget, and as I was on the staff, and full of theories, he asked me if I would teach there. Actually William Gaskill was the director, and *they* agreed that I should teach there. I'd been advocating setting a studio up so I could hardly refuse; but I was embarrassed, and worried. I didn't know anything about training actors, and I was sure that the professionals—many from the Royal Shakespeare, and some who shortly afterwards went into the National Theatre Company—would know far more than I did. I decided to give classes in 'Narrative Skills' (see page 109), hoping I'd be one jump ahead in this area. Because of my dislike of discussion I insisted that everything should be acted out—as at the Writers' Group—and the work became very funny. It was also very different, because I was consciously reacting *against* Stanislavsky. I thought, wrongly, that Stanislavsky's methods implied a naturalistic theatre—which it doesn't, as you can see from the qualifications he introduces as to what sorts of objectives are permissible, and so on. I thought his insistence on the 'given circumstances' was seriously limiting, and I didn't like the 'who, what, where' approach which my actors urged on me, and which I suppose was American in origin (it's described, in Viola Spolin's *Improvisation for the Theatre*, Northwestern University Press, 1963; fortunately I didn't know about this book until 1966, when a member of an audience lent it to me). Lacking solutions, I had to find my own. What I did was to concentrate on relationships between strangers, and on ways of combining the imagination of two people which would be additive, rather than subtractive. I developed status transactions, and word-at-a-time games, and almost all of the work described in this book. I hope this still seems fresh to some people, but actually it dates back to the early sixties and late fifties.

My classes were hysterically funny, but I remembered Stirling's contempt for artists who form 'self-admiration groups' and wondered if we were deluding ourselves. Could the work really be so funny? Wasn't it just that we all knew each other? Even considering the fact that I had some very talented and experienced actors, weren't we just entertaining each other? Was it right that every class should be like a party?

I decided we'd have to perform in front of real audiences, and see if we *were* funny. I took about sixteen actors along to my contemporary theatre class at Morley College, and said we'd like to demonstrate some of the exercises we were developing. I'd thought that I'd be the nervous one, but the actors huddled in the corner and looked terrified. Once I started giving the exercises, they relaxed; and to our amazement we found that when the work was good, the audience laughed far more than we would have done! It wasn't so easy to do work of a high standard in public, but we were delighted at the enthusiasm of the spectators. I wrote to six London colleges and offered them free demonstration classes, and afterwards we received many invitations to perform elsewhere. I cut the number of performers down to four or five and, with strong support from the Ministry of Education, we started touring around schools and colleges. There, we often found ourselves on a *stage*, and we automatically drifted into giving shows rather than demonstrations. We called ourselves 'The Theatre Machine', and the British Council sent us around Europe. Soon we were a very influential group, and the only pure improvisation group I knew, in that we prepared nothing, and everything was like a jazzed-up drama class.

It's weird to wake up knowing you'll be onstage in twelve hours, and that there's absolutely nothing you can do to ensure success. All day you can feel some part of your mind gathering power, and with luck there'll be no interruption to the flow, actors and audience will completely understand each other, and the high feeling lasts for days. At other times you feel a coldness in everyone's eyes, and deserts of time seem to lie ahead of you. The actors don't seem to be able to see or hear properly any more—they feel so wretched that scene after scene is about vomiting. Even if the audience are pleased by the novelty, you feel you're swindling them. After a while a pattern is established in which each performance gets better and better until the audience is like a great beast rolling over to let you tickle it. Then hubris gets you, you lose your humility, you *expect* to be loved, and you turn into Sisyphus. All comedians know these feelings.

As I came to understand the techniques that release creativity in the improviser, so I began to apply them to my own work. What really got me started again was an advert for a play of mine in the paper, a play called *The Martian*. I had never written such a play, so I phoned up Bryan King, who directed the theatre. 'We've been trying to find you,' he said. 'We need a play for next week, does the title *The Martian* suit you?' I wrote the play, and it was well received. Since then I've deliberately put myself in this position. I get myself engaged by a company and write the plays as I'm rehearsing the actors. For example, in eight weeks I did two street theatre plays lasting twenty minutes, plus a three-hour improvised play called *Der Fisch*, plus a children's play lasting an hour—this was for Salvatore Poddine's Tubingen theatre. I don't see that the plays created in this way are inferior to those I struggle over, sometimes for years.

I didn't learn how to direct again until I left the Royal Court Theatre and was invited to Victoria (on Vancouver Island). I directed the Wakefield Mystery Cycle there, and I was so far away from any-one whose criticism I cared about that I felt free to do exactly what I felt like. Suddenly I was spontaneous again; and since then, I've always directed plays as if I was totally ignorant about directing; I simply approach each problem on a basis of common sense and try to find the most obvious solutions possible.

Nowadays everything is very easy to me (except writing didactic things like this book). If we need a cartoon for the programme, I'll draw one. If we need a play I'll write it. I cut knots instead of labor-iously trying to untie them—that's how people see me; but they have no idea of the turgid state I used to be in, or the morass from which I'm still freeing myself.

Getting the Right Relationship

If you want to apply the methods I'm describing in this book, you may have to teach the way that I teach. When I give workshops, I see people frantically scribbling down the exercises, but not noticing what it is I actually do as a teacher. My feeling is that a good teacher can get results using any method, and that a bad teacher can wreck any method.

There seems no doubt that a group can make or break its members, and that it's more powerful than the individuals in it. A great group can propel its members forward so that they achieve amazing things. Many teachers don't seem to think that manipulating a group is their responsibility at all. If they're working with a destructive, bored group, they just blame the students for being 'dull', or uninterested. It's essential for the teacher to blame himself if the group aren't in a good state.

Normal schooling is intensely competitive, and the students are supposed to try and outdo each other. If I explain to a group that they're to work for the other members, that each individual is to be interested in the progress of the other members, they're amazed, yet obviously if a group supports its own members strongly, it'll be a better group to work in.

The first thing I do when I meet a group of new students is (probably) to sit on the floor. I play low status, and I'll explain that if the students fail they're to blame *me*. Then they laugh, and relax, and I explain that really it's *obvious* that they should blame me, since I'm supposed to be the expert; and if I give them the wrong material, they'll fail; and if I give them the right material, then they'll succeed. I play low status physically but my actual status is going up, since only a very confident and experienced person would put the blame for failure on himself. At this point they almost certainly start sliding off their chairs, because they don't want to be higher than me. I have already changed the group profoundly, because failure is suddenly not so frightening any more. They'll want to test me, of course; but I really will apologise to them when they fail, and ask them to be patient with me, and explain that I'm not perfect. My methods are very effective, and other things being equal, most students will succeed, but they won't be trying to win any more. The normal teacher–student relationship is dissolved.

When I was teaching young children, I trained myself to share my eye contacts out among the group. I find this crucial in establishing a 'fair' relationship with them. I've seen many teachers who concentrate their eye contacts on only a few students, and this does affect the *feeling* in a group. Certain students are disciples, but others feel separated, or experience themselves as less interesting, or as 'failures'.

I've also trained myself to make positive comments, and to be as direct as possible. I say 'Good' instead of 'That's enough'. I've actually heard teachers say 'Well, let's see who fails at this one', when introducing an exercise. Some teachers get reassurance when their students fail. We must have all encountered the teacher who gives a self-satisfied smile when a student makes a mistake. Such an attitude is not conducive to a good, warm feeling in the group.

When (in 1964) I read of Wolpe's work in curing phobias, I saw a clear relationship with the ideas I'd got from Stirling, and with the way I was developing them. Wolpe relaxed his phobic patients and then presented them with a very dilute form of the thing that scared them. Someone terrified of birds might be asked to imagine a bird, but one in Australia. At the same time that the image was presented, the patient was relaxed, and the relaxation was maintained (if it wasn't maintained, if the patient started to tremble, or sweat or whatever, then something even less alarming would be presented). Relaxation is incompatible with anxiety; and by maintaining the relaxed state, and presenting images that gradually neared the centre of the phobia, the state of alarm was soon dissipated—in most cases. Wolpe taught his patients to relax, but soon other psychologists were using pentathol to assist the relaxation. However, there has to be an *intention* to relax (muscle-relaxant drugs can be used as a torture!).

If we were *all* terrified of open spaces, then we would hardly recognise this as a phobia to be cured; but it could be cured. My view is that we have a universal phobia of being looked at on a stage, and that this responds very well to 'progressive desensitisation' of the type that Wolpe advocates. Many teachers seem to me to be trying to get their students to conceal fear, which always leaves some traces— a heaviness, an extra tension, a lack of spontaneity. I try to dissipate the fear by a method analogous to Wolpe's, but which I really got from Anthony Stirling. The one finding of Wolpe which I immediately incorporated into my work was the discovery that if the healing process is interrupted by a recurrence of the total fear—maybe a patient being treated for a phobia of birds suddenly finds himself surrounded by fluttering pigeons—then the treatment has to be started again at the bottom of the hierarchy. I therefore constantly return to the very first stages of the work to try to pull in those students who remain in a terrified state, and who therefore make hardly any progress. Instead of seeing people as *untalented*, we can see them as *phobic*, and this completely changes the teacher's relationship with them.

Students will arrive with many techniques for avoiding the pain of failure. John Holt's *How Children Fail* (Penguin, 1969; Pitman, 1970) gives examples of children learning to get round problems, rather than learning to find solutions to problems. If you screw your face up and bite on your pencil to show you're 'trying', the teacher may write out the answer for you. (In my school, if you sat relaxed and *thought*, you were likely to get swiped on the back of the head.) I explain to the students the devices they're using to avoid tackling the problems—however easy the problems are—and the release of tension is often amazing. University students may roll about in hysterical laughter. I take it that the relief comes from understanding that other people use the same manoeuvres as they do.

For example, many students will begin an improvisation, or a scene, in a rather feeble way. It's as if they're ill, and lacking in vitality. They've learned to play for sympathy. However *easy* the problem, they'll use the same old trick of looking inadequate. This ploy is supposed to make the onlookers have sympathy with them if they 'fail' and it's expected to bring greater rewards if they 'win'. Actually this down-in-the-mouth attitude almost guarantees failure, and makes everyone fed up with them. No one has sympathy with an adult who takes such an attitude, but when they were children it probably worked. As adults they're *still* doing it. Once they've laughed at themselves and understood how unproductive such an attitude is, students who look 'ill' suddenly look 'healthy'. The attitude of the group may instantly change.

Another common ploy is to anticipate the problem, and to try and prepare solutions in advance. (Almost all students do this—probably it started when they were learning to read. You anticipate which paragraph will be yours, and start trying to decipher it. This has two great disadvantages: it stops you learning from the attempts of your classmates; and very likely you'll have calculated wrongly, and will be asked to read one of the adjacent paragraphs throwing you into total panic.)

Most students haven't realised—till I show them—how inefficient such techniques are. The idea that a teacher should be interested in such things is, unfortunately, novel to them. I also explain strategies like sitting on the *end* of the row, and how it isolates you from the group, and body positions that prevent absorption (like the 'lit-crit' postures which keep the user 'detached' and 'objective').

In exchange for accepting the blame for failure, I ask the students to set themselves up in such a way that they'll learn as quickly as possible. I'm teaching spontaneity, and therefore I tell them that they mustn't try to control the future, or to 'win'; and that they're to have an empty head and just watch. When it's their turn to take part they're to come out and just do what they're asked to, and *see what happens*. It's this decision not to try and control the future which allows the students to be spontaneous.

If I'm playing with my three-year-old son and I smack him, he looks at me for signals that will turn the sensation into either warmth or pain. A very gentle smack that he perceives as 'serious' will have him howling in agony. A hard 'play' slap may make him laugh. When I want to work and he wants me to continue playing he will give very strong 'I am playing' signals in an attempt to pull me back into his game. All people relate to each other in this way but most teachers are afraid to give 'I am playing' signals to their students. If they would, their work would become a constant pleasure.

NOTE

1. If you have trouble understanding this section, it may be because you're a conceptualiser, rather than a visualiser. William Grey Walter, in *The Living Brain* (Penguin, 1963) calculated that one in six of us are conceptualisers (actually in my view there is a far smaller proportion of conceptualisers among drama students).

I have a simple way of telling if people are visualisers. I ask them to describe the furniture in a room they're familiar with. Visualisers move their eyes as if 'seeing' each object as they name it. Conceptualisers look in one direction as if reading off a list.

Galton investigated mental imagery at the beginning of the century, and found that the more educated the person, the more likely he was to say that mental imagery was unimportant, or even that it didn't exist.

An exercise: fix your eyes on some object, and attend to something at the periphery of your vision. You can *see* what you're attending to, but actually your mind is assembling the object from relatively little information. Now look directly, and observe the difference. This is one way of tricking the mind out of its habitual dulling of the world.

Status

1 The See-saw

When I began teaching at the Royal Court Theatre Studio (1963), I noticed that the actors couldn't reproduce 'ordinary' conversation. They said 'Talky scenes are dull', but the conversations they acted out were nothing like those I overheard in life. For some weeks I experimented with scenes in which two 'strangers' met and interacted, and I tried saying 'No jokes', and 'Don't try to be clever', but the work remained unconvincing. They had no way to mark time and allow situations to develop, they were forever striving to latch on to 'interesting' ideas. If casual conversations really were motiveless, and operated by chance, why was it impossible to reproduce them at the studio?

I was preoccupied with this problem when I saw the Moscow Art's production of *The Cherry Orchard*. Everyone on stage seemed to have chosen the *strongest* possible motives for each action—no doubt the production had been 'improved' in the decades since Stanislavsky directed it. The effect was 'theatrical' but not like life as I knew it. I asked myself for the first time what were the *weakest* possible motives, the motives that the characters I was watching might really have had. When I returned to the studio I set the first of my status exercises.

'Try to get your status just a little above or below your partner's,' I said, and I insisted that the gap should be minimal. The actors seemed to know exactly what I meant and the work was transformed. The scenes became 'authentic', and actors seemed marvellously observant. Suddenly we understood that every inflection and movement implies a status, and that no action is due to chance, or really 'motiveless'. It was hysterically funny, but at the same time very alarming. All our secret manoeuvrings were exposed. If someone asked a question we didn't bother to answer it, we concentrated on why it had been asked. No one could make an 'innocuous' remark without everyone instantly grasping what lay behind it. Normally we are 'forbidden' to see status transactions except when there's a conflict. In reality status transactions continue all the time. In the park we'll notice the ducks squabbling, but not how carefully they keep their distances when they are not.

Here's a conversation quoted by W. R. Bion (*Experience in Groups*, Tavistock Publications, 1968) which he gives as an example of a group not getting anywhere while apparently being friendly. The remarks on the status interactions are mine.

> MRS X: I had a nasty turn last week. I was standing in a queue waiting for my turn to go into the cinema when I felt ever so queer. Really, I thought I should faint or something.

[Mrs X is attempting to raise her status by having an interesting medical problem. Mrs Y immediately outdoes her.]

> MRS Y: You're lucky to have been going to a cinema. If I thought I could go to a cinema I should think I had nothing to complain of at all.

[Mrs Z now blocks Mrs Y.]

> MRS Z: I know what Mrs X means. I feel just like that myself, only I should have had to leave the queue.

[Mrs Z is very talented in that she supports Mrs X against Mrs Y while at the same time claiming to be more worthy of interest, her condition more severe. Mr A now intervenes to lower them all by making their condition seem very ordinary.]

> MR A: Have you tried stooping down? That makes the blood come back to your head. I expect you were feeling faint.

[Mrs X defends herself.]

> MRS X: It's not really faint.

> MRS Y: I always find it does a lot of good to try exercises. I don't know if that's what Mr A means.

[She seems to be joining forces with Mr A, but implies that he was unable to say what he meant. She doesn't say 'Is that what you mean?' but protects herself by her typically high-status circumlocution. Mrs Z now lowers everybody, and immediately lowers herself to avoid counter-attack.]

> MRS Z: I think you have to use your will-power. That's what worries me—I haven't got any.

[Mr B then intervenes, I suspect in a low-status way, or rather trying to be high-status but failing. It's impossible to be sure from just the words.]

> MR B: I had something similar happen to me last week, only I wasn't standing in a queue. I was just sitting at home quietly when . . .

[Mr C demolishes him.]

MR C: You were lucky to be sitting at home quietly. If I was able to do that I shouldn't think I had anything to grumble about. If you can't sit at home why don't you go to the cinema or something?

Bion says that the prevailing atmosphere was of good temper and helpfulness. He adds that 'A suspicion grows in my mind, that there is no hope whatever of expecting co-operation from this group.' Fair enough. What he has is a group where everyone attacks the status of everyone else while pretending to be friendly. If he taught them to play status transactions as *games* then the feeling within the group would improve. A lot of laughter would have been released, and the group might have flipped over from acting as a competitive group into acting as a co-operative one. It's worth noting how much talent is locked away inside these apparently banal people.

We've all observed different kinds of teachers, so if I describe three types of status players commonly found in the teaching profession you may find that you already know exactly what I mean.

I remember one teacher, whom we liked but who couldn't keep discipline. The Headmaster made it obvious that he wanted to fire him, and we decided we'd better behave. Next lesson we sat in a spooky silence for about five minutes, and then one by one we began to fool about—boys jumping from table to table, acetylene-gas exploding in the sink, and so on. Finally, our teacher was given an excellent reference just to get rid of him, and he landed a headmastership at the other end of the county. We were left with the paradox that our behaviour had nothing to do with our conscious intention.

Another teacher, who was generally disliked, never punished and yet exerted a ruthless discipline. In the street he walked with fixity of purpose, striding along and stabbing people with his eyes. Without punishing, or making threats, he filled us with terror. We discussed with awe how terrible life must be for his own children.

A third teacher, who was much loved, never punished but kept excellent discipline, while remaining very human. He would joke with us, and then impose a mysterious stillness. In the street he looked upright, but relaxed, and he smiled easily.

I thought about these teachers a lot, but I couldn't understand the forces operating on us. I would now say that the incompetent teacher was a low-status player: he twitched, he made many unnecessary movements, he went red at the slightest annoyance, and he always seemed like an intruder in the classroom. The one who filled us with terror was a compulsive high-status player. The third was a status expert, raising and lowering his status with great skill. The pleasure attached to misbehaving comes partly from the status changes you make in your teacher. All those jokes on teacher are to make him drop in status. The third teacher could cope easily with any situation by changing his status first.

Status is a confusing term unless it's understood as something one *does*. You may be low in social status, but play high, and vice versa. For example:

> TRAMP: 'Ere! Where are you going?
>
> DUCHESS: I'm sorry, I didn't quite catch . . .
>
> TRAMP: Are you deaf as well as blind?

Audiences enjoy a contrast between the status played and the social status. We always like it when a tramp is mistaken for the boss, or the boss for a tramp. Hence plays like *The Inspector General*. Chaplin liked to play the person at the bottom of the hierarchy and then lower everyone.

I should really talk about dominance and submission, but I'd create a resistance. Students who will agree readily to raising or lowering their status may object if asked to 'dominate' or 'submit'.

Status seems to me to be a useful term, providing the difference between the status you are and the status you play is understood.

As soon as I introduced the status work at the Studio, we found that people will play one status while convinced that they are playing the opposite. This obviously makes for very bad social 'meshing'—as in Bion's therapy group—and many of us had to revise our whole idea of ourselves. In my own case I was astounded to find that when I thought I was being friendly, I was actually being hostile! If someone had said 'I like your play', I would have said 'Oh, it's not up to much', perceiving myself as 'charmingly modest'. In reality I would have been implying that my admirer had bad taste. I experience the opposite situation when people come up, looking friendly and supportive, and say, 'We did enjoy the end of Act One', leaving me to wonder what was wrong with the rest.

I ask a student to lower his status during a scene, and he enters and says:

> A: What are you reading?
>
> B: *War and Peace*.
>
> A: Ah! That's my favourite book!

The class laugh and A stops in amazement. I had told him to lower his status during the scene, and he doesn't see what's gone wrong.

I ask him to try it again and suggest a different line of dialogue.

A: What are you reading?

B: *War and Peace.*

A: I've always wanted to read that.

A now experiences the difference, and realises that he was originally claiming 'cultural superiority' by implying that he had read this immense work many times. If he'd understood this he could have corrected the error.

A: Ah! That's my favourite book.

B: Really?

A: Oh yes. Of course I only look at the pictures . . .

A further early discovery was that there was no way to be neutral. The 'Good morning' that might be experienced as lowering by the Manager, might be experienced as raising by the bank clerk. The messages are modified by the receivers.

You can see people trying to be neutral in group photographs. They pose with arms folded or close to their sides as if to say 'Look! I'm not claiming any more space than I'm entitled to', and they hold themselves very straight as if saying 'But I'm not submissive either!' If someone points a camera at you you're in danger of having your status exposed, so you either clown about, or become deliberately unexpressive. In formal group photographs it's normal to see people guarding their status. You get quite different effects when people don't know they're being photographed.

If status can't even be got rid of, then what happens between friends? Many people will maintain that we don't play status transactions with our friends, and yet every movement, every inflection of the voice implies a status. My answer is that acquaintances become friends when they *agree* to play status games together. If I take an acquaintance an early morning cup of tea I might say 'Did you have a good night?' or something equally 'neutral', the status being established by voice and posture and eye contact and so on. If I take a cup of tea to a friend then I may say 'Get up, you old cow', or 'Your Highness's tea', pretending to raise or lower status. Once students understand that they already play status games with their friends, then they realise that they already know most of the status games I'm trying to teach them.

We soon discovered the 'see-saw' principle: 'I go up and you go down'. Walk into a dressing-room and say 'I got the part' and everyone will congratulate you, but will feel lowered. Say 'They said I was too old' and people commiserate, but cheer up perceptibly. Kings and great lords used to surround themselves with dwarfs and cripples so that they could rise by the contrast. Some modern celebrities do the same. The exception to this see-saw principle comes when you identify with the person being raised or lowered, when you sit on his end of the see-saw, so to speak. If you claim status because you know some famous person, then you'll feel raised when they are: similarly, an ardent royalist won't want to see the Queen fall off her horse. When we tell people nice things about ourselves this is usually a little like kicking them. People really want to be told things to our discredit in such a way that they don't have to feel sympathy. Low-status players save up little tit-bits involving their own discomfiture with which to amuse and placate other people.

If I'm trying to lower my end of the see-saw, and my mind blocks, I can always switch to raising the other end. That is, I can achieve a similar effect by saying 'I smell beautiful' as 'You stink'. I therefore teach actors to switch between raising themselves and lowering their partners in alternate sentences; and vice versa. Good playwrights also add variety in this way. For example, look at the opening of Molière's *A Doctor in Spite of Himself*. The remarks on status are mine.

SGANARELLE: [*Raises himself.*] No, I tell you I'll have nothing to do with it and it's for me to say, I'm the master.

MARTINE: [*Lowers Sganarelle, raises herself.*] And I'm telling you that I'll have you do as I want. I didn't marry you to put up with your nonsensical goings-on.

SGANARELLE: [*Lowers Martine.*] Oh! The misery of married life! How right Aristotle was when he said wives were the very devil!

MARTINE: [*Lowers Sganarelle and Aristotle.*] Just listen to the clever fellow—him and his blockhead of an Aristotle!

SGANARELLE: [*Raises himself.*] Yes, I'm a clever fellow all right! Produce me a woodcutter who can argue and hold forth like me, a man who has served six years with a famous physician and had his Latin grammar off by heart since infancy!

MARTINE: [*Lowers Sganarelle.*] A plague on the idiot!

SGANARELLE: [*Lowers Martine.*] A plague on you, you worthless hussy!

MARTINE: [*Lowers her wedding day.*] A curse on the day and hour when I took it into my head to go and say 'I will'!

SGANARELLE: [*Lowers notary.*] And a curse on the cuckold of a notary who made me sign my name to my own ruin.

MARTINE: [*Raises herself.*] A lot of reason you have to complain,
I must say! You ought to thank Heaven every
minute of your life that you have me for your wife.
Do you think you deserved to marry a woman like
me? [*And so on.*]
(*The Misanthrope and other plays*, translated by
John Wood, Penguin, 1959.)

Most comedy works on the see-saw principle. A comedian is someone paid to lower his own or other people's status. I remember some of Ken Dodd's patter which went something like this: 'I got up this morning and had my bath . . . standing up in the sink . . .' (Laugh from audience.) '. . . and then I lay down to dry off—on the draining-board . . .' (Laughter.) '. . . and then my father came in and said "Who skinned this rabbit?".' (Laughter.) While he describes himself in this pathetic way he leaps about, and expresses manic happiness, thus absolving the audience of the need to pity him. We want people to be very low-status, but we don't want to feel sympathy for them—slaves are always supposed to sing at their work.

One way to understand status transactions is to examine the comic strips, the 'funnies'. Most are based on very simple status transactions, and it's interesting to observe the postures of the characters, and the changes in status between the first and last frames.

Another way is to examine jokes, and analyse their status transactions. For example:

CUSTOMER: 'Ere, there's a cockroach in the loo!

BARMAID: Well you'll have to wait till he's finished, won't you?

Or again:

A: Who's that fat noisy old bag?
B: That's my wife.
B: Oh, I'm sorry . . .
A: You're sorry! How do you think I feel?

2   Comedy and Tragedy

In his essay on laughter Bergson maintained that the man-falling-on-a-banana-skin joke was funny because the victim had suddenly been forced into acting like an automaton. He wrote: 'Through lack of elasticity, through absent-mindedness, and a kind of physical obstinacy: *as a result, in fact, of rigidity or of momentum,* the muscles continued to perform the same movement when the circumstances of the case called for something else. This is the reason for the man's fall, and also of the people's laughter.' Later in the same essay he says: 'What is essentially laughable is what is done automatically.'

In my view the man who falls on the banana skin is funny only if he loses status, and if we don't have sympathy with him. If my poor old blind grandfather falls over I'll rush up and help him to his feet. If he's really hurt I may be appalled. If Nixon had slipped up on the White House steps many people would have found it hysterical. If Bergson had been right then we would laugh at a drowning man, and grand military parades would have the crowds rocking with merriment. A Japanese regiment is said to have masturbated by numbers in a football stadium as an insult to the population of Nanking, but I don't suppose it was funny at the time. Chaplin being sucked into the machine is funny because his style absolves us of the need for sympathy.

Tragedy also works on the see-saw principle: its subject is the ousting of a high-status animal from the pack. Super-intelligent wolves might have invented this form of theatre, and the lupine Oedipus would play high status at all times. Even when he was being led into the wilderness he wouldn't whine, and he'd keep his tail up. If he crumbled into low-status posture and voice the audience wouldn't get the necessary catharsis. The effect wouldn't be tragic, but pathetic. Even criminals about to be executed were supposed to make a 'good end', i.e. to play high status. When the executioner asked Raleigh if he wouldn't rather face the light of the dawn he said something like 'What matter how the head lie, if the heart be right', which is still remembered.

When a very high-status person is wiped out, everyone feels pleasure as they experience the feeling of moving up a step. This is why tragedy has always been concerned with kings and princes, and why we have a special high-status style for playing tragedy. I've seen a misguided Faustus writhing on the floor at the end of the play, which is bad for the verse, and pretty ineffective. Terrible things can happen to the high-status animal, he can poke his eyes out with his wife's brooch, but he must never look as if he could accept a position lower in the pecking order. He has to be *ejected* from it.

Tragedy is obviously related to sacrifice. Two things strike me about reports of sacrifices: one is that the crowd get more and more tense, and then are relaxed and happy at the moment of death; the other is that the victim is *raised* in status before being sacrificed. The best goat is chosen, and it's groomed, and magnificently decorated. A human sacrifice might be pampered for months, and then dressed in fine clothes, and rehearsed in his role at the centre of the great ceremony. Elements of this can be seen in the Christ story (the robe, the crown of thorns, and even the eating of the 'body'). A sacrifice has to be endowed with high status or the magic doesn't work.

3   Teaching Status

Social animals have inbuilt rules which prevent them killing each other for food, mates, and so on. Such animals confront each other, and sometimes fight, until a hierarchy is established, after which there is no fighting unless an attempt is being made to change the 'pecking order'. This system is found in animals as diverse as human beings, chicken, and woodlice. I've known about this ever since I was given a book about social dominance in kittiwake colonies, yet I hadn't immediately thought of applying this information to actor training. This is because normal people are inhibited from seeing that no action, sound, or movement is innocent of purpose. Many psychologists have noted how uncannily perceptive some schizophrenics are. I think that their madness must have opened their eyes to things that 'normal' people are trained to ignore.

In animals the pattern of eye contacts often establishes dominance. A stare is often interpreted as an aggressive act—hence the dangers of looking at gorillas through binoculars. Visitors to zoos feel dominant when they can outstare the animals. I suggest you try the opposite with zoo animals: break eye contact and then glance back for a moment. Polar bears may suddenly see you as 'food'. Owls cheer up perceptibly.

Some people dispute that the held eye contact between 'strangers' is dominant. Kenneth Strongman wrote in the March 1970 issue of *Science Journal*: 'At the time we thought ourselves justified in concluding that a dominance structure of submission from eye contact exists and that this tends to approach hierarchy, particularly when the focus is on initial eye contact. Our reason for considering it to be concerned with dominance was based on a statement made by Argyle and Dean, who suggested that if A wants to dominate B he stares at him appropriately; B can accept this with a submissive expression or by looking away, or can challenge and outstare. However, S. E. Poppleton, a research student at Exeter, has since shown that the relationship between eye-glance submission hierarchies and an independent measure of dominance (provided by Catell's 16PF personality inventory) is an inverse one. Thus he who looks away first is the more dominant.'

One might contrast this with other reports, like that of an experiment at Stanford University where it was found that drivers who had been stared at left traffic lights appreciably faster. Such disagreements indicate the difficulty of actually perceiving status transactions. In my view, breaking eye contact can be high status so long as you don't immediately glance back for a fraction of a second. If you ignore someone your status rises, if you feel impelled to look back then it falls. It's as if the proper state of human beings is high, but that we modify ourselves to avoid conflicts. Posture experts (like Mathias Alexander) teach high-status postures as 'correct'. It's only to be expected that status is established not by staring, but by the reaction to staring. Thus dark glasses raise status because we can't see the submission of the eyes.

I minimise 'status resistance' from my students by getting them to experience various status sensations *before* I discuss the implications, or even introduce the term. I might ask them to say something nice to the person beside them, and then to say something nasty. This releases a lot of laughter, and they are surprised to find that they often achieve the wrong effect. (Some people never really say anything nice, and others never say anything really nasty, but they won't realise this.)

I ask a group to mill about and say 'hallo' to each other. They feel very awkward, because the situation isn't *real*. They don't know what status they should be playing. I then get some of the group to hold all eye contacts for a couple of seconds, while the others try to make and then break eye contacts and then immediately glance back for a moment. The group suddenly looks more like a 'real' group, in that some people become dominant, and others submissive. Those who hold eye contacts report that they feel powerful—and actually look powerful. Those who break eye contact and glance back 'feel' feeble, and look it. The students *like* doing this, and are interested, and puzzled by the strength of the sensations.

I might then begin to insert a tentative 'er' at the beginning of each of my sentences, and ask the group if they detect any change in me. They say that I look 'helpless' and 'weak' but they can't, interestingly enough, say what I'm doing that's different. I don't normally begin every sentence with 'er', so it should be very obvious. Then I move the 'er' into the middle of sentences, and they say that they perceive me as becoming a little stronger. If I make the 'er' longer, and move it

back to the beginning of sentences, then they say I look more important, more confident. When I explain what I am doing, and let them
experiment, they're amazed at the different feelings the length and
displacement of the 'ers' give them. They are also surprised that it's
difficult to get some people to use a short 'er'. There wouldn't seem
to be any problem in putting an 'er' lasting a fraction of a second at the
beginning of each sentence, but many people unconsciously resist.
They say 'um', or they elongate the sound. These are people who
cling to their self importance. The short 'er' is an invitation for people
to interrupt you; the long 'er' says 'Don't interrupt me, even though
I haven't thought what to say yet.'

Again I change my behaviour and become authoritative. I ask them
what I've done to create this change in my relation with them, and
whatever they guess to be the reason—'You're holding eye contact',
'You're sitting straighter'—I stop doing, yet the effect continues.
Finally I explain that I'm keeping my head still whenever I speak, and
that this produces great changes in the way I perceive myself and am
perceived by others. I suggest you try it now with anyone you're with.
Some people find it impossible to speak with a still head, and more
curiously, some students maintain that it's still while they're actually
jerking it about. I let such students practise in front of a mirror, or I
use videotape. Actors needing authority—tragic heroes and so on—
have to learn this still head trick. You can talk and waggle your head
about if you play the gravedigger, but not if you play Hamlet. Officers
are trained not to move the head while issuing commands.

My belief (at this moment) is that people have a preferred status;
that they like to be low, or high, and that they try to manoeuvre
themselves into the preferred positions. A person who plays high
status is saying 'Don't come near me, I bite.' Someone who plays low
status is saying 'Don't bite me, I'm not worth the trouble.' In either
case the status played is a defence, and it'll usually work. It's very
likely that you will increasingly be conditioned into playing the status
that you've found an effective defence. You become a status *specialist*,
very good at playing one status, but not very happy or competent at
playing the other. Asked to play the 'wrong' status, you'll feel 'un-
defended'.

I reassure my students, and encourage them, and let them have
conversations together, trying out different ways of changing their
status. One student might try moving very smoothly (high status)
while his partner moves jerkily (low status).[1] One might keep putting
his hands near his face while he speaks, and the other might try

keeping his hands away from his face. One might try holding his toes pointing inwards (low status), while one sits back and spreads himself (high status).

These are just tricks in order to get the students to experience status changes. If I speak with a still head, then I'll do many other high-status things quite automatically. I'll speak in complete sentences, I'll hold eye contact. I'll move more smoothly, and occupy more 'space'. If I talk with my toes pointing inwards I'm more likely to give a hesitant little 'er' before each sentence, and I'll smile with my teeth covering my bottom lip, and I'll sound a little breathless, and so on. We were amazed to find that apparently unrelated things could so strongly influence each other; it didn't seem reasonable that the position of the feet could influence sentence structure and eye contact, but it is so.

Once students have understood the concepts, and have been coaxed into experiencing the two states, then I get them to play scenes in which: (1) both lower status; (2) both raise status; (3) one raises while the other lowers; (4) the status is reversed during the scene.

I insist that they have to get their status just a *little* above or below their partner's. This ensures that they really 'see' their partner, as they have exactly to relate their behaviour to his. The automatic status skills then 'lock on to' the other actor, and the students are transformed into observant, and apparently very experienced improvisers. Of course, they will have been playing status whenever they improvised, but it would be usually a personal status, not the status of a character. They would be relating to the problem of succeeding in the eyes of the *audience*. These status exercises reproduce on the stage exactly the effects of real life, in which moment by moment each person adjusts his status up or down a fraction.

When actors are reversing status during a scene it's good to make them grade the transitions as smoothly as possible. I tell them that if I took a photograph every five seconds, I'd like to be able to arrange the prints in order just by the status shown. It's easy to reverse status in one jump. Learning to grade it delicately from moment to moment increases the control of the actor. The audience will always be held when a status is being modified.

It isn't necessary for an actor to achieve the status he's trying to play in order to interest an audience. To see someone trying to be high, and failing, is just as delightful as watching him succeed.

Here are some notes made by students who had just been introduced to status work.

'The using of different types of "er" found me swinging unavoidably from feeling now inferior, now superior, then inferior again. I found myself crossing my arms, fidgeting, walking with my hands in my pockets—all movements unnatural to me. I find myself suddenly freezing my body in order to check up on my status.'

'Nothing has been done in class that I didn't believe or "know". But I couldn't have stated it.'

'During that scene with Judith in which she at first touched her head all the time, and then gradually stopped doing it, I couldn't define the change in her movements, and yet for some reason my attitude changed towards her. When she touched her head I tried to be more helpful, reassuring, whereas once she stopped, I felt more distant and businesslike—also a bit more challenged—whereas previously I'd felt nothing but sympathy.'

'I've often been told that an actor should be aware of his body but I didn't understand this until I tried talking with my head still.'

'The most interesting revelation to me was that every time I spoke to someone I could tell if I felt submissive or the opposite. I then tried to play status games in secret with people I knew. Some people I thought I knew very well I wouldn't dare try it with. Other relatively new friends were easy to play status games with.'

'Sense of domination when I hold eye contact. Almost a pride in being able to look at someone else and have them look away. Looking away and back—felt persecuted. As if everyone was trying to crush me underfoot.'

'Status—clothes not important. I was walking to the shower with only a towel over my shoulder when I met a fully dressed student who took on a very low-status look and allowed me to pass on my way.'

'Every time I speak to someone I can now tell if I'm submissive or not.'

'I've always thought that the man I should like to marry should be smarter than me; someone I could look up to and respect. Well, my boy friend is now smarter than me, and I usually respect his knowledge, but often I find his high status a nuisance. Perhaps I should seek someone I consider I'm on the same level with?'

'I felt the dominant figure in the conversation and proceeded to try and subjugate myself to her whims. I did this by the "touch the head and face" method. What happened here is that, while prior to this move I had done most of the talking and directed the conversation, after this . . . I was hard put to get a word in edgeways.'

'I find that when I slow my movements down I go up in status.'

'I felt as if all the world had suddenly been revealed to me. I realise that when I talk to people, my attitude of inner feeling is of almost talking down to them.'

It's a good idea to introduce a bystander into a status scene with instructions to 'try not to get involved'. If you are a 'customer' in a 'restaurant', and someone at the same table quarrels with the 'waiter', then your very subtle status manoeuvrings are a delight to watch.

I increase the confidence of the actors by getting them to play sequences of status exercises. For example, a breakfast scene in which a husband plays low and a wife plays high, might be followed by an office scene in which the husband plays high to a secretary who plays low, leading on to a supper scene in which both wife and husband play low—and so on. Once the status becomes automatic, as it is in life, it's possible to improvise complex scenes with no preparation at all. The status exercises are really crutches to support the actor so that instinctual systems can operate. The actor then feels that everything is *easy*, and he doesn't experience himself as '*acting*' any more than he does in life, even though the actual status he's playing may be one very unfamiliar to him.

Without the status work my improvisation group, the Theatre Machine, could never have toured successfully in Europe; not without preparing the scenes first. If someone starts a scene by saying 'Ah, another sinner! What's it to be, the lake of fire or the river of excrement?' then you can't 'think' fast enough to know how to react. You have to understand that the scene is in Hell, and that the other person is some sort of devil, and that you're dead all in a split second. If you know what status you're playing the answers come automatically.

'Well?'

'Excrement', you say, playing high status, without doing anything you experience as 'thinking' at all, but you speak in a cold voice, and you look around as if Hell was less impressive than you'd been led to believe. If you're playing low status you say 'Which ever you think best, Sir', or whatever. Again with no hesitation, and with eyes full of terror, or wonder.

All this isn't so far away from Stanislavsky as some people might suppose, even though in *Creating a Role* Stanislavsky wrote: '*Play the external plot* in terms of physical actions. For example: enter a room. But since you cannot enter unless you know where you came from, where you are going and why, seek out the external facts of the plot to give you a basis for physical actions.' (From Appendix A.) Some 'method' actors take this to mean that they have to know all the 'given

circumstances' before they can improvise. If I ask them to do something spontaneous they react as if they've been asked to do something
indecent. This is the result of bad teaching. In order to enter a room
all you need to know is what status you are playing. The actor who
understands this is free to improvise in front of an audience with no
given circumstances at all! Interestingly enough Stanislavsky himself
would almost certainly agree. In Chapter Eight of *Creating a Role* he
makes the director, Tortsov, tell the narrator:

' "Go up on the stage and play for us Khlestakov's entrance in the
second act."

' "How can I play it since I don't know what I have to do?" said I
with surprise and objection in my tone.

' "You do not know everything but you do know some things. So
play the little that you know. In other words, execute out of the life of
the part those small physical objectives which you can do sincerely,
truthfully, and in your own person."

' "I can't do anything because I don't know anything!"

' "What do you mean?" objected Tortsov. "The play says '*Enter
Khlestakov*.' Don't you know how to go into a room in an inn?"

' "I do." '

What I think he 'knows' is that he must play a particular status.

One way to teach transitions of status is to get students to leave the
class, and then come in through the real door and act 'entering the
wrong room'. It's then quite normal to see students entering with
head down, or walking backwards, or in some other way that will
prevent them from seeing that it is the wrong room. They want time
to really enter before they start 'acting'. They will advance a couple
of paces, act seeing the audience, and leave in a completely phoney
way.

I remind the students that entering the wrong room is an experience
we all have, and that we always know what to do, since we do 'something'. I explain that I'm not asking the students to 'act', but just to do
what they do in life. We have a radar which scans every new space for
dangers, an early-warning system programmed-in millions of years
ago as a protection against sabre-tooth tigers, or bigger amoebas or
whatever. It's therefore very unusual to refuse to look into the space
you are entering.

As soon as the 'wrong room' exercise becomes 'real' they understand that a change of status is involved. You prepare a status for one
situation, and have to alter it when suddenly confronted by the
unexpected one. I then set the students to predetermine the direction

of the status change, and of course errors are often made. Someone trying to play low status may have to be told to smile, and if he smiles with both sets of teeth (an aggressive smile) he may have to be asked to show the top teeth only. People who want to rise in status may have to be told to turn their backs to us when they leave. Neither smiling nor turning your back is essential but it may help the student get the feeling. In difficult cases it helps to use videotape.

A more complex version of this exercise is really a little play. I invented it at RADA when I was asked if I could push the students into more emotional experiences. It's for one character—let's say he's a teacher, although he could be any profession. He arrives late carrying the register and a pair of glasses. He says something like 'All right, quiet there, now then', treating us as the class. As he is about to read the register he puts the glasses on, and sees not his class, but a meeting of the school Governors. He apologises, dropping in status frantically, and struggles to the door, which sticks. He wrestles with it and after about ten seconds it comes free. The actor feels a very great drop in status when the door jams. It takes him back to feelings he may not have experienced since childhood: feelings of impotence, and of the hostility of objects.

Once outside, the actor either stops the exercise, or if he feels brave, re-enters, and plays the scene again and again. This exercise can turn people into crumbling wrecks in a very short time, and for actors who like to 'pretend' without actually feeling anything, it can be a revelation. One Scandinavian actor who apparently had never really achieved anything because of his self-consciousness, suddenly 'understood' and became marvellous. It was for him a moment of *satori*. The terrifying thing is that there's no limit. For example:

'Why didn't anyone tell me that the room had been changed? I just made a complete fool of myself in front of the Governors.'

(*Puts on glasses. Sees Governors.*)

'Augh! I ... I ... what can I say. Mr Headmaster ... please ... I ... oh ... do excuse me ... The door. I'm afraid ... it sticks ... the damp weather, you ... ah ... so ... so sorry.'

(*Grovels out. Re-enters.*)

'Oh God, it's nice to find someone in the staff-room. Is there any tea on? The most embarrassing thing just happened to me ... I ...'

(*Puts on glasses. Sees Governors.*)

'Oh ... I ... what must you think of me ... I ... I seem to be having some sort of breakdown ... haven't been well lately. So sorry to interrupt ... The ... the door ... THE DOOR! Augh! ... I'm sorry . . . outrageous conduct . . . please understand . . . er . . . er . . .'

> (*Exit. Re-enters.*)

'It's nice of you to see me at such short notice. I know that psychiatrists are very busy . . . I . . .'

> (*Puts on glasses. Sees Governors.*)

'. . . I know it was wrong to commit suicide, God, but . . .'

> (*Puts on glasses. Sees Governors.*)

I wouldn't push anyone into playing this game, and it must be understood by the class that people are allowed to get upset, and are not to be punished by being considered exhibitionistic or cissy.

I repeat all status exercises in gibberish, just to make it quite clear that the things *said* are not as important as the status *played*. If I ask two actors to meet, with one playing high, and one playing low, and to reverse the status while talking an imaginary language, the audience laugh amazingly. We don't know what's being said, and neither do the actors, but the status reversal is enough to enthral us. If you've seen great comedians working in a language you don't understand you'll know what I mean.

I get the actors to learn short fragments of text and play every possible status on them. For example, A is late, and B has been waiting for him.

> A: Hallo.
> B: Hallo.
> A: Been waiting long?
> B: Ages.

The implication is that B lowers A, but any status can be played. If both play high then A might stroll on with 'all the time in the world' and say 'Hallo' as if he wasn't late at all. B might hold eye contact and say 'Hallo' with emphasis. A might look away airily and say 'Been waiting long? with a sigh as if B were being 'difficult'. 'Ages,' says B, staring at him, or walking off as if expecting A to follow. If both are to play low, then A might arrive running; B might stand up, bend the head forwards and give a low-status smile. 'Hallo,' says A breathlessly, showing embarrassment that B has stood. 'Hallo,' replies B, also a little breathless. 'Been waiting long?' asks A with anxiety. 'Ages,' says B with a weak laugh as if making a feeble joke.

Here's a dialogue taking place in 'Sir's' office.

> SIR: Come in. Ah, sit down Smith. I suppose you know why I sent for you?
> SMITH: No, Sir.
>
> (*Sir pushes a newspaper across the desk.*)

SMITH: I was hoping you wouldn't see that.
SIR: You know we can't employ anyone with a criminal record.
SMITH: Won't you reconsider?
SIR: Good-bye, Smith.
SMITH: I never wanted your bloody job anyway.
(*Exit Smith.*)

If Smith plays high, then saying 'Won't you reconsider' gives him an enormous resistance to work against. When Sir says 'Good-bye, Smith' low status it produces a gripping scene. For Smith to say 'I didn't want your bloody job anyway' low status, it may be necessary for him to burst into tears.

One interesting complication in such a scene is that Smith will have to play low status to the space, even when playing high status to Sir, or it'll look like his office. Conversely, Sir must play high status to the space, even when playing low status to Smith. If he doesn't he'll look like an intruder. 'Move about,' I say. 'Answer the telephone. Walk over to the window.'

Status is played to anything, objects as well as people. If you enter an empty waiting-room you can play high or low status to the furniture. A king may play low status to a subject, but not to his palace.

An actor is waiting on stage for someone to enter and play a scene with him. 'What status are you playing?' I ask. He says, 'I haven't started yet.' 'Play low status to the bench,' I say.

He looks around him as if he was in a park that he suspects may be private. Then he 'sees' a pigeon, and mimes feeding it, rather unconvincingly. 'Play low status to the pigeon,' I say, and immediately his mime improves, and the scene is believable. More 'pigeons' arrive, and one lands on the bench and starts pecking at the bread he's holding. Another lands on his arm, and then shits on him. He wipes the mess off surreptitiously. And so on. He doesn't need another actor to play status scenes with. He can do it with anything in the environment.

I give students a very strong feeling of 'status' by making them use only the way they look and sound to ward off attacks. I call it 'non-defence', but really it's one of the best of all defences. Imagine two siblings, one of whom (A) lives in the flat of the other (B). B enters and asks if any letters have arrived for him. A says that there is one on the sideboard. B picks it up and sees it's been opened. A is always opening B's letters which causes conflict between them. The scene will probably develop something like this:

> B: Why did you open my letter?
> A: Is it open?
> B: You always open my letters.
> A: I don't know who did it.
> B: No one else has been here!

B will probably start to push A about, and I'll have to stop the scene for fear that they might hurt each other.

I start the scene again, but tell A that he is to admit everything, while playing low status.

> B: Did you open my letter?
> A: Yes.

B stops the attack. He pauses.

> B: Yes?
> A: Yes.
> B: Well, what did you do it for?
> A: I wanted to see what was inside.

B is checked again. He may step backwards. He may even retreat to the furthest wall and lean against it. I encourage him to be angry, and to close in on A.

> B: How dare you open my letters?
> A: You're right to be angry. I'm a shit.
> B: I told you never to open my letters.
> A: I always do it.
> B: You do?

B finds it increasingly difficult to press home his attack. If he starts to shake A, then A must cry and keep nodding his head, and saying 'You're right, you're right.' B can of course override his instincts—human beings do unfortunately have this ability—but the more he attacks, the more strongly a mysterious wind seems to be trying to blow him away. If A makes an error, and rises in status, then B closes in, but if the low status is maintained then B has to consciously 'force' his anger.

> B: Well, don't open them again.
> A: I poke my nose into everything.

I've seen the low-status player leap about with joy and roll over and over on the floor after playing such a scene. It's exhilarating to be controlling the movements of the other person as if he were a puppet. When I explained that the more A accepted B's dominance the more powerfully B was deflected, B said, 'That's right. I thought, "Mother put him up to it." '

Non-defence is exploited by the wolf who exposes his neck and underbelly to a dominant wolf as a way of ending a losing battle. The top Wolf wants to bite, but can't. Some Congolese soldiers dragged two white journalists out of a jeep, shot one and were about to shoot the other when he burst into tears. They laughed and kicked him back to the jeep and let him drive away, while they waved and cheered. It was more satisfying to see the white man cry than to shoot him.

Once non-defence has been mastered together with a low-status attitude, I teach it as a high-status exercise. The same kind of dialogue occurs:

> B: Did you open my letter?
> A: Yes. (Quite calmly, and sipping his coffee as if no attack was being made on him.)
> B: Yes? (Momentarily nonplussed.)
> A: I always open your letters. (Dismissively.) (And so on.)

At first hardly anyone can carry off such a scene. They pretend to be high status, but you can see that they're actually crumbling. I explain that they are making concealed low-status movements. An arm climbs up to the back of the chair as if wanting to flee from the aggressor, or to hold on for support. A foot starts to tap as if it wanted to go.

The best solution I've found is to weight the situation heavily in favour of A. For example, I might set the scene in A's house, with B a guest who arrived late the night before, and now meets his host for the first time at breakfast. I make B's position worse by setting him the problem of asking A for his daughter's hand in marriage. Once A's position is reinforced in this way he should be able to maintain his high status while making no verbal defence at all.

> A: You must be John . . .
> B: Er . . . yes.
> A: Cynthia tells me you want to marry her . . .
> B: That's right.
> A: Oh, by the way, a letter came for you this morning.
> B: It's been opened.
> A: I open everyone's letters.
> B: But it was addressed to me.
> A: It's from your mother. Some of it I thought most unsuitable. You'll see I crossed some paragraphs out . . . (And so on.)

4 Insults

If you can get the students to insult each other playfully, then the status work will become easier. Playing scenes with custard pies might be equally liberating, but I've never had the opportunity. Once you can accept being insulted (the insult is the verbal equivalent of the custard pie), then you experience a great elation. The most rigid, self-conscious, and defensive people suddenly unbend.

It's no good just asking the students to insult each other. It's too personal. If you've just called someone 'kipper feet' it's disconcerting to suddenly notice that he's flat-footed. If your ears stick out then it's upsetting to be called 'cloth ears'. On the other hand it is important for an actor to accept being insulted. The stage becomes an even more 'dangerous' area if you can't admit your disabilities. The young George Devine cried once because the audience laughed when the character he was playing was referred to as thin. I remember a flat-chested actress being destroyed on stage because an adolescent shouted out that she was a man. The actor or improviser must accept his disabilities, and allow himself to be insulted, or he'll never really feel *safe*.

My solution is to remove all responsibility for the choice of insult from the person doing the insulting. I divide the class into two halves, and get each group to write out a list of names that would insult people: fool, slut, pig, arsehole, jerk, meatface, dumbhead, flatfoot, pigeyes, skinny twat, bugeyes, buckteeth, cowflop, monkeyface, swine, rathead, shitnose, bullshitter, faggot. Only half the class know who suggested a particular insult, and each suggestion has already been stamped with half the class's approval.

I put the lists aside and get the students to play 'shop'.

'Can I help you?'

'Yes, I'd like a pair of shoes.'

'Would these do?'

'I'd like another colour.'

'I'm afraid this is the only colour we have, Sir.'

'Ah. Well, perhaps a hat.'

'I'm afraid that's my hat, Sir.'

And so on—very boringly, with both actors 'blocking' the transaction in order to make the scene more 'interesting' (which it doesn't).

I explain that I don't want them to make the scene 'interesting', that they are just to buy and sell something. They start again.

'Can I help you?'

'Just browsing.'

'No you're not,' I say. 'Buy something.'

'I want a hat.'

'How about this one, Sir?'

'Buy it,' I say.

'I'll buy it.'

'Two pounds ninety, Sir.'

'Here.'

'I'm afraid I don't have any change, Sir.'

'Yes you do,' I insist.

I have to struggle with the actors before they will agree just to buy something and sell something. Then I get them to play the scene again, but adding the insults. I give them a list each, and get them to add an insult to the end of each sentence. This idea delights everyone, but it's very boring.

'Can I help you, fool?'

'Yes, bugeyes!'

'Do you want a hat, slut?' (And so on.)

I explain that insulting is of no interest. What we really want to see is someone being insulted. The interest we have in custard pies is in seeing them hit people. I tell them to repeat every insult in disbelief and outrage. As soon as they do this the performers get deeply involved and are often impossible to stop. People who are bound physically relax into a greater physical freedom. Gestures flow instead of being suddenly jerked to a stop.

'Can I help you, pig?'

'Pig! Why I . . . Flat-footed pig yourself!'

'Me! Flat-footed pig! You call me a flat-footed pig, you . . . you arsehole!'

'Arsehole!'

'Buy something!' I shout.

'I want a hat, buckteeth!'

'Buckteeth! Try this for size, jerk!'

'Jerk! Jerk! *You* call *me* jerk! I'll take it—Cowflop!'

'Cowflop!' (And so on.)

The insults must remain an ornamentation to the scene, they mustn't become the scene itself. Once this is understood they can be applied to any situation. If you keep changing the lists then the most terrible things will have been said to everybody. I then give one actor a list, and let the other actor make up his own, and I set up scenes with several people. For example master–servant teams can meet, and insult in this way. But there must be some purpose they're trying to achieve as well as 'being insulted'. In my experience this game is very 'releasing'. The status lowering is so drastic, and at the same time so pleasurable, that ordinary status scenes hold fewer terrors.

In the average school the teachers are supposed to inhibit their pupils, and the kind of healing openness typical of therapy groups simply isn't possible, but the game is useful even with censored lists, or even in gibberish. Gibberish imposes an acceptance of the insult, or no one can understand what's happening. The technique is to repeat the last sound of any gibberish sentence.

'Gort intok horntow lipnol.'

'Lipnol! Lipnol! Grant hork lop sonto inkutu!'

'Inkutu! Die gorno inkutu! Krankon!'

'Krankon!' (And so on.)

This insult game can be played between two groups who slowly approach each other, but the teacher must ensure that every insult is received. Enormous energy is released, with individuals running forwards to hurl their insults, and then being dragged back by their friends. The target of the insults should be the opposing group, not individual members. The game usually ends with actors standing face to face and screaming at each other, and everyone having a very good time. If they've got 'high' on the game, you can make them repeat it in mime. It makes a good 'aside' exercise if actors who are insulted repeat the word to the audience.

5 Status Specialists

If you wish to teach status interactions, it's necessary to understand that however willing the student is consciously, there may be very strong subconscious resistances. Making the student safe, and getting him to have confidence in you, are essential. You then have to work together with the student, as if you were both trying to alter the behaviour of some *third* person. It's also important that the student who succeeds at playing a status he feels to be alien should be instantly rewarded, praised and admired. It's no use just giving the exercises and *expecting* them to work. You have to understand where the resistance is, and devise ways of getting it to crumble. Many teachers don't recognise that there's a problem because they only exploit the 'preferred' status. In a bad drama school it's possible to play your 'preferred' status all the time, since they cast you to type, exploiting what you can do, instead of widening your range. In the professional theatre actors divide up roughly into high-status and low-status specialists. The actors' directory *Spotlight* used to have the high-status specialists at the front (called 'straight'), followed by the low-status specialists (called 'character actors'), followed by children, and then dogs. This isn't as bad as it sounds, but it's symptomatic of the tendency for actors to overspecialise. A proper training for actors would teach all types of transaction.

Some problems: there are students who will report no change of sensation when they alter their eye-contact patterns. If you observe them closely you'll see that the ones who always play low status in life won't ever hold eye contact long enough to feel dominant. When high-status specialists break eye contact and glance back, they'll be holding the glance back for at least a second, which is too long. You may have to precisely control the length of time that they look before they experience the change of sensation. Then they'll say, 'But it feels wrong.' This feeling of wrongness is the one they have to learn as being correct.

I remember a girl who always played high status in improvisations, and who had never experienced safety and warmth as a performer. When I asked her to put a short 'er' in front of each sentence she used the long 'eeeerrrrr' but denied she was doing it. When I asked her to move her head as she talked she moved it in an abstract way, as if watching a fly circling in front of her. I asked her to play low status with an expert low-status improviser, but she held on to herself tightly with her arms and crossed her legs as if refusing to let her partner 'invade' her. I asked her to unfold and then to tilt her head and suddenly she was transformed—we wouldn't have recognised her. She became soft and yielding and really seemed to enjoy the feelings that flooded into her, and she acted with feeling and rapport for the first time. Now that she's learned to play low status with a low-status partner she can learn to play it with a high-status partner.

Another student refused to play high status in anything but a wooden manner. He said that he lived in a working-class area and that he didn't want to be stuck-up. I explained that I wasn't trying to remove his present skills, which were very necessary, but only to add a few new ones. He believed that it was necessary to play low status within his working-class community, not realising that you can play high or low in any situation. His problem is that he plays low status *well* and he won't experiment with other skills.

I asked him to play a scene in which he was to tell his father he had VD. I chose the scene in order to stir him up, and involve his real feelings. All young men have anxieties in that area. He acted out a scene with no conviction at all, and tried to think up 'clever things' to say.

'I'll give you the dialogue,' I said. 'Enter. Go to the window. Look out, then turn and say you've got VD.'

He did this. He looked out of the window and immediately made trivial movements, and dropped down in status.

I stopped him. I explained that if he turned from the window, looked at his father and didn't move his head, then he'd experience exactly the sensations he was trying to avoid. I said that he mustn't try to suppress the head movements but that he must be aware when he does them, and then somehow feel so dominant that he no longer needs to make them. When he repeats the scene it's his father who breaks eye contact and starts to crumble. From this beginning the student can learn to play characters of any social class, and make them high or low.

6 Space

I can't avoid talking about 'space' any longer, since status is basically territorial. Space is very difficult to talk about, but easy to demonstrate.

When I was commissioned to write my first play I'd hardly been inside a theatre, so I watched rehearsals to get the feel of it. I was struck by the way space flowed around the actors like a fluid. As the actors moved I could feel imaginary iron filings marking out the force fields. This feeling of space was strongest when the stage was uncluttered, and during the coffee breaks, or when they were discussing some difficulty. When they *weren't* acting, the bodies of the actors continually readjusted. As one changed position so all the others altered their postures. Something seemed to flow between them. When they were 'acting' each actor would pretend to relate to the others, but his movements would stem from himself. They seemed 'encapsulated'. In my view it's only when the actor's movements are related to the space he's in, and to the other actors, that the audience feel 'at one' with the play. The very best actors pump space out and suck it in, or at least that's what it feels like. When the movements are not spontaneous but 'intellectual' the production may be admired, but you don't see the whole audience responding in empathy with the movements of the actors.

Here's Stanislavsky describing a performance by Salvini, an actor who obviously used space in the way I mean:

'Salvini approached the platform of the Doges, thought a little while, concentrated himself and, unnoticed by any of us, took the entire audience of the great theatre into his hands. It seemed that he did this with a single gesture—that he stretched his hand without looking into the public, grasped all of us in his palm, and held us there as if we were ants or flies. He closed his fist, and we felt the breath of death; he opened it, and we felt the warmth of bliss. We were in his power, and we will remain in it all our lives. . . .'

The movement teacher Yat Malmgren told me that as a child he'd discovered that he didn't end at the surface of his body, but was actually an oval 'Swiss cheese' shape. To me, this is 'closed-eye' space, and you experience it when you shut your eyes and let your body feel outwards into the surrounding darkness. Yat also talked about people who were cut off from sensing areas of themselves. 'He has no arms,' he would say, or 'She has no legs', and you could see what he meant. When I investigated myself I found many areas that I wasn't ex-periencing, and my feelings are still defective. What I did find was another shape besides the 'Swiss cheese' shape: a parabola sweeping ahead of me like a comet's tail. When I panic, this parabola crushes in. In stage fright space contracts into a narrow tunnel down which you can just about walk without bumping into things. In cases of extreme stage fright the space is like a plastic skin pressing on to you and making your body rigid and bound. The opposite of this is seen when a great actor makes a gesture, and it's as if his arm has swept right over the heads of the people sitting at the back of the audience.

Many acting teachers have spoke of 'radiations', and they often sound like mystics. Here's Jean-Louis Barrault:

'Just as the earth is surrounded by an atmosphere, the living human being is surrounded by a magnetic aura which makes contact with the external objects without any concrete contact with the human body. This aura, or atmosphere, varies in depth according to the vitality of human beings. . . .

'The mime must first of all be aware of this boundless contact with things. There is no insulating layer of air between the man and the outside world. Any man who moves about causes ripples in the ambient world in the same way a fish does when it moves in the water.' (*The Theatre of Jean-Louis Barrault*, Barrie and Rockcliff, 1961.)

This isn't very scientific, but like all magical language it does com-municate a way an actor can 'feel'. If I stand two students face to face and about a foot apart they're likely to feel a strong desire to change their body position. If they don't move they'll begin to feel love or hate as their 'space' streams into each other. To prevent these feelings they'll modify their positions until their space flows out relatively unhindered, or they'll move back so that the force isn't so powerful. High-status players (like high-status seagulls) will allow their space to flow *into* other people. Low-status players will avoid letting their space flow into other people. Kneeling, bowing and prostrating one-self are all ritualised low-status ways of shutting off your space. If we wish to humiliate and degrade a low-status person we attack him while refusing to let him switch his space off. A sergeant-major will stand a recruit to attention and then scream at his face from about an inch away. Crucifixion exploits this effect, which is why it's such a power-ful symbol as compared to, say, boiling someone in oil.

Imagine a man sitting neutrally and symmetrically on a bench. If he crosses his left leg over his right then you'll see his space flowing over to the right as if his leg was an aerofoil. If he rests his right arm along the back of the bench you'll see his space flowing out more strongly. If he turns his head to the right, practically all his space will be flowing in this same direction. Someone who is sitting neutrally in the 'beam' will seem lower-status. Every movement of the body modifies its space. If a man who is sitting neutrally crosses his left wrist over his right the space flows to his right, and vice versa. It's very obvious that the top hand gives the direction, but the class are amazed. The difference seems so trivial, yet they can see it's a quite strong effect.

The body has reflexes that protect it from attack. We have a 'fear-crouch' position in which the shoulders lift to protect the jugular and the body curls forward to protect the underbelly. It's more effective against carnivores than against policemen jabbing at your kidneys, but it evolved a long time ago. The opposite to this fear crouch is the 'cherub posture', which opens all the planes of the body: the head turns and tilts to offer the neck, the shoulders turn the other way to expose the chest, the spine arches slightly backwards and twists so that the pelvis is in opposition to the shoulders exposing the under-belly—and so on. This is the position I usually see cherubs carved in, and the opening of the body planes is a sign of vulnerability and tenderness, and has a powerful effect on the onlooker. High-status people often adopt versions of the cherub posture. If they feel under attack they'll abandon it and straighten, but they won't adopt the fear crouch. Challenge a low-status player and he'll show some tend-ency to slide into postures related to the fear crouch.

When the highest-status person feels most secure he will be the most relaxed person, as for example in the opening scenes of Kozintsev's film of *King Lear*. A solemn ceremony is arranged, the daughters take their places, an atmosphere of expectancy is built up, and then Lear (Juri Jarvet) enters as if he owns the place, warms his hands at the fire, and 'makes himself at home'. The effect is to enormously *elevate* Lear in status. Lears who strain to look powerful and threatening in this opening scene miss the point, which is that Lear is so confident, and trustful, that he willingly divides his kingdom and sets in motion his own destruction.

Status can also be affected by the shape of the space you are in. The corners of couches are usually high-status, and high-status 'winners' are allowed to take them. If you leave a car in the middle of a great wilderness there is a moment when you 'move out of the space of the car'. In the wilderness the effect is very strong, for people always like to be beside objects. Thrones are usually set against walls and often have a canopy set high up below the ceiling—possibly a relic of the need to swing up into trees in emergencies.

Imagine an empty beach. The first family to arrive can sit anywhere, but they'll either take up position against some rocks, or sit a third of the way in—supposing it's all equally sandy. In my part of England, where there are many small beaches, the next family to appear might well move on to the next beach, regarding the first one as 'claimed'. If they do move in they'll stake out 'their part of the beach', *away* from the first group. If they sat close to the first group then they'd have to make friends, which could be difficult. If they sat close without making friends, then the first group would react with alarm. 'Close' is a concept related to the amount of space available. Once the beach fills up with people you can sit very close to the original family. The space people demand around them contracts as more people are added. Finally as the beach reaches saturation people stare at the sky, or roll in to face their friends, or cover their faces with newspaper or whatever.

People will travel a long way to visit a 'view'. The essential element of a good view is distance, and preferably with nothing human in the immediate foreground. When we stand on a hill and look across fifty miles of emptiness at the mountains, we are experiencing the pleasure of having our space flow out unhindered. As people come in sight of a view, it's normal for their posture to improve and for them to breathe better. You can see people remarking on the freshness of the air, and taking deep breaths, although it's the same air as it was just below the brow of the hill. Trips to the sea, and our admiration of mountains are probably symptoms of overcrowding.

Approach distances are related to space. If I approach someone on open moorland I have to raise an arm and shout 'excuse me' as soon as I'm within shouting distance. In a crowded street I can actually brush against people without having to interact.

Imagine that two strangers are approaching each other along an empty street. It's straight, hundreds of yards long and with wide pavements. Both strangers are walking at an even pace, and at some point one of them will have to move aside in order to pass. You can see this decision being made a hundred yards or more before it actually 'needs' to be. In my view the two people scan each other for signs of status, and then the lower one moves aside. If they think they're equal, both move aside, but the position nearest the wall is actually the strongest. If each person believes himself to be dominant a very curious thing happens. They approach until they stop face to face, and do a sideways dance, while muttering confused apologies. If a little old half-blind lady wanders into your path this 'mirror' dance doesn't happen. You move out of her way. It's only when you think the other person is challenging that the dance occurs, and such incidents are likely to stick in the mind. I remember doing it in a shop doorway with a man who took me by my upper arms and moved me gently out of his path. It still rankles. Old people who don't want to give way, and who cling to the status they used to have, will walk along the street hugging the wall, and 'not noticing' anyone who approaches them. If, as an experiment, you also hug the wall very funny scenes occur when you stop face to face—but the sideways dance doesn't happen because you're conscious of what you're doing. Old people in, say, Hamburg, often collide with young Britishers in the street, because they expect the young to step aside for them. Similarly, a high-status stripper will walk stark naked into a stagehand who stands in her way. In the Russian *Hamlet* film there's a moment where Hamlet finds his way momentarily obstructed by a servant and he smashes him down. When you watch a bustling crowd from above it's amazing that they don't all bump into each other. I think it's because we're all giving status signals, and exchanging subliminal status challenges all the time. The more submissive person steps aside.

This means that when two improvisers pass on a bare stage it may be possible to say where they are, even though they may not have decided on a location. The class will agree that the actors look as if they're in a hospital corridor, or in a crowded street, or passing on a narrow pavement. We judge this from the distance at which they make the first eye contact, and from the moment that they 'switch off' from each other before passing. The class may not know why they imagine the actors in a particular environment, but there is often a general agreement. When actors and directors misjudge social distances, or distort them for 'dramatic effect' the audience will, at some level, know that the work is not truthful.

One way to teach a student an appreciation of social distance is to get him to hand out leaflets in the street. You can't just thrust your hand out at people, you have to establish that you're giving out leaflets, and then present one at the right moment. When you get it wrong people either ignore you, or show alarm. Another way is to get the students, working in pairs, to identify strangers in the street as if they knew them. I get one student to do the recognising 'Hi! How are you? How's the family? Same old job then', and so on, while the other student acts bored, and says 'Come on, we'll be late', and generally expresses impatience. Most people find this approach very convincing, and sometimes extremely interesting scenes take place, but if the students are nervous, they will probably mistime the initial approach. Then it looks as if they are invisible. You can see them greeting people who sweep past as if they didn't exist. The great advantage in working in the street is that you can't dismiss real people's reactions as 'untruthful'.

Another way of opening people's eyes to the way the body positions assert dominance or submission by controlling space is to ask two people who have established a spatial relationship between themselves to freeze, and let the other students study them. Many students still won't understand, but if you take the two 'statues', lift them, together with their chairs, and place them on the opposite sides of each other, the change is dramatic. Their 'space' which seemed so 'natural' looks weird, and everyone can see how carefully they had adjusted their movements to fit in with each other.

I ask students (for homework!) to watch groups of people in coffee bars, and to notice how everyone's attitude changes when someone leaves or joins a group. If you watch two people talking, and then wait for one to leave, you can see how the person remaining has to alter his posture. He had arranged his movements to relate to his partner's, and now that he's alone he *has* to change his position in order to express a relationship to the people around him.

7 Master-Servant

One status relationship that gives immense pleasure to audiences is the master–servant scene. A dramatist who adapts a story for the stage will often add a servant, especially if it's a comedy; Sophocles gave Silenus as a slave to the Cyclops, Molière gave Don Juan a servant, and so on. The master–servant scene seems to be funny and entertaining in all cultures—even people who have never seen a manservant have no difficulty in appreciating the nuances.

The relationship is not necessarily one in which the servant plays low and the master plays high. Literature is full of scenes in which the servant refuses to obey the master, or even beats him and chases him out of the house. The whole point of the master–servant scene is that both partners should keep see-sawing. Dramatists go to ludicrous lengths to devise situations in which the servant actually has to pretend to be the master, and the master to pretend to be the servant!

If I ask two students to play a master–servant scene they will almost always look like a parent helping a child, or one friend helping another friend, or at best, as if some incompetent person is standing in for the real servant who's off sick. Once they've been trained the servant can throttle the master while remaining visibly the servant. This is very pleasing to the audience, even though they may have no idea of the forces operating.

I teach that a master–servant scene is one in which both parties act as if all the space belonged to the master. (Johnstone's law!) An extreme example would be the eighteenth-century scientist Henry Cavendish, who is reported to have fired any servant he caught sight of! (Imagine the hysterical situations: servants scuttling like rabbits, hiding in grandfather clocks and ticking, getting stuck in huge vases.) People who are not literally masters and servants may act out the roles, henpecked husbands and dominant wives for example. The contrasts between the status played between the characters and the status played to the space fascinates the audience.

When the masters are not present, then the servants can take full possession of the space, sprawl on the furniture, drink the brandy, and so on. You may have noticed how 'shifty' chauffeurs look when their masters are away. They can smoke, chat together and treat the cars as their 'own', but being in the street they feel 'exposed'. They have to keep a 'weather eye out'. When the master is present, the servant must take care at all times not to dominate the space. One might imagine that since the servants have work to do, everything possible should be done to see that they're kept 'fresh' and at ease, but a servant is not a worker in this sense. You can work for someone without being 'their servant'. A servant's primary function is to elevate the status of the master. Footmen can't lean against the wall, because it's the master's wall. Servants must make no unnecessary noise or movement, because it's the master's air they're intruding on.

The preferred position for a servant is usually at the edge of the master's 'parabola of space'. This is so that at any moment the master can confront him and dominate him. The exact distance the servant stands from the master depends on his duties, his position in the hierarchy, and the size of the room.

When the servant's duties take him into close proximity with the master he must show that he invades the master's space 'unwillingly'. If you have to confront the master in order to adjust his tie you stand back as far as possible, and you may incline your head. If you're helping with his trousers you probably do it from the side. Crossing in front of the master the servant may 'shrink' a little, and he'll try to keep a distance. Working behind the master, brushing his coat, he can be as close as he likes, and visibly higher, but he mustn't stay out of sight of the master unless his duties require it (or unless he is *very* low status).

The servant has to be quiet, to move neatly, and not to let his arms or legs intrude into the space around him. Servants' costumes are usually rather tight so that their bodies take up a minimum of space. Other things being equal, the servant should be near a door so that he can be instantly dismissed without having to walk round the master. You can see servants edging surreptitiously into this position.

It's always interesting for the audience when the master tries to coax the servant out of his role.

'Ah, Perkins, sit down, will you.'

'In . . . in your chair, Sir?'

'Certainly certainly, what will you have?'

'Er . . . er . . .'

'Whisky? Soda?'

'Anything you wish, Sir.'

'Oh come on, man, you must have some preference. Don't sit on the edge of the chair, Perkins, relax, make yourself comfortable. I'd like your advice, actually.'

And so on. It's interesting because the audience knows that if the servant does step out of his role, there'll be trouble.

'How dare you take a cigar, Perkins!'

'But Sir, you told me to make myself at home, Sir!'

If the master and the servant agree to step out of their roles everyone else will be furious—as when Queen Victoria made friends with John Brown.

I get my students to mime dressing and undressing each other as masters and servants. It's very easy to see when the space is wrong, and they suddenly 'catch on'. I also play scenes with nice masters and horrible servants, and nasty masters with flustered servants. You can improvise quite long plays by putting together a structure of such scenes (this is how the Commedia dell' Arte scenarios worked). For example: (1) nice master, nasty servant; (2) nasty master, nice servant; (3) both teams interrelate and quarrel; (4) Team One prepares for duel; (5) Team Two prepares for duel; (6) the duel.

On a good night the Theatre Machine could improvise a half-hour comedy based on this structure. Sometimes the servants have to fight the actual duel, sometimes the duel is fought on piggyback with the servants as horses, and so on.

It's very easy to invent master–servant games, but there are some that are particularly important for public improvisers. One is 'keeping the servant on the hop'. In this game the master objects to everything the servant is, or says, or does. The servant accepts the master's statement, and then deflects it.

'Smith! Why are you wearing that ridiculous uniform?'

'It's your birthday, Sir.'

This is a correct answer. 'I'm not wearing a uniform, Sir' rejects the master's statement, and is therefore incorrect. 'You told me to, Sir' is also wrong because it's implying that the challenge shouldn't have been made.

You can always recognise a correct reply, because the master 'boggles' for a moment, as his mind readjusts.

'Your coffee, Sir.'

'Where's the sugar?'

'It's in, Sir.'

A correct answer, since the servant has accepted that the master takes sugar, and that there isn't any visible. To say 'What about your diet, Sir?' or 'You don't take sugar, Sir' would be less correct, and feebler.

Another game involves the servant getting himself into trouble.

'Why are you wearing that uniform, Smith?'

'I burned the other one, Sir.'

Or:

'Where's the sugar?'

'I've eaten the last lump, Sir.'

This game also generates its own content.

'Good morning, Jenkins.'

'I'm afraid it's not morning, Sir. I forgot to wake you.'

'Augh! Four o'clock in the afternoon. Don't you know what day it is?'

'Your coronation, Sir.'

There is a *lazzi* that I use in teaching this game. It's a particular pattern of master–servant dialogue in which the servant is so guilty that he 'overconfesses'. I got it from Molière.

'Ah Perkins! I have a bone to pick with you!'

'Not the rhubarb patch, Sir.'

'What about the rhubarb patch?'

'I let the goat in by mistake, Sir.'

'You let my goat eat my rhubarb! You know I have a passion for rhubarb! What will we do with all the custard we ordered?'

'I'm planting some more, Sir.'

'So I should hope. No! It's much worse than mere rhubarb!'

'Oh, Sir! The dog!'

'My dog!'

'Yes, Sir. I couldn't stand it following me around and sniffing me and messing everywhere, and, and it wetting me when you made me stand to attention at parties, and them all laughing. That's why I did it, Sir!'

'Did what?'

'Why, nothing, Sir.'

'Did what? What did you do to poor Towser?'

'I ... I ...'

'Go on!'

'Poisoned it, Sir.'

'You poisoned my dog!'

'Don't hit me, Sir.'

'Hit you! Hanging would be too good for you. Why it's worse than the thing I wanted you for in the first place. You'd better make a clean breast of it.'

'But what have I done?'

'You've been found out, Perkins.'

'Oh no, Sir.'

'Oh yes!'

'Oh, Sir.'

'Scoundrel!'

'She shouldn't have told you, Sir.'

'What?'

'She got me in the bathroom, Sir. She swore she'd scream and tell you that I'd attacked her, Sir. She tore her clothes off, Sir.'

'What! What!'

The literary value may not be high, but audiences laugh a lot.

Getting an actor to play both parts in a master–servant scene can accelerate the skills. When the actor is wearing a hat he's the master, then he removes it and leaps into the position in which he's been imagining the servant, and plays the servant role. The moment he can't think what to say he changes roles. He can throttle himself, and beat himself up, or praise himself, and he 'blocks' the action far less. It's actually *easier* to play master–servant scenes as solos. The mind has an ability to split itself readily into several people—Frederick Perls got people to play 'top dog' and 'underdog' in a similar way.

An excellent way to play master–servant scenes is to let one actor do both voices, the other mouthing the words that are supposed to be his. This sounds very difficult, but it's actually easier to sustain long scenes in this way. At first the actor who's mouthing the words will play a passive role. It's necessary to prod him into developing the action. If he picks up a chair and threatens the master with it, then the master will have to say something appropriate, like 'Where's the money you owe me, Sir?' Perhaps the master will beat the servant up and do all the screams and pleas for mercy himself.

If you experiment with master–servant scenes you eventually realise that the servant could have a servant, and the master could have a master, and that actors could be instantly assembled into pecking orders by just numbering them. You can then improvise very complicated group scenes on the spur of the moment.

I introduce pecking orders as clown games, oversimplifying the procedures, and creating complex absurdities which 'cartoon' real life. Orders and blame are passed one way along the hierarchy, excuses and problems are passed the other way. So far as possible each person is to interact with the one next to him in rank. Audiences never seem to tire of dialogue like this:

> 1: Chair!
> 2: Chair!
> 3: Get a chair!
> 4: Yes, Sir.
> 1: What's happening?
> 2: I'll just check, Sir. Where's the chair?
> 3: Number Four's getting it, Sir.
> 4: Beg pardon, but I can't find one, Sir.
> 3: He can't find one!
> 2: 'Sir!' How dare you address me without calling me 'Sir'?

3: Yes, Sir! Number Four reports that there is no chair, Sir!

1: What's going on here, Number Two?

2: There's no chair, Sir.

1: No chair! This is monstrous! Have someone crouch so that I can sit on them!

2: Number Three, have Number Four crouch so that Number One can sit on him.

4: Permission to speak, Sir! (And so on.)

The patterns become even clearer if you give each actor a long balloon with which to hit people. If Number One hits Number Two, Number Two apologises to him, and hits Number Three, and so on. Number Four, who can't hit anyone ducks, or cries, or bites his lip, or dies, or whatever. Each person can also try to make faces at anyone 'above' him, without getting caught (if possible). If Number One sees Number Three make a face at Number Two, he informs Number Two, and so on. This may look very tedious on the page, but these simple rules produce amazing permutations.

One of the craziest 'clown games' is a version of 'taking the hat'. I've seen spectators collapsing with laughter. I start the game by taking four students and numbering them one to four. Each wears a soft trilby hat. First, Number One takes Number Two's hat and throws it at his feet. Number Two reacts with horror and embarrassment and shrieks for Number Three to pick the hat up and replace it. Number Two then takes Number Three's hat—and so on, except that Number Four will have to put his own hat on.

I then tell Number One that although he prefers to take Number Two's hat, he can in fact take anybody's. Number Two similarly prefers to take Number Three's, but he can also take Number Four's.

Once this pattern is almost learnt, I let people weave about and try not to get their hats taken. And I *insist* that the hats must be thrown at the feet. People have a strong impulse to throw or kick the hats right away, which breaks up the group and spoils the crazy patterns. If you can keep the actors 'high' on the game they will now be using their bodies like excellent physical comedians, they will have a marvellous 'rapport' with each other, and absolutely no trace of self-consciousness. I make them play a scene while continuing this insane activity. I send them outside and get them to enter as if burgling a house in which people are asleep upstairs. Or I get them to pack for the holidays, or interact with another pecking order who are also 'taking hats'. Number One will probably have to throw insane fits of rage to get anything done, but it's more important that the scene is played than the hat game 'demonstrated'. You can't even *teach* this game unless you yourself are 'high' and expressing great drive and energy.

Actors should become expert at each stage of a pecking order. There will be actors who can at first only play one role really well. Videotape is useful in explaining to them where their behaviour is inappropriate.

Number One in a pecking order has to make sure that everything is functioning properly. Anything that irritates him must be suppressed. At all times everything must be organised for his personal content-ment. He can also add his own rules, insisting that absolute silence should be maintained at all times, or that the word 'is' should be abolished from the language, or whatever. Desmond Morris, in *The Human Zoo* (Cape, 1969; Corgi, 1971) gives 'ten golden rules' for people who are Number Ones. He says, 'They apply to all leaders, from baboons to modern presidents and prime ministers.' They are:

1. You must clearly display the trappings, postures and gestures of dominance.

2. In moments of active rivalry you must threaten your subordinates aggressively.

3. In moments of physical challenge you (or your delegates) must be able forcibly to overpower your subordinates.

4. If a challenge involves brain rather than brawn you must be able to outwit your subordinates.

5. You must suppress squabbles that break out between your subordinates.

6. You must reward your immediate subordinates by permitting them to enjoy the benefits of their high ranks.

7. You must protect the weaker members of the group from undue persecution.

8. You must make decisions concerning the social activities of your group.

9. You must reassure your extreme subordinates from time to time.

10. You must take the initiative in repelling threats or attacks arising from outside your group.

Number Four has to keep Number Three happy while avoiding the attention of One or Two. If addressed by One or Two he must avoid any appearance of wanting to usurp Three's position. If the general speaks to a private we should expect the private to keep glancing at the sergeant. If the general lowers the sergeant the private may be secretly delighted but he'll have to hide it, and at the time he might be expected to find it embarrassing. Number Four has to be an expert at making excuses, and in evading responsibility. He must also be inventing problems to pass up the pecking order.

Basically, One imposes aims and tries to get them fulfilled, while Four discovers that the house is on fire, or the enemy approaching, or that there's only three minutes' oxygen left, and so on. Two and Three are mostly concerned with maintaining their respective positions, and with the communication of information up and down the line.

More naturalistic pecking-order work can be introduced as 'status towers'. Someone begins with some low-status activity, and each person who enters the scene plays a step higher. Or you can start at the top and add each person one step down.

It is the lack of pecking-order that makes most crowd scenes look unconvincing. The 'extras' mill about trying to look 'real', and the spaces between them are quite phoney. In films where Mafia bandits wait on a hillside while their leader confers with someone, you can see that the director has spaced them out 'artistically', or has just said 'spread yourself out'. By just numbering people in hierarchies so that they knew what status they were, such errors could be avoided.

8 Maximum Status Gaps

In life, status gaps are often exaggerated to such an extent that they become comical. Heinrich Harrer met a Tibetan whose servant stood holding a spitoon in case the master wanted to spit. Queen Victoria would take her position and sit, and there *had* to be a chair. George the Sixth used to wear electrically heated underclothes when deerstalking, which meant a gillie had to follow him around holding the battery.

I train actors to use minimum status gaps, because then they have to assess the status of their partners accurately, but I also teach them to play maximum status-gap scenes. For example, I ask the actors to play a scene in which a master is as high in status as possible, and the servant as low as possible. At first they'll play ineptly. The master looks uncomfortable, and the servant intrudes on the master's space.

I start the scene again and say that the moment the master feels the slightest irritation he's to snap his fingers—the servant will then commit suicide. I'll have to prod the master into action because he'll be reluctant to exercise his power. The moment the master looks irritated I say 'Kill him!' and send in more servants until the stage is littered with bodies. Everyone laughs a lot, but often the servants have no idea why they're being killed. I ask the master to explain the reasons, but I stress that he doesn't need to be fair. The servants usually think the master is being harsh, but the audience are amazed that servants survive so long, since everything they do is inept. Servants are killed because they wave their arms about, because they clump about, because they're disrespectful, or because they misunderstand the master's requirements.

Now I give the servants *three* lives, so they die at the third snap of the fingers. Amazingly you'll see them doing exactly the same thing after a finger snap as before it. 'Do something different,' I shout, 'he's about to kill you again.' The servants seem amazingly unadaptable—this is because they're demonstrating their role as servants rather than attending to the needs of the master. At first they survive for just a few seconds, but soon they're surviving for minutes, and the masters begin to feel amazingly pampered as they're thrust up in status by their servants.

Once a maximum-gap master–servant scene is established, I send in a third person who has to placate the master, and cope with the servants as well.

In one form of this game you reverse the expected status. If an executioner is trying to play as low as possible, then he'll be too nervous to roll the last cigarette, he'll apologise for the untidiness, he'll ask for an autograph, or he'll accidentally shoot himself in the foot. The suicide on the ledge who plays high status may argue the rescuer into jumping off. It's very easy to create scenes this way.

'Excuse me, Miss . . .'
'Next cashier please. I'm just going off duty.'
'Er . . . no, no . . . I'm not a customer.'
'If you'll just join the queue over there, Sir . . .'
'I've got a note. Here.'
'Four shirts, two pants, six socks?'
'No, no . . . er . . . here, this one.'
'Hand over the money? This is a stick-up!'
'Not so loud.'
'Well, how much did you want?'
'All of it!'
'Don't be absurd!'
'Yeah, well, just a few quid then, to tide us over.'
'I shall have to refer this to Mr Carbuncle.'
'50p, then!'

Maximum-status-gap exercises produce 'absurd' improvisations. (I don't like the term 'theatre of the absurd', because the best 'absurd' plays present 'equivalents' for reality, and aren't nonsensical, and many conventional writers have written 'existential' plays. 'Absurd' plays are based on maximum-status-gap transactions.)

9 Text

Although this short essay is no more than an introduction, by now it will be clear to you that status transactions aren't only of interest to the improviser. Once you understand that every sound and posture implies a status, then you perceive the world quite differently, and the change is probably permanent. In my view, really accomplished actors, directors, and playwrights are people with an intuitive understanding of the status transactions that govern human relationships. This ability to perceive the underlying motives of casual behaviour can also be taught.

In conclusion, but as a coda, rather than a summing-up, I'd suggest that a good play is one which ingeniously displays and reverses the status between the characters. Many writers of great talent have failed to write successful plays (Blake, Keats, Tennyson, among others) because of a failure to understand that drama is not primarily a literary art. Shakespeare is a great writer even in translation; a great production is great even if you don't speak the language. A great play is a virtuoso display of status transactions—*Waiting for Godot*, for example. The 'tramps' play friendship status, but there's a continual friction because Vladimir believes himself higher than Estragon, a thesis which Estragon will not accept. Pozzo and Lucky play maximum-gap master–servant scenes. The 'tramps' play low status to Lucky, and Pozzo often plays low status to the tramps—which produces thrilling effects. Here's a section where the 'tramps' are asking why Lucky holds the bags instead of resting them on the ground.

POZZO: ... Let's try and get this clear. Has he got the right to? Certainly he has. It follows that he doesn't want to. There's reasoning for you. And why doesn't he want to? (*Pause.*) Gentlemen, the reason is this.

VLADIMIR: (*To Estragon.*) Make a note of this.

POZZO: He wants to impress me so that I'll keep him.

ESTRAGON: What?

POZZO: ... In reality, he carries like a pig. It's not his job.

VLADIMIR: You want to get rid of him?

POZZO: He imagines that when I see him indefatigable I'll
regret my decision. Such is his miserable scheme. As
though I were short of slaves! (*All three look at
Lucky.*) Atlas, son of Jupiter!

If you observe the status, then the play is fascinating. If you ignore
it the play is tedious. Pozzo is not really a very high-status master,
since he fights for status all the time. He owns the land, but he doesn't
own the space.

POZZO: . . . I must be getting on. Thank you for your
society. (*He reflects.*) Unless I smoke another pipe
before I go. What do you say? (*They say nothing.*)
Oh, I'm only a small smoker, a very small smoker,
I'm not in the habit of smoking two pipes one on
top of the other, it makes (*Hand to heart, sighing*) my
heart go pit-a-pat. (*Silence.*) But perhaps you don't
smoke? Yes? No? It's of no importance. (*Silence.*)
But how am I to sit down now, without affectation,
now that I have risen? Without appearing to—how
shall I say—without appearing to falter. (*To
Vladimir.*) I beg your pardon? (*Silence.*) Perhaps
you didn't speak? (*Silence.*) It's of no importance.
Let me see . . .
(*He reflects.*)

ESTRAGON: Ah! That's better.
(*He puts the bones in his pocket.*)

VLADIMIR: Let's go.

ESTRAGON: So soon?

POZZO: One moment! (*He jerks the rope.*) Stool! (*He points
with his whip. Lucky moves the stool.*) More! There!
(*He sits down. Lucky goes back to his place*) Done it!
(*He fills his pipe.*)

It must be clear, I think, that even the stage directions relate to
status. Every 'silence' is lowering to Pozzo. I remember a reviewer
(Kenneth Tynan) making fun of Beckett's pauses, but this just shows
a lack of understanding. Obviously Beckett's plays need careful pacing,
but the pauses are part of the pattern of dominance and submission.
Godot earns its reputation as a boring play only when directors try to
make it 'significant', and ignore the status transactions.

I don't myself see that an educated man in this culture necessarily
has to understand the second law of thermodynamics, but he certainly

should understand that we are pecking-order animals and that this affects the tiniest details of our behaviour.

Note

1. The high-status effect of slow motion means that TV heroes who have the power of superhuman speed are shown slowed down! Logic would suggest that you should speed the film up, but then they'd be jerking about like the Keystone Cops, or the bionic chicken.

Spontaneity

'I was given the part of poor Armgard, so I stood in front of the class and as I began with "Here he cannot escape me, he must hear me", I suddenly noticed a warm friendly feeling in the region of the stomach, like a soft hotwater bottle in a cold bed, and when I got to "Mercy, Lord Governor! Oh, pardon, pardon", I was already on my knees, tears streaming from my eyes and nose, and sobbing to such an extent that I could only finish the passage "My wretched orphans cry for bread" with supreme difficulty. The fishhead was in favour of a more restrained performance and her cutting voice drove me to the back of the class room with words of "Un-German hysterical conduct". It was a nightmare. I almost died of shame and prayed for an earthquake or an air raid to deliver me from the derision and shock . . . apart from the nagging voice all went still, the others stared at me as though they had unwittingly harboured a serpent in their midst. The rest of my days with Weise were torture. I was afraid of the others and myself for I could never be certain that I wouldn't again throw myself down in tears because of the orphans. . . .' (Hildegarde Knef, *The Gift Horse*, André Deutsch, 1971.)

It's possible to turn unimaginative people into imaginative people at a moment's notice. I remember an experiment referred to in the *British Journal of Psychology*—probably in the summer of 1969 or 1970—in which some businessmen who had showed up as very dull on work-association tests were asked to imagine themselves as happy-go-lucky hippy types, in which persona they were retested, and showed up as far more imaginative. In creativity tests you may be asked to suggest different ways of using a brick; if you say things like 'Build a house', or 'Build a wall', then you're classified as unimaginative—if you say 'Grind it up and use it for diarrhoea mixture', or 'Rub off warts with it', then you're imaginative. I'm oversimplifying, but you get the general idea.

Some tests involve picture completion. You get given a lot of little squares with signs in them, and you have to add something to the sign. 'Uncreative' people just add another squiggle, or join up a 'C' shape to make a circle. 'Creative' people have a great time, parallel lines become the trunk of a tree, a 'V' on its side becomes the beam of a lighthouse, and so on. It may be a mistake to think of such tests as showing people to be creative, or uncreative. It may be that the tests are recording different activities. The person who adds a timid squiggle may be trying to reveal as little as possible about himself. If we can persuade him to have fun, and not worry about being judged, then maybe he can approach the test with the same attitude as a 'creative' person, just like the tired businessmen when they were pretending to be hippies.

Most schools encourage children to be *unimaginative*. The research so far shows that imaginative children are disliked by their teachers. Torrance gives an eye-witness account of an 'exceptionally creative boy' who questioned one of the rules in the textbook: 'The teacher became irate, even in the presence of the principal. She fumed, "So! You think you know more than this book!" ' She was also upset when the boy finished the problems she set almost as quickly as it took to read them. 'She couldn't understand how he was getting the correct answer and demanded that he write down all of the steps he had gone through in solving each problem.'

When this boy transferred to another school, his new principal telephoned to ask if he was the sort of boy 'who has to be squelched rather roughly'. When it was explained that he was 'a very wholesome, promising lad who needed understanding and encouragement' the new principal exclaimed 'rather brusquely, "Well, he's already said too much right here in my office!" ' (E. P. Torrance, *Guiding Creative Talent*, Prentice-Hall, 1962.)

One of my students spent two years in a classroom where the teacher had put a large sign over the blackboard. It said 'Get into the "Yes, Sir" attitude.' No doubt we can all add further anecdotes. Torrance has a theory that 'many children with impoverished imaginations have been subjected to rather vigorous and stern efforts to eliminate fantasy too early. They are afraid to think.' Torrance seems to understand the forces at work, but he still refers to attempts to eliminate fantasy *too early*. Why should we eliminate fantasy at all? Once we eliminate fantasy, then we have no artists.

Intelligence is proportional to population, but talent appears not to be related to population numbers. I'm living in a city at the edge of the Rocky Mountains; the population is much greater than it was in Shakespearian London, and almost everyone here is literate, and has had many thousands of dollars spent on his education. Where are the poets, and playwrights, and painters, and composers? Remember that there are hundreds of thousands of 'literate' people here, while in Shakespeare's London very few people could read. The great art of this part of the world was the art of the native peoples. The whites flounder about trying to be 'original' and failing miserably.

You can get a glimmer of the damage done when you watch people trying out pens in stationers' shops. They make feeble little scribbles for fear of giving something away. If an Aborigine asked us for a sample of Nordic art we'd have to direct him to an art gallery. No Aborigine ever told an anthropologist, 'Sorry, Baas, I can't draw.' Two of my students said they couldn't draw, and I asked, 'Why?' One said her teacher had been sarcastic because she'd painted a blue snowman (every child's painting was pinned up on the walls except hers). The other girl had drawn trees up the sides of her paintings (like Paul Klee), and the teacher drew a 'correct' tree on top of hers. She remembered thinking 'I'll never draw for you again!' (One reason given for filling in the windows of the local schools here is that it'll help make the children more attentive!)

Most children can operate in a creative way until they're eleven or twelve, when suddenly they lose their spontaneity, and produce imitations of 'adult art'. When other races come into contact with our culture something similar happens. The great Nigerian sculptor Bamboya was set up as principal of an art school by some philanthropic Americans in the 1920s. Not only did he fail to hand on his talents, but his own inspiration failed him. He and his students could still carve coffee tables for the whites, but they weren't *inspired* any more.

So-called 'primitive painters' in our own culture sometimes go to art school to improve themselves—and lose their talent. A critic told me of a film school where each new student made a short film unaided. These, he said, were always interesting, although technically crude. At the end of the course they made a longer, technically more proficient film, which hardly anyone wanted to see. He seemed outraged when I suggested they should close the school (he lectured there); yet until recently our directors didn't get any training. Someone asked Kubrick if it was usual for a director to spend so much care on lighting each shot and he said, 'I don't know. I've never seen anyone else light a film.'

You have to be a very stubborn person to remain an artist in this culture. It's easy to play the role of 'artist', but actually to create something means going against one's education. I read an interview once in which Grandma Moses was complaining that people kept urging her to improve her snow scenes by putting blue in them, but she insisted that the snow she saw was white, so she wouldn't do it. This little old lady could paint *because* she defied the 'experts'. Even after his works had been exhibited in court as proof that he wasn't in his right mind, Henri Rousseau still had the stubbornness to go on painting!

We see the artist as a wild and aberrant figure. Maybe our artists are the people who have been constitutionally unable to conform to the demands of the teachers. Pavlov found that there were some dogs that he couldn't 'brainwash' until he'd castrated them, and starved them for three weeks. If teachers could do that to us, then maybe they'd achieve Plato's dream of a republic in which there are no artists left at all.

Many teachers think of children as immature adults. It might lead to better and more 'respectful' teaching, if we thought of adults as atrophied children. Many 'well adjusted' adults are bitter, uncreative frightened, unimaginative, and rather hostile people. Instead of assuming they were born that way, or that that's what being an adult entails, we might consider them as people damaged by their education and upbringing.

2

Many teachers express surprise at the switch-off that occurs at puberty, but I don't, because first of all the child has to hide the sexual turmoil he's in, and secondly the grown-ups' attitude to him completely changes.

Suppose an eight-year-old writes a story about being chased down a mouse-hole by a monstrous spider. It'll be perceived as 'childish' and no one will worry. If he writes the same story when he's fourteen it may be taken as a sign of mental abnormality. Creating a story, or painting a picture, or making up a poem lay an adolescent wide open to criticism. He therefore has to fake everything so that he appears 'sensitive' or 'witty' or 'tough' or 'intelligent' according to the image he's trying to establish in the eyes of other people. If he believed he was a transmitter, rather than a creator, then we'd be able to see what his talents really were.

We have an idea that art is self-expression—which historically is *weird*. An artist used to be seen as a medium through which something else operated. He was a servant of the God. Maybe a mask-maker would have fasted and prayed for a week before he had a vision of the Mask he was to carve, because no one wanted to see *his* Mask, they wanted to see the God's. When Eskimos believed that each piece of bone only had one shape inside it, then the artist didn't have to 'think up' an idea. He had to wait until he knew what was in there—and this is crucial. When he'd finished carving his friends couldn't say 'I'm a bit worried about that Nanook at the third igloo', but only, 'He made a mess getting that out!' or 'There are some very odd bits of bone about these days.' These days of course the Eskimos get booklets giving illustrations of what will sell, but before we infected them, they were in contact with a source of inspiration that we are not. It's no wonder that our artists are aberrant characters. It's not surprising that great African sculptors end up carving coffee tables, or that the talent of our children dies the moment we expect them to become adult. Once we believe that art is self-expression, then the individual can be criticised not only for his skill or lack of skill, but simply for being what he is.

Schiller wrote of a 'watcher at the gates of the mind', who examines ideas too closely. He said that in the case of the creative mind 'the intellect has withdrawn its watcher from the gates, and the ideas rush in pell-mell, and only then does it review and inspect the multitude.' He said that uncreative people 'are ashamed of the momentary passing madness which is found in all real creators . . . regarded in isolation, an idea may be quite insignificant, and venturesome in the extreme, but it may acquire importance from an idea that follows it; perhaps in collation with other ideas which seem equally absurd, it may be capable of furnishing a very serviceable link.'

My teachers had the opposite theory. They wanted me to reject and discriminate, believing that the best artist was the one who made the most elegant choices. They analysed poems to show how difficult 'real' writing was, and they taught that I should always know where the writing was taking me, and that I should search for better and better ideas. They spoke as if an image like 'the multitudinous seas incarnadine' could have been worked out like the clue to a crossword puzzle. Their idea of the 'correct' choice was the one anyone would have made if he had thought long enough.

I now feel that imagining should be as effortless as perceiving. In order to recognise someone my brain has to perform amazing feats of analysis: 'Shape . . . dark . . . swelling . . . getting closer . . . human . . . nose type X15, eyes type E24B . . . characteristic way of walking . . . look under relative . . .' and so on, in order to turn electromagnetic radiation into the image of my father, yet I don't experience myself as 'doing' anything at all! My brain creates a whole universe without my having the least sense of effort. Of course, if I say 'Hi Dad', and the approaching figure ignores me, then I'd do something that I perceive as 'thinking'. 'That's not the coat he usually wears,' I think, 'This man is shorter.' It's only when I believe my perceptions to be in error that I have to 'do' anything. It's the same with imagination. Imagination is as effortless as perception, unless we think it might be 'wrong', which is what our education encourages us to believe. Then we experience ourselves as 'imagining', as 'thinking up an idea', but what we're really doing is faking up the sort of imagination we think we ought to have.

When I read a novel I have no sense of effort. Yet if I pay close attention to my mental processes I find an amazing amount of activity. 'She walked into the room . . .' I read, and I have a picture in my mind, very detailed, of a large Victorian room empty of furniture, with the bare boards painted white around what used to be the edge of the carpet. I also see some windows with the shutters open and sunlight streaming through them. 'She noticed some charred papers in the grate . . .' I read, and my mind inserts a fireplace which I've seen in a friend's house, very ornate. 'A board creaked behind her . . .' I read, and for a split second I see a Frankenstein's monster holding a wet teddy bear. 'She turned to see a little wizened old man . . .', instantly, the monster shrivels to Picasso with a beret, and the room darkens and fills with furniture. My imagination is working as hard as the writer's, but I have no sense of doing anything, or 'being creative'.

A friend has just read the last paragraph and found it impossible to imagine that she's being creative when she reads. I tell her I'll invent a story especially for her. 'Imagine a man walking along the street,' I say. 'Suddenly he hears a sound and turns to see something moving in a doorway . . .' I stop and ask her what the man is wearing.

'A suit.'

'What sort of suit?'

'Striped.'

'Any other people in the street?'

'A white dog.'

'What was the street like?'

'It was a London street. Working-class. Some of the buildings have been demolished.'

'Any windows boarded up?'

'Yes. Rusty corrugated iron.'

'So they've been boarded up a long time?'

She's obviously created much more than I have. She doesn't pause to think up the answers to my questions, she 'knows' them. They flashed automatically into her consciousness.

People may seem uncreative, but they'll be extremely ingenious at rationalising the things they do. You can see this in people who obey post-hypnotic suggestions, while managing to explain the behaviour ordered by the hypnotist as being of their own volition.

People maintain prejudices quite effortlessly. For example, in this conversation (R. B. Zajonc, *Public Opinion Quarterly*, Princeton, 1960, Vol. 24, 2, pp. 280–96):

MR X: The trouble with Jews is that they only take care of their own group.

MR Y: But the record of the community chest shows that they give more generously than non-Jews.

MR X: That shows that they are always trying to buy favour and intrude in Christian affairs. They think of nothing but money; that's why there are so many Jewish bankers.

MR Y: But a recent study shows that the per cent of Jews in banking is proportionally much smaller than the per cent of non-Jews.

MR X: That's it. They don't go for respectable businesses. They would rather run nightclubs.

In a way this bigot is being very creative.

I knew a man who was discovered stark naked in a wardrobe by an irate husband. The wife screamed, 'I've never seen this man before in my life.' 'I must be in the wrong flat,' said my friend. These reactions aren't very satisfactory, but they didn't have to be 'thought up', they sprang to mind quite automatically.

I sometimes shock students who have been trained by strict 'method' teachers.

'Be sad,' I say.

'What do you mean, be sad?'

'Just be sad. See what happens.'

'But what's my motivation?'

'Just be sad. Start to weep and you'll know what's upset you.'

The student decides to humour me.

'That isn't very sad. You're just pretending.'

'You asked me to pretend.'

'Raise your arm. Now, why are you raising it?'

'You asked me to.'

'Yes, but why might you have raised it?'

'To hold on to a strap in the Tube.'

'Then that's why you raised your arm.'

'But I could have given any reason.'

'Of course; you could have been waving to someone, or milking a giraffe, or airing your armpit . . .'

'But I don't have time to choose the best reason.'

'Don't choose anything. Trust your mind. Take the first idea it gives you. Now try being sad again. Hold the face in a sad position, fight back the tears. Be unhappier. More. More. *Now* tell me why you're in this state?'

'My child has died.'

'Did you think that up?'

'I just knew.'

'There you are, then.'

'My teacher said you shouldn't act adjectives.'

'You shouldn't act adjectives without justifying them.'

If an improviser is stuck for an idea, he shouldn't search for one, he should trigger his partner's ability to give 'unthought' answers.

If someone starts a scene by saying 'What are you doing here?' then his partner can instantly say, without thinking, 'I just came down to get the milk, Sir.'

'Didn't I tell you what I'd do if I caught you again?'

'Oh Sir, don't put me in the refrigerator, Sir.'

If you don't know what to do in a scene, just say something like, 'Oh my God! What's that?'

This immediately jerks images into your partner's mind: 'Mother!' he says, or 'That dog's messed the floor again', or 'A secret staircase!' or whatever.

3

At school any spontaneous act was likely to get me into trouble. I learned never to act on impulse, and that whatever came into my mind first should be rejected in favour of better ideas. I learned that my imagination wasn't 'good' enough. I learned that the first idea was unsatisfactory because it was (1) psychotic; (2) obscene; (3) unoriginal.

The truth is that the *best* ideas are often psychotic, obscene and unoriginal. My best known play—a one-acter called *Moby Dick*—is about a servant who keeps his master's one remaining sperm in a goldfish bowl. It escapes, grows to monstrous size, and has to be hunted down on the high seas. This is certainly a rather obscene idea to many people, and if I hadn't thrown away everything that my teachers taught me, I could never have written it. These teachers, who were so sure of the rules, didn't produce anything themselves at all. I was one of a number of playwrights who emerged in the late 1950s, and it was remarkable that only one of us had been to a university—that was John Arden—and he'd studied architecture.

Let's take a look at these three categories.

Psychotic Thought

My feeling is that sanity is actually a pretence, a way we *learn* to behave. We keep this pretence up because we don't want to be rejected by other people—and being classified insane is to be shut out of the group in a very complete way.

Most people I meet are secretly convinced that they're a little crazier than the average person. People understand the energy necessary to maintain their own shields, but not the energy expended by other people. They understand that their own sanity is a performance, but when confronted by other people they confuse the person with the role.

Sanity has nothing directly to do with the way you think. It's a matter of presenting yourself as *safe*. Little old men wander around London hallucinating visibly, but no one gets upset. The same behaviour in a younger, more vigorous person would get him shut away. A Canadian study on attitudes to mental illness concluded that it was when someone's behaviour was perceived as 'unpredictable' that the community rejected them. A fat lady was admiring a painting at a private view at the Tate when the artist strode over and bit her. They threw him out, but no one questioned his sanity—it was how he always behaved.

I once read about a man who believed himself to have a fish in his jaw. (The case was reported in *New Society*.) This fish moved about, and caused him a lot of discomfort. When he tried to tell people about the fish, they thought him 'crazy', which led to violent arguments. After he'd been hospitalised several times—with no effect on the fish— it was suggested that perhaps he shouldn't tell anyone. After all it was the quarrels that were getting him put away, rather than the delusion.

Once he'd agreed to keep his problem secret, he was able to lead a normal life. His sanity is like our sanity. We may not have a fish in our jaw, but we all have its equivalent.

When I explain that sanity is a matter of interaction, rather than of one's mental processes, students are often hysterical with laughter. They agree that for years they have been suppressing all sorts of thinking because they classified it as insane.

Students need a 'guru' who 'gives permission' to allow forbidden thoughts into their consciousness. A 'guru' doesn't necessarily teach at all. Some remain speechless for years, others communicate very cryptically. All reassure by example. They are people who have been into the forbidden areas and who have survived unscathed. I react playfully with my students, while showing them that there are just as many dead nuns or chocolate scorpions inside my head as there are in anybody's, yet I interact very smoothly and sanely. It's no good *telling* the student that he isn't to be held responsible for the content of his imagination, he needs a teacher who is living proof that the monsters are not real, and that the imagination will not destroy you. Otherwise the student will have to go on *pretending* to be dull.

At one time I went from a class of mental patients in the morning to a class of drama students in the afternoon. The work of the drama students was far more bizarre, because they weren't so scared of what their minds might do. The mental patients mistook even the normal working of the imagination as proof of their insanity.

I remember the psychologist David Stafford-Clark criticising Ken Campbell at a public meeting. Ken had said that he encouraged his actors to act like lunatics, because then people would find them amusing. Stafford-Clark was upset at the idea that mad people should be thought 'funny', but that's hardly Ken's fault. Laughter is a whip that keeps us in line. It's horrible to be laughed at against your will. Either you suppress unwelcome laughter or you start controlling it. We suppress our spontaneous impulses, we censor our imaginations, we learn to present ourselves as 'ordinary', and we destroy our talent—then no one laughs at us. If Shakespeare had been worried about establishing his sanity, he could never have written *Hamlet*, let alone *Titus Andronicus*; Harpo couldn't have inflated a rubber glove and milked it into the coffee cups;[1] Groucho would never have threatened to horse-whip someone—if he had a horse; W. C. Fields would never have leapt out of the aeroplane after his whisky bottle; Stan Laurel would never have snapped his fingers and ignited his thumb.

We all know instinctively what 'mad' thought is: mad thoughts are those which other people find unacceptable, and train us not to talk about, but which we go to the theatre to see expressed.

Obscenity

I find many things obscene, in the sense of repulsive or shocking. I find the use of film from real massacres in the titles of TV shows pretty nasty. I find the way people take pills and smoke cigarettes, and generally screw themselves up, rather awful. The way parents and teachers often treat children nauseates me. Most people think of obscene things as sexual like pubic hair, obscene language, but I'm more shocked by modern cities, by the carcinogens in the air and in the food, by the ever-increasing volume of radioactive materials in the environment. In the first seven months of 1975 the cancer rate in America seems to have jumped by 5.2 per cent, but few noticed—the information didn't have 'news value'.

Most people's idea of what is or isn't obscene *varies*. In some cultures certain times are set aside when the normal values are reversed—the 'Lord of Misrule', Zuni clowning, many carnivals—and something similar happens even in this culture, or so I'm told, at office parties for example. People's tolerance of obscenity varies according to the group they're with, or the particular circumstances (*'pas devant les enfants'*). People can laugh at jokes told at a party that they wouldn't find funny on a more formal occasion. It seems unfortunate to me that the classroom is often considered a 'formal' area in this sense.

The first school I taught at had one woman teacher. When she went out shopping at lunchtime, the men pulled their chairs round and told dirty stories non-stop. Down in the playground, as usual, the children were swopping similar stories, or writing 'shit' or 'fuck' on the walls, always correctly spelt; yet the staff considered the children 'dirty little devils', and punished them for saying things which were far milder than things the teachers themselves would say, and enjoy laughing at. When these children grow up, and perhaps crack up, then they'll find themselves in therapy groups where they'll be encouraged to say all the things that the teacher would have forbidden during school.[2]

Foulkes and Anthony (in *Group Psychotherapy*, Penguin, 1972) say that a therapeutic situation is one 'in which the patient can freely voice his innermost thoughts towards himself, towards any other person, and towards the analyst. He can be confident that he is not being judged, and that he is fully accepted, whatever he may be, or whatever he may disclose.' Later they add: 'We encourage the relaxation of censorship. We do this by letting the patient members understand that they are not only permitted, but expected to say anything that comes to mind. We tell them not to allow any of their usual inhibitory considerations to stand in the way of voicing the ideas that come to them spontaneously.'

I was at school more than twenty years ago, but in education the more things change the more they are the same. (Recent research suggests that the old 'monitor' system may be one of the most efficient teaching methods!) Here are some answers that headmasters gave to a questionnaire about sex education in their schools. (Reported in the *New Statesman*, 28 February 1969.)

'I'm against all "frank discussion" of these matters.'

'Those who are determined to behave like animals can doubtless find out the facts for themselves.'

'I am sick, sick of the talk about sex. I'll have none of it in my school.'

'Everything that needs to be done in my school is done individually, and in private by a missionary priest.'

Notice the use of 'my school' rather than 'our school'. Recently a young girl burned to death because she was ashamed to run naked from a burning house. To some extent her teachers are to blame. Here's Sheila Kitzinger on some effects of middle-class prudery.

'In Jamaica I discovered that the West Indian peasant woman rarely feels discomfort in the perineum, or minds the pressure of the baby's head as it descends. But from the case studies of English middle-class women it appears that many of them worry about dirtying the bed and are often shocked by sensations against the rectum and the vagina in labour—sensations which they may find excruciating. They feel distressed, in fact, at just those sensations which the peasant woman meets with equanimity.

'Some women find relaxation of the abdominal wall difficult, and especially so when they experience any pain. They have been taught to "hold their tummies in", and sometimes it goes against the grain to release these muscles.' (Sheila Kitzinger, *The Experience of Childbirth*, Gollancz, 1962.) She adds that women with prolonged labours tended to be 'inhibited, embarrassed by the processes taking place in their bodies, ladylike in the extreme, and endured what they were undergoing stoically as long as they were able, without expressing their anxieties. It was not these women's bodies that were causing them difficulties; they were being held up by the sort of people they were. They were not able to *give* birth.'

When I have been teaching in universities, I haven't experienced any problem with censorship—at least not on 'sexual' grounds—and I'm not saying that fear of obscenity is the most important factor in making people reject the first ideas that come to them, but it does help though, if improvisation teachers are not puritanical, and can allow the students to behave as *they* want to behave. The best situation is one in which the class is seen as a party, rather than a formal teacher-pupil set-up. If it isn't possible to let students speak and act with the same freedom they have outside the school, then it might be better not to teach them drama at all. The most repressed, and damaged, and 'unteachable' students that I have to deal with are those who were the star performers at bad high schools. Instead of learning how to be warm and spontaneous and giving, they've become armoured and superficial, calculating and self-obsessed. I could show you many many examples where education has clearly been a destructive process.

My feeling isn't that the group should be 'obscene', but that they should be aware of the ideas that are occurring to them. I don't want them to go rigid and blank out, but to laugh, and say 'I'm not saying that' or whatever.

Originality

Many students block their imaginations because they're afraid of being unoriginal. They believe they know exactly what originality is, just as critics are always sure they can recognise things that are avant-garde.

We have a concept of originality based on things that already exist. I'm told that avant-garde theatre groups in Japan are just like those in the West—well of course, or how would we know what they were? Anyone can run an avant-garde theatre group; you just get the actors to lie naked in heaps or outstare the audience, or move in extreme slow motion, or whatever the fashion is. But the real avant-garde aren't imitating what other people are doing, or what they did forty years ago; they're solving the problems that *need* solving, like how to get a popular theatre with some worth-while content, and they may not look avant-garde at all!

The improviser has to realise that the more obvious he is, the more original he appears. I constantly point out how much the audience like someone who is direct, and how they always laugh with pleasure at a really 'obvious' idea. Ordinary people asked to improvise will search for some 'original' idea because they want to be *thought* clever. They'll say and do all sorts of inappropriate things. If someone says

'What's for supper?' a bad improviser will desperately try to think up something original. Whatever he says he'll be too slow. He'll finally drag up some idea like 'fried mermaid'. If he'd just said 'fish' the audience would have been delighted. No two people are exactly alike, and the more obvious an improviser is, the more himself he appears. If he wants to impress us with his originality, then he'll search out ideas that are actually commoner and less interesting. I gave up asking London audiences to suggest where scenes should take place. Some idiot would always shout out either 'Leicester Square public lavatories' or 'outside Buckingham Palace' (never '*inside* Buckingham Palace'). People trying to be original always arrive at the same boring old answers. Ask people to give you an original idea and see the chaos it throws them into. If they said the first thing that came into their head, there'd be no problem.

An artist who is inspired is being *obvious*. He's not making any decisions, he's not weighing one idea against another. He's accepting his first thoughts. How else could Dostoyevsky have dictated one novel in the morning and one in the afternoon for three weeks in order to fulfil his contracts? If you consider the volume of work produced by Bach then you get some idea of his fluency (and we've lost half of it), yet a lot of his time was spent rehearsing, and teaching Latin to the choirboys. According to Louis Schlosser, Beethoven said: 'You ask me where I get my ideas? That I can't say with any certainty. They come unbidden, directly, I could grasp them with my hands.' Mozart said of his ideas: '*Whence* and *how* they come, I know not; nor can I force them. Those that please me I retain in the memory, and I am accustomed, as I have been told, to hum them.' Later in the same letter he says: 'Why my productions take from my hand that particular form and style that makes them *Mozartish,* and different from the works of other composers, is probably owing to the same cause which renders my nose so large or so aquiline, or in short, makes it Mozart's, and different from those of other people. For I really do not study or aim at any originality.'

Suppose Mozart *had* tried to be original? It would have been like a man at the North Pole trying to walk north, and this is true of all the rest of us. Striving after originality takes you far away from your true self, and makes your work mediocre.

4

Let's see how these theories work out in practice. Suppose I say to a student, 'Imagine a box. What's in it?' Answers will flash into his mind uninvited. Perhaps:

'Uncle Ted, dead.'

If he said this then people would laugh, and he'd seem good-natured and witty, but he doesn't want to be thought 'insane', or callous. 'Hundreds of toilet rolls', says his imagination, but he doesn't want to appear preoccupied with excretion. 'A big, fat, coiled snake'? No—too Freudian. Finally after a pause of perhaps two whole seconds he says 'Old clothes' or 'It's empty', and feels unimaginative and defeated.

I say to a student, 'Name some objects.'

He tenses up. 'Er . . . pebble . . . er . . . beach . . . cliff . . . er . . . er . . .'

'Have you any idea why you've blocked?' I ask.

'I keep thinking of "pebble".'

'Then say it. Say whatever occurs to you. It doesn't have to be original.' Actually it would be very original to keep saying the same word: 'Pebble. Another pebble. A big pebble. A pebble with a hole in it. A pebble with a white mark. The pebble with a hole in it again.'

'Say a word', I say to someone else.

'Er . . . er . . . cabbage,' he says looking alarmed.

'That's not the word you first thought of.'

'What?'

'I saw your lips move. They formed an "O" shape.'

'Orange.'

'What's wrong with the word orange?'

'Cabbage seemed more ordinary.'

This student wants to appear *un*imaginative. What sort of crippling experiences must he have gone through before he came to me?

'What's the opposite of "starfish"? '

He gapes.

'Answer, say it,' I shout, because I can see that he did think of something.

'Sunflower,' he says, amazed because he didn't know that was the idea that was about to come out of him.

A student mimes taking something off a shelf.

'What is it?' I ask.

'A book.'

'I saw your hand reject an earlier shape. What did you want to take?'

'A tin of sardines.'

'Why didn't you?'

'I don't know.'

'Was it open?'

'Yes.'

'All messy?'

'Yes.'

'Maybe you were opting for a pleasanter object. Mime taking something else off a shelf.'

His mind goes blank.

'I can't seem to think of anything.'

'Do you know why?'

'I keep thinking of the sardines.'

'Why don't you take down another tin of sardines?'

'I wanted to be original.'

I ask a girl to say a word. She hesitates and says 'Pig.'

'What was the first word you thought of?'

'Pea.'

'Tell me a colour.'

Again she hesitates.

'Red.'

'What colour did you think of first?'

'Pink.'

'Invent a name for a stone.'

'Ground.'

'What was the name you first thought of?'

'Pebble.'

Normally the mind doesn't know that it's rejecting the first answers because they don't go into the long-term memory. If I didn't ask her immediately, she'd deny that she was substituting better words.

'Why don't you tell me the first answers that occur to you?'

'They weren't significant.'

I suggest to her that she didn't say 'Pea' because it suggested urination, that maybe she rejects pink because it reminds her of flesh. She agrees, and then says that she rejected 'Pebble' because she didn't want to say three words beginning with 'P'. This girl isn't really slow, she doesn't *need* to hesitate. Teaching her to accept the first idea will make her seem far more inventive.

The first time I meet a group I might ask them to mime taking a hat off, or to mime taking something off a shelf, or out of their pocket. I won't watch them while they do it; I'll probably look out of the window. Afterwards I explain that I'm not interested in what they did, but in how their minds worked. I say that either they can put their hand out, and see what it closes on; or else they can think first, decide what they'll pick up, and then do the mime. If they're worried about failing, then they'll *have* to think first; if they're being playful, then they can allow their hand to make its own decision.

Suppose I decide to pick up something. I can put my hand down and pick up something dangly. It's an old, used rubber contraceptive, which isn't something I would have chosen to pick up, but it is what my hand 'decided' to close on. My hand is very likely to pick up something I don't want, like a steaming horse-turd, but the audience will be delighted. They don't want me to think up something respectable to mime, like a bucket or a suitcase. I ask the class to try doing the mime both with and without 'thinking' so that they can sense the difference. If I make people produce object after object, then very likely they'll stop bothering to think first, and just swing along being mildly interested in what their hands select. Here's a sequence that was filmed, so I remember it pretty well. I said:

'Put your hand into an imaginary box. What do you take out?'
'A cricket ball.'
'Take something else out.'
'Another cricket ball.'
'Unscrew it. What's inside?'
'A medallion.'
'What's written on it?'
' "Christmas 1948." '
'Put both hands in. What have you got?'
'A box.'
'What's written on it?'
' "Export only." '
'Open it and take something out.'
'A pair of rubber corsets.'
'Put your hands in the far corners of the box. What have you got?'
'Two lobsters.'
'Leave them. Take out a handful of something.'
'Dust.'
'Feel about in it.'
'A pearl.'
'Taste it. What's it taste of?'
'Pear drops.'

'Take something off a shelf.'

'A shoe.'

'What size?'

'Eleven.'

'Reach for something behind you.'

He laughs.

'What is it?'

'A breast . . .'

Notice that I'm helping him to fantasise by continually changing the 'set' (i.e. the category) of the questions.

5

There are people who prefer to say 'Yes', and there are people who prefer to say 'No'. Those who say 'Yes' are rewarded by the adventures they have, and those who say 'No' are rewarded by the safety they attain. There are far more 'No' sayers around than 'Yes' sayers, but you can train one type to behave like the other.[3]

'Your name Smith?'

'No.'

'Oh . . . are you Brown, then?'

'Sorry.'

'Well, have you seen either of them?'

'I'm afraid not.'

Whatever the questioner had in mind has now been demolished and he feels fed up. The actors are in total conflict.

Had the answer been 'Yes', then the feeling would have been completely different.

'Your name Smith?'

'Yes.'

'You're the one who's been mucking about with my wife then?'

'Very probably.'

'Take that, you swine.'

'Augh!'

Fred Karno understood this. When he interviewed aspiring actors he'd poke his pen into an empty inkwell and pretend to flick ink at them. If they mimed being hit in the eye, or whatever, he'd engage them. If they looked baffled, and 'blocked' him, then he wouldn't.

There is a link with status transactions here, since low-status players tend to accept, and high-status players to block. High-status players will block any action unless they feel they can control it. The high-status player is obviously afraid of being humiliated in front of an audience, but to block your partner's ideas is to be like the drowning man who drags down his rescuer. There's no reason why you can't play high status, and yet yield to other people's invention.

'Is your name Smith?'

'And what if it is?'

'You've been making indecent suggestions to my wife.'

'I don't consider them indecent!'

Many teachers get improvisers to work in conflict because conflict is interesting but we don't actually need to teach competitive behaviour; the students will already be expert at it, and it's important that we don't exploit the *actors'* conflicts. Even in what seems to be a tremendous argument, the actors should still be *co-operating*, and coolly developing the action. The improviser has to understand that his first skill lies in releasing his partner's imagination. What happens in my classes, if the actors stay with me long enough, is that they learn how their 'normal' procedures destroy other people's talent. Then, one day they have a flash of *satori*—they suddenly understand that all the weapons they were using against other people they also use inwardly, against themselves.

'Working' Someone

Bill Gaskill used to make one actor responsible for the content and development of the scene, while his partner just 'assisted'.

'Have you got it?'

'Here it is, Sir.'

'Well, unwrap it.'

'Here you are, Sir.'

'Well, help me put it on.'

'There, Sir. I think it's a good fit.'

'And the helmet.'

'How's that, Sir?'

'Excellent. Now close the faceplate and start pumping. I shall give give three tugs on the rope when I find the wreck. Can't be more than twenty fathoms.'

If you concentrate on the task of involving your assistant in some action, then a scene evolves automatically. In my view the game is most elegant when the audience have no idea that one actor is working the other.

'Good morning.'

'Good morning.'

'Yes . . . shall I sit here?'

'Oh, yes, Sir.'

The first actor sits at a slant in the chair and opens his mouth. The second actor 'catches on' and mimes pumping the chair higher, like a dentist.

'Having some trouble, Sir?'

'Yes. It's one of these molars.'

'Hmm. Let's see now. Upper two occlusal . . .'

'Aaaauuuggghh!'

'My goodness, that is sensitive.'

The trick is not to think of getting the assistant to do things, but of ways of getting each other into trouble.

'The regular dentist is on holiday, is he?'

'Yes, Sir.'

'I must say, you seem rather young.'

'Just out of dental school, Sir.'

'Will you have to extract it? I mean, is it urgent?'

'I'll say it's urgent, Sir. Another day or so and that would have exploded.'

The audience will be convinced that it's the dentist who is controlling the scene. When improvisers are anxious, each person tries to 'carry' the whole scene by himself. Putting the responsibility all on to one person helps them work more calmly.[4]

Blocking and Accepting

Blocking is a form of aggression. I say this because if I set up a scene in which two students are to say 'I love you' to each other, they almost always accept each other's ideas. Many students do their first interesting, unforced improvisations during 'I love you' scenes.

If I say 'start something' to two inexperienced improvisers, they'll probably talk, because speech feels safer than action. And they'll block any possibility of action developing.

'Hallo, how are you.'

'Oh, same as usual. Nice day, isn't it.'

'Oh I don't think so.'

If one actor yawns his partner will probably say 'I do feel fit today.' Each actor tends to resist the invention of the other actor, playing for time, until he can think up a 'good' idea, and then he'll try to make his partner follow it. The motto of scared improvisers is 'when in doubt, say "NO".' We use this in life as a way of blocking action.

Then we go to the theatre, and at all points where we would say 'No' in life, we want to see the actors yield, and say 'Yes'. Then the action we would suppress if it happened in life begins to develop on the stage.

If you'll stop reading for a moment and think of something you wouldn't want to happen to you, or to someone you love, then you'll have thought of something worth staging or filming. We don't want to walk into a restaurant and be hit in the face by a custard pie, and we don't want to suddenly glimpse Grannie's wheelchair racing towards the edge of the cliff, but we'll pay money to attend enactments of such events. In life, most of us are highly skilled at suppressing action. All the improvisation teacher has to do is to reverse this skill and he creates very 'gifted' improvisers. Bad improvisers block action, often with a high degree of skill. Good improvisers develop action:

'Sit down, Smith.'
'Thank you, Sir.'
'It's about the wife, Smith.'
'She told you about it has she, Sir?'
'Yes, yes, she's made a clean breast of it.'

Neither actor is quite sure what the scene is about but he's willing to play along, and see what emerges.

At first students don't realise when they're blocking or yielding, and they're not very good at recognising when it's happening with other students. Some students prefer to yield (these are 'charming' people) but most prefer to block, even though they may have no idea exactly what they are doing. I often stop an improvisation to explain how the blocking is preventing the action from developing. Videotape is a great help: you replay the transaction, and it's obvious to everyone.

A: Augh!
B: What's the matter?
A: I've got my trousers on back to front.
B: I'll take them off.
A: No!

The scene immediately fizzles out. A blocked because he didn't want to get involved in miming having his trousers taken off, and having to pretend embarrassment, so he preferred to disappoint the audience.

I ask them to start a similar scene, and to avoid blocking if possible.

A: Augh!
B: (*Holding him*) Steady!
A: My back hurts.
B: No, it doesn't . . . Yes, you're right.

B has noticed his error in blocking, which resulted from his wishing to stick to the trouser idea. A then blocks his own idea by shifting to another.

> A: I'm having trouble with my leg.
> B: I'm afraid I'll have to amputate.
> A: You can't do that, Doctor.
> B: Why not?
> A: Because I'm rather attached to it.
> B: (*Losing heart*) Come, man.
> A: I've got this growth on my arm too, Doctor.

During this scene B gets increasingly fed up. Both actors experience the other as rather difficult to work with. They can say 'The scene isn't working', but they still don't consciously realise why. I've written down the dialogue while they were playing the scene, and I go through it, and explain exactly how they were interacting, and why B was looking more and more depressed.

I get them to start the scene again, and this time they've understood.

> A: Augh!
> B: Whatever is it, man?
> A: It's my leg, Doctor.
> B: This looks nasty. I shall have to amputate.
> A: It's the one you amputated last time, Doctor.

(This is not a block because he's accepted the amputation.)

> B: You mean you've got a pain in your wooden leg?
> A: Yes, Doctor.
> B: You know what this means?
> A: Not woodworm, Doctor!
> B: Yes. We'll have to remove it before it spreads to the rest of you.
>   (*A's chair collapses.*)
> B: My God! It's spreading to the furniture! (And so on.)

The interest to the audience lies in their admiration and delight in the actors' attitude to each other. We so seldom see people working together with such joy and precision.

Here's another scene I noted down.

> A: Is your name Smith?
> B: Yes.
> A: I've brought the . . . car.

I interrupt and ask him why he hesitated. A says he doesn't know, so I ask him what he was going to say. He says 'Elephant'.

'You didn't want to say "elephant" because there was one mentioned in the last scene.'

'That's right.'

'Stop trying to be original.'

I make them restart the scene.

> A: I've brought the elephant.
>
> B: For the gelding?
>
> A: (*Loudly*) No!

The audience groan and cry out with disappointment. They were enthralled with the possibilities latent in a scene about gelding an elephant, the elephant suddenly fizzing down to nothing at the first cut, or cutting the trunk off by mistake, or a severed penis chasing the actors about the room. But of course this is why A felt impelled to block. He didn't want to be involved in anything so obscene or psychotic. He resisted the very thing that the audience longed to see.

I call anything that an actor does an 'offer'. Each offer can either be accepted, or blocked. If you yawn, your partner can yawn too, and therefore *accept* your offer.

A block is anything that prevents the action from developing, or that wipes out your partner's premise.[5] If it develops the action it isn't a block. For example:

'Your name Smith?'

'What if it is, you horrible little man!'

This is not a block, even though the answer is antagonistic. Again:

'I've had enough of your incompetence, Perkins! Please leave.'

'No, Sir!'

This isn't a block either. The second speaker has accepted that he's a servant, and he accepts the situation, one of annoyance between himself and his employer.

If a scene were to start with someone saying 'Unhand me, Sir Jasper, let me go', and her partner said 'All right, do what you like, then', this is probably a block. It would get a laugh but it would create bad feeling.

Once you have established the categories of 'offer', 'block' and 'accept' you can give some very interesting instructions. For example, you can ask an actor to make *dull* offers, or *interesting* offers, or to '*overaccept*', or to '*accept and block*' and so on.

You can programme two actors so that A offers and accepts, and B offers and blocks.

> A: Hallo, are you a new member?
>
> B: No, I've come to fix the pipes. You got a leak somewhere?

> A: Yes, oh, thank goodness. There's three feet of water in the basement.
>
> B: Basement? You ain't got a basement.
>
> A: No, well, er, the boiler-room. It's just down a few steps. You've not brought your tools.
>
> B: Yes I have. I'm miming them.
>
> A: Oh, silly of me. I'll leave you to it then.
>
> B: Oh no. I need an assistant. Hand me that pipe wrench. (And so on.)

Sometimes both actors can block as well as offer. Bad improvisers do this all the time, of course, but when you *tell* people to block each other their morale doesn't collapse so easily. This again suggests to me that blocking is aggressive. If the order comes from me, the actors don't take it personally.

> A: Are you nervous?
>
> B: Not at all. I can see that *you* are.
>
> A: Nonsense. I'm just warming my fingers up. You're taking the piano exam, are you?
>
> B: I'm here for my flying lesson.
>
> A: In a bathing costume?
>
> B: I always wear a bathing costume.
>
> Me: You've accepted the bathing costume.
>
> (*laughter*.)

An *interesting* offer can be 'The house is on fire!', or 'My heart! Quick, my pills!' but it can also be something non-specific. 'All right, where's the parcel?' or 'Shall I sit here, Doctor?' are interesting offers, because we want to know what will happen next. Even 'All right, begin' is OK. Your partner can beat you on the head with a balloon, and you thank him, and the audience are delighted.

Here's an example in which A makes dull offers, while B makes interesting offers.

> A: (Dull offer.) Good morning!
>
> B: (Accepts.) Good morning. (Makes interesting offer.) Great heavens! Frank! Did they let you out? Have you escaped?
>
> A: (Accepts.) I hid in the laundry van. (Makes dull offer.) I see you've had the place redecorated.
>
> B: (Accepts, makes interesting offer.) Yes ... but ... look ... about the money. You'll get your share. It wasn't my idea to cut you out. I've ... I've got a good business here ...

A: (Accepts, makes dull offer.) Yes, it's a step up in
the world.

B: (Accepts, makes interesting offer.) It was different
in the old days ... I ... I didn't mean to rat on
you Charlie ...

The actors have automatically become involved in some sort of
gangster scene, but all they actually worry about is the category the
offers fit into. The scene 'looks after itself'.

Scenes spontaneously generate themselves if both actors offer and
accept alternately.

'Haven't we met before?'

'Yes, wasn't it at the yacht club?'

'I'm not a member.'

(Accepts the yacht club. A bad improviser would say 'what yacht
club?')

'Ah, I'm sorry.'

'School!'

'That's right. I was in the first form and you were one of the school
leavers.'

'Pomeroy!'

'Snodgrass!'

'After all these years!'

'What do you mean, after all these years? It seems only yesterday
that you were beating me up every lunchtime.'

'Oh well ... boys will be boys. Was it you we held out of the
windows by your feet?'

'Butterfingers.'

'I see you're still wearing the brace.'

Good improvisers seem telepathic; everything looks prearranged.
This is because they accept all offers made—which is something no
'normal' person would do. Also they may accept offers which weren't
really intended. I tell my actors never to think up an offer, but instead
to assume that one has already been made. Groucho Marx understood
this: a contestant at his quiz game 'froze' so he took the man's pulse
and said, 'Either this man's dead or my watch has stopped.' If you
notice that you are shorter than your partner you can say 'Simpkins!
Didn't I forbid you ever to be taller than me?'—which can lead on to
a scene in which the servant plays on all fours, or a scene in which the
master is starting to shrink, or a scene in which the servant has been
replaced by his elder brother, or whatever. If your partner is sweating,
fan yourself. If he yawns, say 'Late, isn't it?'

Once you learn to accept offers, then accidents can no longer interrupt the action. When someone's chair collapsed Stanislavsky berated him for not continuing, for not apologising to the character whose house he was in. This attitude makes for something really amazing in the theatre. The actor who will accept anything that happens seems supernatural; it's the most marvellous thing about improvisation: you are suddenly in contact with people who are unbounded, whose imagination seems to function without limit.

By analysing everything into blocks and acceptances, the students get insight into the forces that shape the scenes, and they understand why certain people seem difficult to work with.

These 'offer-block-accept' games have a use quite apart from actor training. People with dull lives often think that their lives are dull by chance. In reality everyone chooses more or less what kind of events will happen to them by their conscious patterns of blocking and yielding. A student objected to this view by saying, 'But you don't choose your life. Sometimes you are at the mercy of people who push you around.' I said, 'Do you avoid such people?' 'Oh!' she said, 'I see what you mean.'

6

Here are some games I've used with my students.

'Two Places'

You can play very funny scenes in which one character plays, for example, waiting at a bus stop, while another character claims that the stage is his living-room, and so on. Such scenes exploit blocking very successfully. (This game comes from the Royal Court Writers' Group, circa 1959.)

'Presents'

I invented a rather childish game, which is now often used with small children, but works really well with grown-ups, if you coax them through their initial resistance.

I divide people into pairs and call them A and B. A gives a present to B who receives it. B then gives a present back, and so on. At first each person thinks of giving an interesting present, but then I stop them and suggest that they can just hold their hands out, and see what the other person chooses to take. If you hold out both hands about three feet apart, then obviously it will be a larger present, but you don't have to determine what your gift is. The trick is to make the thing you are *given* as interesting as possible. You want to 'overaccept' the offer. Everything you are given delights you. Maybe you wind it up and let it walk about the floor, or you sit it on your arm and let it fly off after a small bird, or maybe you put it on and turn into a gorilla.

An important change of thinking is involved here. When the actor concentrates on making the thing he *gives* interesting, each actor seems in competition, and feels it. When they concentrate on making the gift they *receive* interesting, then they generate warmth between them. We have strong resistances to being overwhelmed by gifts, even when they're just being mimed. You have to get the class enthusiastic enough to go over the 'hump'. Then suddenly great joy and energy are released. Playing in gibberish helps.

'Blind Offers'

An inexperienced improviser gets annoyed because his partners misunderstand him. He holds out his hand to see if it's raining, and his partner shakes it and says 'Pleased to meet you.' 'What an idiot', thinks the first actor, and begins to sulk. When you make a blind offer, you have no intention to communicate at all. Your partner accepts the offer, and you say 'Thank you.' Then *he* makes an intentionless gesture, and you accept that, and *he* says 'Thank you' and so on.

A strikes a pose.
B photographs him.
A says 'Thank you.'
B stands on one leg, and bends the other.
A straddles the bent leg and 'nails a horseshoe on it'.
B thanks him and lies on the ground.
A mimes shovelling earth over him.
B thanks him . . . And so on.

Don't underestimate the value of this game. It's a way of interacting that the audience love to see. They will watch fascinated, and every time someone says 'Thank you', they laugh!

It's best to offer a gesture which moves away from the body. When you've made a gesture, you then freeze in the position until your partner reacts.

Once the basic technique has been mastered, the next step is to get the actors to play the game while discussing some quite different subject.

'A touch of autumn in the air today, James,' says A, stretching his hand out. 'Yes, it is a little brisk,' says B, peeling a glove off A's hand. B then lies on the floor. 'Is the Mistress at home?' says A, wiping his feet on B . . . and so on. The effect is startling, because each actor seems to have a telepathic understanding of the other's intentions.

'It's Tuesday'

This game is based on 'overaccepting'. We called it 'It's Tuesday' because that's how we started the game. If A says something matter of fact to B, like 'It's Tuesday', then maybe B tears his hair, and says 'My God! The Bishop's coming. What'll he do when he sees the state everything's in?' or instead of being upset he can be overcome with love because it's his wedding day. All that matters is that an inconsequential remark should produce the maximum possible effect on the person it's said to.

> A: It's Tuesday.
>
> B: No . . . it can't be . . . It's the day predicted for my
> death by the old gypsy!

(It doesn't matter how crummy the idea is, what matters is the intensity of the reaction.) Now B turns white, clutches his throat, staggers into the audience, reels back, bangs his head on the wall, somersaults backwards, and 'dies' making horrible noises, and saying at his last gasp:

> B: Feed the goldfish.

A now plays 'It's Tuesday' on the goldfish remark. Maybe he expresses extreme jealousy:

> A: That's all he ever thought about, that goldfish.
> What am I to do now? Haven't I served him
> faithfully all these years? (*Weeps on knee of
> audience member.*) He's always preferred that
> goldfish to me. Do forgive me, Madam. Does . . .
> does anyone have a Kleenex? Fifty years' supply of
> ants' eggs, and what did he leave to me—not a
> penny. (*Throws spectacular temper tantrum.*) I shall
> write to Mother.

This last remark introduces new material, so that B now plays 'It's Tuesday' on that.

> B: (*Recovering*) Your mother! You mean Milly is still
> alive?

He then plays passionate yearning, until he can't take the emotion any further and throws in another 'ordinary' remark. Any remark will do. 'Forgive me Jenkins, I got rather carried away.' Maybe Jenkins can then do a five-minute 'hate' tirade: 'Forgive you? After the way you hounded her? Turning her out into the snow that Christmas Eve . . .' and so on.

Three or four sentences can easily last ten minutes, when expanded a little, and the audience are astounded and delighted. They don't expect improvisers, or actors for that matter, to take things to such extremes.

I would classify 'It's Tuesday' as a 'make boring offers, and overaccept' game.

'Yes, But . . .'

This is a well known 'accept-and-block' game (described in Viola Spolin, *Improvisation for the Theatre*). (Its twin game 'Yes, and . . .' is an 'accept-and-offer' game.) I'll describe it because there are two ways of playing which produce opposite results, and which tell one a lot about the nature of spontaneity.

A asks questions that B can say 'Yes' to. B then says 'But . . .' and then whatever occurs to him. To play the game badly, B should think of his reply *before* he begins to speak.

'Excuse me, is that your dog?'
'Yes, but I'm thinking of selling him.'
'Will you sell him to me?'
'Yes, but he's expensive.'
'Is he healthy?'
'Yes, but you can take him to a vet to check him out if you like.' (And so on.)
Probably the audience do not laugh, and probably the actors don't enjoy the experience much. This is because the more logical, rational part of the mind is in control.

If you reply 'Yes, but . . .' with enthusiasm, as soon as the question is put to you, and then say whatever comes into your head, the scenes are quite different. I'll play it with myself now, typing as quickly as possible.

'Don't I know you?'
'Yes, but I'm going.'
'You took my money!'
'Yes, but I've spent it.'
'You're a swine.'
'Yes, but everyone knows that.'
This time an audience would probably laugh. It's worth teaching both ways of playing the game. It can demonstrate to uptight people

exactly how cautious they usually are. Also it's very funny to launch
out strongly on 'Yes, but . . .', and then *have* to complete the sentence
off the top of your head.

Verse

If the students are in a really happy mood, I might
ask them to improvise in verse. At first they're appalled. I'll already
have made them play scenes in gibberish, and as impromptu operas,
but they'll have been turned off verse by school, while at the same time
retaining an exaggerated respect for it.

To me the most enjoyable thing about verse is its spontaneity. You
can 'fake up' verse by deciding what to write, and then thinking up
the rhymes, but if you're asked to improvise it you just have to abandon conscious control, and let the words come of their own accord.

I start to talk in verse, and explain that it doesn't matter whether
the verse is good or bad, and that anyway we're going to start with
the worst possible verse:

> 'Tom and Else take your places,
> A happy smile on your faces,
> Don't start wondering what to say
> Or we will never start today!
> We'll have Tom come in and propose
> 'Cause Else's pregnant, I suppose . . .'

The worse the verse I speak, the more encouraged the actors are.
I get them to stop thinking ahead, and just say a line, and trust to luck
that there'll be something to rhyme with it. If they're in trouble and
can't think what to say, they're not to rack their brain, and try and
force their inspiration. I get them to say 'prompt' and then either I
shout something out, or one of the audience does.

Once a scene starts, the verse has to control the content and the
action. Someone says:

> 'At last I've got you in my clutches:
> I'll keep you here and take your crutches.'

He won't make any attempt to mime taking crutches away from his
partner though, until I yell 'Take the crutches!' Then his partner
falls over and says:

> 'Oh, please Sir Jasper, let me go!
> You must not treat a cripple so . . .'
> 'Oh no! I'll not be robbed of my revenge!
> I'll sacrifice you here in old Stonehenge.'

He makes no attempt to sacrifice her, I have to tell him:

'Do it—it's what you said!
Everyone wants to see her dead.'
'Lie down on yonder block and pray . . . prompt?'
'I'll kill her at the break of day . . .' suggests someone in the audience.

No one in their right senses would think up a scene about sacrificing a cripple at Stonehenge, but the verse precipitates it. My job is to get the actors to go where the verse takes them. If you don't care what you say, and you go with the verse, the exercise is exhilarating. But if an actor suddenly produces a really witty couplet, you'll see him suddenly 'dry' as his standard rises, and he tries to produce 'better' verse.

7

Reading about spontaneity won't make you more spontaneous, but it may at least stop you heading off in the opposite direction; and if you play the exercises with your friends in a good spirit, then soon all your thinking will be transformed. Rousseau began an essay on education by saying that if we did the opposite of what our own teachers did we'd be on the right track, and this still holds good.

The stages I try to take students through involve the realisation (1) that we struggle against our imaginations, especially when we *try* to be imaginative; (2) that we are not responsible for the content of our imaginations; and (3) that we are not, as we are taught to think, our 'personalities', but that the imagination is our true self.

NOTES
1. I don't know who originated the rubber glove gag, but in his book *King of Comedy* (Peter Davies, 1955) Mack Sennett attributes it to Felix Adler.
2. Teachers are obliged to impose a censorship on their pupils, and in consequence schools provide an anti-therapeutic environment. In *Interacting with Patients* (Macmillan, New York, 1963), a work intended for nurses, Joyce Samhammer Hays and Kenneth Larson describe therapeutic and non-therapeutic ways of interacting. Here are their first ten 'therapeutic techniques'.

Therapeutic techniques	*Examples*
Using silence:	
Accepting:	Yes.
	Uh Hmm.
	I follow what you said.
	Nodding.

Giving recognition:	Good morning, Mr S.
	You've tooled a leather wallet.
	I notice that you've combed your hair.
Offering self:	I'll sit with you a while.
	I'll stay here with you.
	I'm interested in your comfort.
Giving broad openings:	Is there something you'd like to talk about?
	What are you thinking about?
	Where would you like to begin?
Offering general leads:	Go on.
	And then?
	Tell me about it.
Placing the event in time or in sequence:	What seemed to lead up to . . .?
	Was this before or after . . .?
	When did this happen?
Making observations:	You appear tense.
	Are you uncomfortable when you . . .
	I notice you are biting your lips.
	It makes me uncomfortable when you . . .
Encouraging description of perceptions:	Tell me when you feel anxious.
	What is happening?
	What does the voice seem to be saying?
Encouraging comparison:	Was this something like . . .?
	Have you had similar experiences?

Obviously the book has psychiatric nurses in mind, but it's interesting to compare it to teacher–pupil interactions. Here are the first ten 'non-therapeutic techniques'.

Non-therapeutic techniques	*Examples*
Reassuring:	I wouldn't worry about . . .
	Everything will be all right.
	You're coming along fine.
Giving approval:	That's good.
	I'm glad that you . . .
Rejecting:	Let's not discuss . . .
	I don't want to hear about . . .
Disapproving:	That's bad.
	I'd rather you wouldn't . . .
Agreeing:	That's right.
	I agree.
Disagreeing:	That's wrong.
	I definitely disagree with . . .
	I don't believe that.
Advising:	I think you should . . .
	Why don't you . . .?
Probing:	Now tell me about . . .
	Tell me your life history.

Challenging:	But how can you be President of the United States?
	If you're dead, why is your heart beating?
Testing:	What day is this?
	Do you know what kind of a hospital this is?
	Do you still have the idea that . . .?

I'm doing the book an injustice by quoting out of context, but it's widely available, and it analyses many interactions. Schools make it difficult for teachers to interact therapeutically. Thinking back to my own schooling, I remember how isolated the teachers were, how there were only certain areas in which you could communicate with them at all. If teachers were allowed to interact in a therapeutic manner, then the adjective 'school-teachery' would not be disparaging.

3. When I meet a new group of students they will usually be 'naysayers'. This term and its opposite, 'yeasayers', come from a paper by Arthur Couch and Kenneth Kenison, who were investigating the tendency of people answering questionnaires to be generally affirmative, or generally negative in attitude. They wrote in Freudian terms:

'We have arrived at a fairly consistent picture of the variables that differentiate yeasayers from naysayers. Yeasayers seem to be "id-dominated" personalities, with little concern about or positive evaluation of an integrated control of their impulses. They say they express themselves freely and quickly. Their "psychological inertia" is very low, that is, very few secondary processes intervene as a screen between underlying wish and overt behavioural response. The yeasayers desire and actively search for emotional excitement in their environment. Novelty, movement, change, adventure—these provide the external stimuli for their emotionalism. They see the world as a stage where the main theme is 'acting out' libidinal desires. In the same way, they seek and respond quickly to internal stimuli: their inner impulses are allowed ready expression . . . the yeasayer's general attitude is one of *stimulus acceptance,* by which we mean a pervasive readiness to respond affirmatively or yield willingly to both outer and inner forces demanding expression.

'The "disagreeing" naysayers have the opposite orientation. For them, impulses are seen as forces requiring control, and perhaps in some sense as threats to general personality stability. The naysayer wants to maintain inner equilibrium; his secondary processes are extremely impulsive and value maintaining forces. We might describe this as a state of high psychological inertia—impulses undergo a series of delays, censorships, and transformations before they are permitted expression. Both internal and external stimuli that demand response are carefully scrutinised and evaluated: these forces appear as unwelcome intruders into a subjective world of "classical" balance. Thus, as opposed to the yeasayers, the naysayers' general attitude is one of *stimulus rejection—* a pervasive unwillingness to respond to impulsive or environmental forces.' ('Yeasayers and Naysayers', *Journal of Abnormal and Social Psychology,* Vol. 160, No. 2, 1960.)

4. My impro group used to set up a 'say "Yes" ' game using a tape

recorder. We would record a one-sided dialogue, and then play the tape during a show, and get an actor who did not know what was on the tape to improvise with it. It means you have to accept the tape or fail totally, since the tape can't adapt to you. One tape ran like this:

'Hallo. (*Pause.*) No, no, me, I'm down here. On the footpath. (*Pause.*) I'm an ant. (*Pause.*) Pick me up, will you? (*Pause.*) Go careful. (*Pause.*) We want to surrender. (*Pause.*) We're fed up with being stepped on, bloody great things. Dictate your terms. (*Pause.*) Excuse me interrupting. Can you see what I'm holding? (*Pause.*) Hold me up to your eye. (*Pause*). Closer. (*Pause.*) Now. Pick up Willy. Put your hand down and he'll climb on. Feel him. (*Pause.*) Put him on your shoulder. (*Pause.*) You may feel him climbing up into your ear. What's that Willy? He says there's a lot of wax here. (*Pause.*) Right now you may hear a sort of crinkling noise. (*Pause.*) That's Willy blowing up a paper bag. Any trouble from you and he'll burst it against your eardrum. (*Pause.*) (*Huge explosion.*) Do it again Willy, just to show him. (*Explosion. Pause.*) Well? What have you got to say, ant-murderer? (*Pause.*) We'll talk later. Get moving. Walk. Left, right, left, right . . .'

5. A Japanese text compares two actors who block each other to 'two mantids eating each other. They fight with each other; if one puts out a hand it is eaten off; if one puts out a leg, it is eaten off, so that it is natural that in the end they destroy each other.' (*The Actor's Analects,* translated by Charles J. Dunn and Bunzo Torigoe, Columbia University Press, 1969.)

A problem for the improviser is that the audience are likely to reward blocking at the moment it first appears.

'Your name Smith?'

'No!'

(*Laughter.*)

They laugh because they enjoy seeing the actors frustrated, just as they'll laugh if the actors start to joke. Jokey TV or radio programmes usually stop for a song, or some animation, every few minutes. The improviser, who is committed to performing for longer periods, gags or blocks at his peril, although the immediacy of the audience's laughter is likely to condition him to do just this. Once the performers have been lured into gagging or blocking, the audience is already on the way towards irritation and boredom. More than laughter they want *action*.

Narrative Skills

I

Playboy: *Knife in the Water* was an original, and unusual
screenplay. Where did you get the idea for it?

Polanski: It was the sum of several desires in me. I loved the
lake area in Poland and I thought it would make a
great setting for a film. I was thinking of a film with
a limited number of people in it as a form of
challenge. I hadn't ever seen a film with only three
characters, where no one else even appeared in the
background. The challenge was to make it in a way
that the audience wouldn't be aware of the fact that
no one else had appeared even in the background.
As for the idea, all I had in mind when I began the
script was a scene where two men were on a sailboat
and one fell overboard. But that was a starting-point,
wouldn't you agree?

Playboy: Certainly, but a strange one. Why were you thinking
about a man falling out of a sailboat?

Polanski: There you go, asking me how to shrink my head again.
I don't *know* why. I was interested in creating a mood,
an atmosphere, and after the film came out, a lot of
critics found all sorts of symbols and hidden
meanings in it that I hadn't even thought of. It
made me sick. (*Playboy,* December, 1971.)

I started my work on narrative by trying to make the improvisers
conscious of the implications of the scenes they played. I felt that an
artist ought to be 'committed', and that he should be held responsible for the effects of his work—it seemed only common sense. I got
my students to analyse the content of *Red Riding Hood* and *The
Sleeping Beauty* and *Moby Dick* and *The Birthday Party,* but this made
them even more inhibited. I didn't realise that if the people who
thought up *Red Riding Hood* had been aware of the implications, then
they might never have written the story. This was at a time when I
had no inspiration as a writer at all, but I didn't twig that the more I
tried to understand the 'real' meaning, the less I wrote. When Pinter

directs his own plays he may say 'We may assume that what the author intended here is . . .'—and this is a sensible attitude: the playwright is one person and the director another, even when they share the same skull.

When I ran the Royal Court's script department, I used to read about fifty plays a week, and many of them seemed to betray their author's conscious intention. At one time there was a glut of plays about homosexual lovers whose happiness, or even lives, are destroyed by the opposition of ignorant bigots. I didn't see these as pro-homosexual although I'm sure their authors did. If I wrote such a play my homosexuals would live happily ever after, just as my Goldilocks would end up living in a commune with the bears. Recent films in which the good lawman comes to grief when he tries to fight the system (*Walking Tall, Serpico*) have the moral 'Don't stick your neck out', but this may not be what their directors intend. In the old days the honest sheriff was triumphant; nowadays he's crippled, or dead. Content lies in the *structure*, in what happens, not in what the characters say.

Even at the level of geometrical signs 'meaning' is *ambiguous*. A cross, a circle, and a swastika contain a 'content' quite apart from those which we *assign* to them. The swastika is symmetrical but unbalanced: it's a good sign for power, it has a clawiness about it (cartoonists drew swastika spiders scrabbling over the face of Europe). The circle is stiller, is a much better sign for eternity, for completeness. The cross can stand for many things, for a meeting-place, for a crossroads, for a kiss, for a reed reflected in a lake, for a mast, for a sword—but it isn't meaningless just because the interpretations aren't one-for-one. Whatever a cross suggests to us it won't have the same associations as a circle, which makes a much better sign for a moon, for example, or for pregnancy. Moby Dick may be a symbol for the 'life-force', or for 'evil' and we can add anything it suggests to us, but the area of legitimate association is limited. There are things the white whale *doesn't* symbolise, as well as things it does, and once you start combining signs together in a narrative the whole thing becomes too complex. A story is as difficult to interpret as a dream, and the interpretation of a dream depends on who's doing the interpreting. When *King Lear* really gets going—the mad King, the man pretending to be mad, the fool paid to be mad, and the whole mass of overlapping and contradictory associations—what can the spectator sensibly do but be swept away on the flood, and *experience* the play, instead of trying to think what it 'means'.

My decision was that content should be ignored. This wasn't a conclusion I wished to reach, because it contradicted my political thinking. I hadn't realised that every play makes a political statement, and that the artist only needs to worry about content if he's trying to fake up a personality he doesn't actually have, or to express views he really isn't in accord with. I tell improvisers to follow the rules and see what happens, and not to feel in any way responsible for the material that emerges. If you improvise spontaneously in front of an audience you have to accept that your innermost self will be revealed. The same is true of any artist. If you want to write a 'working-class play' then you'd better *be* working class. If you want your play to be religious, then *be* religious. An artist has to accept what his imagination gives him, or screw up his talent.

Alex Comfort once filmed some of my work, and he seemed surprised when I told him that my students never attacked me physically. He'd been explaining that I was really operating as a therapist, that I was coaxing students into areas that would normally be 'forbidden', and that spontaneity means abandoning some of your defences.

I didn't have an answer at the time, except to say 'Well, they don't', but my refusal to attribute any importance to content may be the answer. If my students produce disturbing material I link it with ideas of my own, or with something someone else has produced, and I stop them feeling isolated or 'peculiar'. Whatever dredges up from their unconscious I'll accept, and treat as 'normal'. If I seized on the content of scenes as revealing secrets about the student, then I'd be perceived as a threat. They'd have to 'love' me, or 'hate' me. I'd have negative and positive transference states to contend with—which would be a hindrance.

Once you decide to ignore content it becomes possible to understand exactly what a narrative is, because you can concentrate on *structure*.

My dictionary says a story is 'a sequence of events that have, or are alleged to have happened, a series of events that are or might be narrated ... a person's account of his life or some portion of it ... a narrative of real or, more usually fictitious events, designed for the entertainment of the hearer . . .' and so on. Even a small child knows that a story isn't just a series of events, because he says 'And is that the end?' If we say 'A story is a series of events that might be narrated' then we beg the question, which is: 'Why do we narrate one series of events but not another?'

I had to decide what a story was, and present a theory that an improviser could use on the spur of the moment in any situation. Obviously, the 'seventeen basic plots' approach would be too limiting. I needed a way to handle anything that cropped up.

Suppose I make up a story about meeting a bear in the forest. It chases me until I come to a lake. I leap into a boat and row across to an island. On the island is a hut. In the hut is a beautiful girl spinning golden thread. I make passionate love to the girl . . .

I am now 'storytelling' but I haven't told a *story*. Everyone knows it isn't finished. I could continue forever in the same way: Next morning I am walking around the island when an eagle seizes me and carries me high into the sky. I land on a cloud and find a path leading to Heaven. To one side of the path I notice a lake with three swans. One of the swans suddenly disappears, and an old man stands in his place . . .

The trouble with such a sequence is that there's no place where it can stop, or rather, that it can stop *anywhere*; you are unconsciously waiting for another activity to start, not free association, but *re-incorporation*.

Let's begin the story again: I escape from a bear by rowing across to an island. Inside a hut on the island is a beautiful girl bathing in a wooden tub. I'm making passionate love to her when I happen to glance out of the window. If I now see the bear rowing across in a second boat, then there was some point in mentioning him in the first place. If the girl screams 'My lover!' and hides me under the bed, then this is better storytelling, since I've not only reintroduced the bear, but I've also linked him to the girl. The bear enters the hut, unzips his skin, and emerges as the grey old man who makes love to the girl. I creep out of the hut taking the skin with me so that he can't change back into a bear. I run down to the shore and row back to the mainland, towing the second boat behind me (reintroducing the boats). Then I see the old man paddling after me in the tub. He seems incredibly strong and there's no escape from him. I wait for him among the trees, and pull the bearskin around myself. I become a bear and tear him to pieces—thus I've reincorporated both the man and the skin. I row back to the island and find the girl has vanished. The hut has become very old and the roof is sagging in, and trees that were young saplings are now very tall. Then I try to remove the skin and I find it's sealed up around me.

At this point a child would probably say 'And is that the end?' because clearly some sort of pattern has been completed. Yet at no time have I thought about the *content* of the scene. I presume it's about sexual anxieties and fear of old age, or whatever. Had I 'known' this, then I wouldn't have constructed that particular story, but as usual the content has looked after itself, and anyway is only of interest to critics or psychologists. What matters to me is the ease with which I 'free-associate' and the skill with which I reincorporate.

Here's a 'good night' story made up by me and Dorcas (age six).

'What do you want a story about?' I asked.

'A little bird,' she said.

'That's right. And where did this little bird live?'

'With Mummy and Daddy bird.'

'Mummy and Daddy looked out of the nest one day and saw a man coming through the trees. What did he have in his hand?'

'An axe.'

'And he took the axe and started chopping down all the trees with a white mark on. So Daddy bird flew out of the nest, and do you know what he saw on the bark of his tree?'

'A white mark.'

'Which meant?'

'The man was going to cut down their tree.'

'So the birds all flew down to the river. Who did they meet?'

'Mr Elephant.'

'Yes. And Mr Elephant filled his trunk with water and washed the white mark away from the tree. And what did he do with the water left in his trunk?'

'He squirted it over the man.'

'That's right. And he chased the man right out of the forest and the man never came back.'

'And is that the end of the story?'

'It is.'

At the age of six she has a better understanding of storytelling than many university students. She links the man to the birds by giving him an axe. She links up the water left in the trunk with the wood-cutter, whom she remembers we'd shelved. She isn't concerned with content but any narrative will have some (about insecurity, I suppose).

I say to an actress, 'Make up a story.' She looks desperate, and says, 'I can't think of one.'

'Any story,' I say. 'Make up a silly one.'

'I can't,' she despairs.

'Suppose I think of one and you guess what it is.'

At once she relaxes, and it's obvious how very tense she was.

'I've thought of one,' I say, but I'll only answer "Yes", "No", or "Maybe".'

She likes this idea and agrees, having no idea that I'm planning to say 'Yes' to any question that ends in a vowel, 'No' to any question that ends in a consonant, and 'Maybe' to any question that ends with the letter 'Y'.

For example, should she ask me 'Is it about a horse?' I'll answer 'Yes' since 'hors*e*' ends in an 'E'.

'Does the horse have a bad le*g*?'

'No.'

'Does it run awa*y*?'

'Maybe . . .'

She can now invent a story easily, but she doesn't feel obliged to be 'creative', or 'sensitive' or whatever, because she believes the story is *my* invention. She no longer feels wary, and open to hostile criticism, as of course we all are in this culture whenever we do anything spontaneously. Her first question is:

'Has the story got any people in it?'

'No.'

'Has it got animals in it?'

'No.'

'Has it got buildings in it?'

'Yes.' (I'm having to drop my rule about consonants, or she'd get too discouraged.)

'Does the building have anything to do with the story?'

'Maybe.'

'Does it have aeroplanes in it?'

'No.'

'Fish?'

'No.'

'Insects?'

'Yes.'

'Do the insects play a large part in the story?'

'Maybe.'

'Do they live underground?'

'No.'

'Do they start out as harmless?'

'No.'

'Do the insects take over the world?'

'Yes.'

'Are they as big as elephants?'

'No.'

'Do they take any poison?'

'No!'

'Is it a gradual process, this taking over of the world?'

'No.'

'Were there many insects?'

'No.'

'Do the insects gain anything by destroying the world?'

'Yes.'

'Do they reign utterly alone?'

'Yes.'

'Do they destroy the world in a foul manner?'

'No.'

'Does the story begin with their existing?'

'No.'

'But there aren't any people in this bloody story. So it must start with the insects. Have the insects been reigning alone in the world for a long time?'

'Yes.'

'Do they live in the buildings that used to be the people's buildings?'

'Yes.'

'And then they suddenly decide to destroy the world?'

'Yes.'

'And they don't die. And when they eat everything in sight they become larger?'

'Yes.'

'And then they can't fit into the buildings again?'

'Yes.'

'And is that the end of the story?'

'It is.'

If she got more than two 'Nos' in a row I sometimes said 'Yes' to encourage her, and in the end I said 'yes' all the time because she was getting discouraged. We used to play this game at parties, and people who claim to be unimaginative would think up the most astounding stories, so long as they remained convinced that they weren't *responsible* for them. The great joke was to lure somebody into inventing a story about a midget dentist sexually assaulting Siamese twins, or whatever, wait until he accused you of having really perverted minds, and then explain triumphantly that he had created the story himself. Faubion Bowers once wrote an article on this game, in, I think, *Playboy*.

To some extent such stories are due to chance, but you can see in the last example that a story is struggling to get out. She doesn't ask 'Are the insects harmless?', she says 'Do they start out as harmless?' so that you know she has the intention of creating some destructive force. She also wants them to be big. She says 'Are they as big as elephants?' and gets the answer 'No', but she still ends up getting them gigantic, since they eat so much that they can't fit into the buildings. She's been lured into constructing one of the basic myths of our culture, the apparently harmless force that destroys the environment—and itself. Notice how she shapes the story by recapitulation. She links the buildings and the insects, and she reintroduces the buildings again at the end. She says, 'Is that the end?' because she knows she's linked up the story. It must be obvious that when someone insists that they 'can't think up a story', they really mean that they 'won't think up a story'—which is OK by me, so long as they understand it's a refusal, rather than a 'lack of talent'.

2

The improviser has to be like a man walking backwards. He sees where he has been, but he pays no attention to the future. His story can take him anywhere, but he must still 'balance' it, and give it shape, by remembering incidents that have been shelved and reincorporating them. Very often an audience will applaud when earlier material is brought back into the story. They couldn't tell you why they applaud, but the reincorporation does give them pleasure. Sometimes they even cheer! They admire the improviser's grasp, since he not only generates new material, but remembers and makes use of earlier events that the audience itself may have temporarily forgotten.

It seems obvious to teach storytelling as two separate activities. I get the actors to work in pairs, with Actor A telling a story for thirty seconds, and then with Actor B finishing it for thirty seconds. Actor A is to provide disconnected material, and Actor B is somehow to connect it.

> A: It was a cold winter's night. The wolves howled in the trees. The concert pianist adjusted his sleeves and began to play. An old lady was shovelling snow from her door . . .
>
> B: . . . When she heard the piano the little old lady began shovelling at fantastic speed. When she

reached the concert hall she cried, 'That pianist is my son!' Wolves appeared at all the windows, and the pianist sprang on to the piano, thick fur growing visibly from under his clothes.

Or again:

A: An old lady sits in her lighthouse very worried because the sea has dried up and there are no ships for her light to warn. In the middle of the desert a tap has been dripping since the beginning of time. In the heart of the jungle, in a little hut, an old man sits cross-legged . . .

B: . . . 'I can't stand that dripping sound,' he cries, leaping up and making a great journey to the centre of the desert. Nothing he can do will stop the tap dripping. 'At least I can turn it on,' he cries. Immediately the desert flourishes, the seas fill up again, and the old lady is very happy. She travels to the jungle to thank the old man, and ever afterwards keeps a picture of him and his hut above the mantelpiece in the lighthouse.

And again:

A: A man sits in a cave surrounded by pieces of bicycles. There is a fire outside the cave, and a woman is sending up smoke signals. Some children are playing in the river. An aeroplane passes over the valley and breaks the sound barrier . . .

B: . . . The sonic boom makes the children look up. They see the smoke signals. 'Daddy mended the bicycles,' they shout. When they run back to the cave a strange sight meets their eyes: not bicycles, but a flying-machine made out of all the pieces. Leaping on, they all pedal into the air, and fly around the valley all day.

Sometimes Actor A will try to make it 'easy' for Actor B. This actually makes it more difficult.

A: There was a little old lady in Putney who ran a fish-and-chip shop. All the people liked her, especially the local cats, because she used to give them scraps of fish. Also she didn't charge much, not to poor people, so they saved up and bought her a birthday present . . .

B: There's nothing for me to do. She's joined it all up herself.

Me: True!

I'm not saying that this method produces great literature, but you can get people inventing stories who previously claimed they could never think of any.

Once people have learned to play each stage of this game with no effort or anxiety, I let them play both halves themselves. I say 'Free-associate', and then when they've produced unconnected material, I say 'Connect', or 'Reincorporate'.

A knowledge of this game is very useful to a writer. First of all it encourages you to write whatever you feel like; it also means that you look *back* when you get stuck, instead of searching *forwards*. You look for things you've shelved, and then reinclude them.

If I want people to free-associate, then I have to create an environment in which they aren't going to be punished, or in any way held responsible for the things their imagination gives them. I devise techniques for taking the responsibility away from the personality. Some of these games are very enjoyable and others, at first encounter, are rather frightening; people who play them alter their view of themselves. I protect the students, encourage them and reassure them that they'll come to no harm, and then coax them or trick them into letting the imagination off its leash.

One way to bypass the censor who holds our spontaneity in check is to distract him, or overload him. I might ask someone to write out a paragraph on paper (without premeditation) while counting backwards aloud from a hundred. I'll try it now as I'm typing:

'Extra. I fall through the first storey of the car park. The driver throughout the night thought the soft concrete slit his genitals thoughtfully. Nurse Grimshaw fell further . . .'

I got to sixty until I felt my brain was going to explode. It's like trying to write after a severe concussion. Try it. It's very surprising to see what something in you 'wants' to write when it gets the chance.

You might try drawing a picture with two hands at once. The trick is to keep your attention equally divided, rather than switching quickly from hand to hand. Also you shouldn't decide what to draw; just sit down with a blank mind and draw as quickly as possible. This regresses your mind to about five years of age. Curiously, each hand seems to draw with the same level of skill.

3

Lists

If I tell a student, 'Say a word', he'll probably gawp. He wants a context in which his answer will be 'right'. He wants his answer to bring credit to him, that's what he's been taught answers are for.

'Why can't you just say whatever comes into your head?'

'Yes, well, I don't want to speak nonsense.'

'Any word would have done. A spontaneous reply is never nonsense.' This puzzles him.

'All right,' I say, 'just name me a list of objects, but as quick as you can.'

'Er . . . cat, dog, mouse, trap, dark cellar . . .'

He trails off, because he feels that the list is somehow revealing something about himself. He wants to keep his defences up. When you act or speak spontaneously, you reveal your real self, as opposed to the self you've been trained to present.

Nonsense results from a scrambling process, and takes time. You have to consider your thought, decide whether it gives you away, and then distort it, or replace it with something else. The student's 'trap' and 'dark cellar' were threatening to release some anxiety in him. If he'd continued with the list, speaking as quickly as possible, he'd have revealed himself as not quite so sane and secure as he pretends. I'll try typing out some nonsense as fast as I can and see what I get.

'The lobster bites the foot. Freda leaps skyward, back falling prone on to the long breakwater. Archie Pellingoe the geologist leaping up around down and upon her lovingly chews her alabaster sandwich . . .'

This is still partly scrambled, because I can't type quickly enough. I managed to censor some of it, but I wasn't able to remove all the sexual content. I veered away from the lobster suspecting the image to be vaguely erotic, but it got worse. The only way I could have made it meaningless would be to type more slowly, and to substitute other images. This is what my students do all the time. I ask them for an idea and they say '. . . oh . . . aahh . . . um . . .' as if they couldn't think of one. The brain constructs the universe for us, so how is it possible to be 'stuck' for an idea? The student hesitates not because he doesn't have an idea, but to conceal the inappropriate ones that arrive uninvited.

I make my students improvise lists of objects to make them understand that there are two processes they can use. You can make rational jumps from one object to the next: 'Dog, cat, milk, saucer, spoon, fork . . .' or you can improvise a non-associative list. I'll type out one as quickly as I can. 'Duck, rhomboid, platypus, elephant's egg, cactus, Johnnie Ray, clock face, East Acton . . .' It's like emptying all sorts of garbage from your mind that you didn't know was there. Try it. It's more difficult than you think, but it stops people caring what comes out of their minds. I'll try again. 'Dead nun, postbox, cat-o-nine-tails, cement hopper, mouse-juice, Pope Urban the Eighth, a blob, giant opera singer, piece of lettuce, a kazoo, a vivisected clown, a lump of interstellar dust, limpet shell, moving lava, red minibus, stamen, sickle-cell anaemia . . .'

A sequential list feels like one you 'think up'. A non-sequential list seems to arrive by itself. One day I'm sure there'll be an explanation for the two processes. Students choose the first way, and have to be coaxed into attempting the second. They feel as if they're being bombarded with the thoughts of someone else. They can't understand why such bizarre lists should occur to them. I tell them that it's perfectly natural, and that hypnagogic images come in the same way.

Associating Images

One of the earliest games we played at the studio involved associating images. We developed it from word-association games and we found that if someone gives an image suddenly, this will automatically trigger off another image in his partner's mind. Someone says 'A lobster . . .' and someone answers 'With a flower in its claw', and the juxtaposition does imply a content: 'A torn photograph . . .' '. . . An empty room'; 'Basket of eggs . . .' '. . . Cement mixer'. Afterwards you can see that a lobster with a flower in its claw is a good symbol of insensitivity, for someone locked out of the world of feeling, and so on, yet none of these associations were conscious at the moment that the pairing image jerked out.

Here's some genuine nonsense assembled by C. E. Shannon and based on word-probabilities:

'The head and frontal attack on an English writer that the character of this point is therefore another method for the letters that the time of whoever told the problem for an unexpected . . .' and so on. This is *not* the sort of thing spewed out by the unconscious.

'Characters'

One way to trigger off narrative material is to put the students in groups of three, and have them invent a name for a character, and see if they can agree on what he's like. For example:

'Betty Plum.'

'Big breasts.'

'Yes. A barmaid.'

'Er . . .'

'Well, she has worked as a barmaid . . .'

'Yes.'

'Lives in a room with blue curtains.'

'A stuffed toy dog on the dresser . . .'

'Which she keeps her nightdress in.'

'Nylon.'

The group continue until they know who she lives with, her taste in music, her secret ambition, the sorrow in her life, etc. The important thing is that the students should *really* agree, they shouldn't just make compromises. As soon as one person disagrees they wipe the character out, and start on another. Soon they learn to develop a character much further, and in a way that satisfies all of them. 'George Honeywell—keeps bees—smokes a pipe—married—*was* married—in love with the daughter of the tobacconist—wears a soft cap—he's a voyeur—likes dogs . . .' And so on.

Automatic Writing

Automatic writing is one way of getting students to understand that there is 'something inside them besides themselves'. Normally this skill is rare, but I have invented a method that works for most people; actually I suppose I should call it 'automatic reading'. Here's how I coaxed a poem from a volunteer at a public lecture.

'Mime taking a book from a shelf,' I said.

'Yes.'

'What colour is it?'

'Blue.'

'Did you have to think up the colour or did you see it?'

'It was blue.'

'Open it at the flyleaf. Can you see the name of the publisher?'

'It's faint.'

'Spell it.'

'H . . . o . . . d . . . Hodson.'

'And the name of the book?'

'*In* . . .'

'Yes.'

'*The* . . .'

'Yes . . . try to spell it.'

'C . . . *country*.'

'*In the Country* . . . author?'

'Alex . . . ander Pope.'

'Open it till you come to a page of verse. What's the page number?'

'Thirty-nine.'

'Find me a line of verse.'

'So that we . . .'

'Are you seeing it or inventing it?'

'Seeing it.'

'Next word.'

'It's blurred.'

'I've given you a magnifying-glass . . .'

I continued drawing the poem out of her, until she'd 'read' two verses. Then I stopped because she was finding the experience frightening. So did the audience, because it really didn't seem to be a poem *she* was inventing, yet someone was inventing it.

> So that we can be happy
> Together in our loves
> Since you were away
> I have been alone.
>
> Having been so close
> I cannot live again
> Many years will pass
> Till I live again.

The personality will often try to resist this method by saying 'It's in Russian', or 'It's too tiny to read the print', and so on. I say 'There's something written in English in the margin' or 'I'm shrinking you down to the size of the book', or something suitable. It's easy to switch from 'automatic reading' to my form of 'automatic writing'. You just look at a blank sheet of paper, and 'see' a word, and then write it where you 'saw' it. I've filled many exercise books using this method, partly to see where it led me, and partly to know what happens if you go past the point where you feel impelled to stop. I've learned a lot about myself this way. Again there's a great gap between what I would choose to write, and what actually emerges. Here's a bit that sounds like a statement about the imagination.

The great dragon dare not stir
The trainer watches kindly but
At the slightest movement taps it on the nose
The eyes glint fire and yet the muscles dare
Not exert themselves nor let the flame burst forth
Which would engulf the city in one flash.
The trainer speaks of kindness and consoles
And says he is the dragon's only friend
Sometimes the dragon purrs but oh the pain
Of never moving those enormous limbs.

Here's another one, not at all like 'my' writing.

Windmills
The vanes split apart
   All the mechanism rusts
Growing children talk
   Words turn to dust.

Look where the ocean
   Clogged with oil stands
Still struggling seabird
   Below on black sand.

Where on the headland
   Does a lighthouse blaze now?
The endless waves mount
   Desire fails below.

'Dreams'

A game we got from America uses relaxation to bypass the censor. It's used by psychologists, and I've seen dire warnings about other people using it. Most psychologists who use games rely very heavily on the discoveries of people working in the theatre, and my guess is that the 'guided dream' came from the theatre in the first place. (Frederick Perls says he was once a pupil of Max Reinhardt!) Anyway, I think the warnings are due to the same kind of fear that Mask work and hypnosis inspire. It's true that if someone is hovering on the edge of insanity one little push may topple him over, but a bus trip can be just as disturbing as anything that happens in a theatre class.

If I get you to lie down, close your eyes and relax, and report what your imagination gives you, then you'll probably go into a deep state of absorption, and instead of 'thinking things up' the experiences will seem to be really happening to you. Afterwards, if I ask 'Did you feel the floor?' then you'll probably say, 'There wasn't any floor.' If I say, 'Did you experience your body?' you'll probably answer, 'I wasn't in my body' or 'I was in the body I had in the story.'

I begin by suggesting something like 'You're on a beach?'

'Yes.'

'Is it sandy or stony?'

'Sandy.'

'Did you think that up?'

'No, I just knew.'

It's very likely that the student will want to stay on the beach and not be moved. I ask if he can see anything, or anyone, but he'll usually be alone. I tell him he's lain on the beach a long time, and then I suggest that he moves to the water, or away from it. If I don't tell him he's been there a long time, he'll probably refuse to 'get up'. The sort of story I'll expect to get may involve him walking along the shore, passing a cave. I may suggest he looks in the cave, or wades into the ocean, but probably he'll prefer to go on walking. Maybe he walks up to the top of the cliffs and looks down. Then I stop him.

Most people will have a good experience with this game, and sometimes it's like paradise. It can also be pretty hellish. I watch their breathing, and if they seem alarmed I take them out, or steer them towards something less alarming. I coax them near to threatening areas: I'll suggest they enter the cave or swim in the ocean, but I won't push them.

Once the basic technique is mastered, I let students try it again. This time they'll be bolder. They'll encounter other people, they'll have adventures, but I'll still guide them away from 'bad trips'. I'm using the game to demonstrate to the student that he can be effortlessly creative, not to teach him that his imagination is terrifying and should be suppressed! People can get upset playing the game, but if they weep you can cuddle them, which makes them feel better. When people abreact I always establish that (1) it's good for them; (2) they'll feel marvellous in half an hour; (3) it 'happens to everybody'.

Advanced students, whom you know well, may want to set off on deeper and more fearful journeys. That's all right when they know what they're doing. One way is to have them cuddled by other students while they play the game. If they start to express great alarm, take them out, be calm, tell them to open their eyes, rock them if necessary. Two people can go on a journey together, each trying to have the same fantasy. The essential thing is not that the student should abreact, but that he should have the experience of imagining something 'effortlessly', and 'choicelessly'. He should understand through this game that he doesn't have to *do* anything in order to imagine, any more than he needs to *do* anything in order to relax or perceive.

Here's a dream in which I was the questioner, and the 'victim' a drama student.

'What sort of stories do you like?'

'Science fiction. Well . . . Tolkien. Stories like *The Hobbit*.'

'OK. Imagine a lake surrounded by mountains.'

'Yes.'

'You are swimming in the lake.'

'Yes.'

'Can you see any fish?'

'Yes.'

'Large ones?'

'No.'

'Shoals of little ones turning and darting?'

'Yes.'

'There is one particular fish. What do you do with it?'

'I catch it.'

'You swim back to the shore and three hooded figures are waiting for you. What do you give them?'

'The fish.'

'And what do they give you in exchange?'

'A stick.'

'What do you do with it?'

'I point it at an oak tree and it vanishes.'

'And then?'

'I point it at the three hooded figures and they vanish too.'

'You set out through the woods. Does the path lead up or down?'

'Up.'

'What do you hear? Is it from your right or your left?'

'Left. Someone crying.'

'You look down into a clearing and see a woman surrounded by . . .?'

'Little men.'

'What's she wearing? Anything?'

'She's naked.'

'The little men see you?'

'They're coming at me waving sticks.'

'The woman calls to them?'

'She says it's not me who did it.'

'Was it someone from the castle?'

'Yes, he threw her out naked into the forest.'

'Do you help her?'

'Yes.'

'Do you go up the path?'

'I put my cloak round her and we set off to the castle.'

'It gets dark?'

'Yes.'

'And you are going to sleep?'

'We cover ourselves with leaves and we lie about eight feet apart.'

'You're fast asleep when you wake up to feel her touching you.'

'Yes.'

'What's she after?'

'The stick.'

'Does she get it?'

'Yes.'

'She points it at you and what happens?'

'It goes all grey and wintry.'

'What do you see in the mist?'

'A huge oak tree, and three hooded figures leaping about and shouting.'

At this point the story has obviously ended (because of a brilliant reincorporation), and we roll about on the floor roaring with laughter. We're very pleased to have co-operated so effortlessly.

You'll notice that my suggestions are mostly in the form of questions. He said 'Yes' to most of them, because we had a good rapport, and I knew what to ask. Such 'dreams' are intensely *real* to the person lying down, and pretty vivid to the questioner. This happened years ago, but I still have the 'vision' of the story sharp in my mind. I could easily draw illustrations to every part of it. To be a good questioner you have to enter something like the same trance state as the person answering.

'Experts'

When Vahktangov, one of Stanislavsky's favourite pupils, was directing *Turandot* he asked the wise men to set themselves impossible problems. When they were onstage they were always to be secretly trying to solve problems like 'How do you make a fly the size of an elephant?'

I adapted this idea to use in 'interviews'. One actor plays a TV interviewer, and his partner becomes an 'expert' who has to convince us that he's an authority on his subject.

The best way to think up the questions is to start a sentence without knowing how it's going to end. You say: 'Good evening . . . We are fortunate enough to have Professor Trout in the studio with us, who has just returned from Africa where he has been teaching hippopotamuses to . . .' You have no idea what to say next, but almost anything will do: '. . . to do handstands' or '. . . to yodel'. If you try to 'think up' impossible questions, it's very difficult. Once you start the sentence 'How do you turn a pig into . . .' it's very easy to conclude it '. . . a fire station'.

If you are asked, 'How do you teach hippopotamuses to knit?' you are likely to hedge: 'Well now, we have, as you know, a large number of these hippopotamuses which the Government has assembled in the hope that they will eventually boost Kenya's export trade. We're hoping to sell about ten thousand pullovers a year soon.' You waffle on like that, hoping that a nice idea will occur to you, but this isn't a good way of really amazing an audience. It's much better to give *any* answer. The interviewer's job is to hold the 'expert' to the problem of answering.

'Yes, but how exactly did you teach them?'

'It was the carrot and the whip really.'

'But what techniques?'

The 'expert' has agreed to answer the problem as part of the game, and he understands that the interviewer is trying to help him in demanding an immediate answer. Once he 'jumps in', and stops hedging, the game is simple.

"Well, I demonstrated the stitches. Then I gave them sharpened telegraph poles and about a mile of barbed wire.'

'Didn't they have trouble holding onto the poles?'

'Yes, well they would. They lack the opposed thumb. They do have quite good co-ordination though, and are very suited to activities of a repetitive nature.'

'But how exactly did they hold the poles?'

'Ah! Leather pole-holders strapped on to the forearms, or, er, in common parlance, feet.'

'But the pullovers, weren't they rather uncomfortable?'

'Terrible. We were starting with barbed wire and telegraph poles just to give them the general idea. If you try with wool right away, they keep snapping it.'

'Quite.'

'It's all a matter of grading. You get 'em on to rope, and then string, and finally they'll be doing crochet.'

'Do you have any examples of their work?'

'I'm wearing it. Every article of my clothing was knitted by the Kilimanjaro Hippo Co-operative.' (And so on.)

It's a little difficult on the printed page to show how pleasurable the game is. It's not so much what is said, but the expert's eagerness to supply instant answers. The audience know that *they*'d hedge, and beat about the bush, and they have a great respect for a performer who doesn't try any evasions. Sometimes such interviews are hysterically funny. It's very good if the interviewer refers to 'charts' that he imagines on the wall, and asks the 'expert' to explain them, or if the activity can be demonstrated. If you've been teaching mushrooms to yodel, the interviewer can say, 'I believe you've brought some of your soloists with you this evening.' Anyone from the audience would hastily deny this. It's so nice when the expert says 'Yes' and calls them in, or mimes taking them out of his pocket.

'Verbal Chase'

Students can become better at playing 'Experts' if they play a 'verbal chase' game first.

For example: Suppose I say 'Imagine a box.' A student can predict that the next thing I will say is something like 'What's in it?' Instead I say 'Who put you in there?' 'My father,' he says, anticipating a further question like 'Why did he put you there?' Instead I say 'What have you got in there with you?'. He replies 'A toilet'. I don't know what he anticipates now, but certainly not what I do say, which is 'What's written on the outside of the box?' 'Ladies!' he says, collapsing with laughter.

We all laugh, I suppose because of the implied homosexuality. If I were to point this out, then the student would feel the need to guard against me. Instead, I ignore the content, and concentrate on trying to jerk the answers out of the student as quickly as possible.

I say to another student: 'You're in a street. What street are you in?'

'Main street.'

'What's the shop?'

'A fishmonger's.'

'What does the fishmonger point at you?'

'A pistol.'

'What comes out?'

'Vinegar.'

Again everyone laughs and is very pleased. Answering such questions is easy. Asking them is very difficult, because you have to change the 'set' of the questions each time. Here's a sequence recorded in connection with a TV show. I was working with a girl student I'd just met for the first time.

'Where are you?'

'Here!'

'You're not. Where are you?'

'In a box.'

'Who put you there?'

'Mummy.'

'She's not really your mummy. Who is she?'

'She's my aunt.'

'What's her secret plan?'

'To kill me.'

'What with?'

'A knife.'

'She sticks the knife where?'

This question freaks her, because it's so sexual.

'In . . . in . . . in my stomach.'

'She cuts it open and takes out a handful of papery . . .'

'Boxes.'

'On the boxes is written . . .?'

' "Help!" '

'Who wrote it?'

'I did.'

'Who's in the box? Crawling out?'

'A spider.'

'A spider marked . . .?'

' "YES".'

'The spider does what?'

'It eats me.'

'Inside the spider you meet?'

'My father.'

'Holding?'

'A . . . a . . . a . . . elephant.'

'By the . . .'

'Tail.'

Everyone falls about with laughter, as if we'd been telling jokes, and they understand that some sort of sequence has come to an end. A student who becomes an expert questioner, that is, who becomes very ingenious at changing the 'set' of the questions, becomes a better improviser. Speed is important, so that the questions and answers are a little too fast for 'normal' thought.

Some questioners start doing all the work. For example:

'You're walking along a road.'

'Yes.'

'You meet a giant.'

'Yes.'

'You fall into a pool and are eaten by crocodiles.'

'Yes.'

'Er . . . er . . .'

This could be rephrased, and would then work.

'You're walking along—what?'

'A road.'

'A giant does what to you?'

'Throws me into a pond.'

'What do the crocodiles bite?'

The more 'insane' the questions, the better in jerking spontaneous answers from the 'victim'.

'Word at a Time'

If I ask someone to invent the first line of a short story, he'll unconsciously rephrase the question. He'll tense up, and probably say 'I can't think of one.' He'll really act as if he's been asked for a *good* first line. Any first line is really as good as any other, but the student imagines that he's being asked to think up dozens of first lines, then imagine the type of stories they might give rise to, and then assess the stories to find the best one. This is why he looks appalled and mumbles '. . . oh . . . dor . . . um . . .'

Even if I ask some people for the first *word* of a short story they'll panic and claim that they 'can't think of one', which is really amazing. The question baffles them because they can't see how to use it to display their 'originality' . . . A word like 'the' or 'once' isn't good enough for them.

If I ask one student for the first word of a story, and another for the second word, and another for the third word, and so on, then we could compose a story in this way:

'There' . . . 'was' . . . 'a' . . . 'man' . . . 'who' . . . 'loved' . . . 'making' . . . 'people' . . . 'happy'.

One version of the game—which I still play occasionally—involved telling a story around a circle as quickly as possible. Sometimes we did it to a beat. Anyone who 'blocked' we threw out until only two people were left. You can make the game tougher by having each person who speaks point to the person who is to say the next word, there's no way to anticipate when your turn will come.

Anyone who tries to control the future of the story can only succeed in ruining it. Every time you add a word, you know what word you would like to follow. Unless you can continually wipe your ideas out of your mind you're paralysed. You can't adapt to the words said by other people.

'We . . . (went for a walk) . . .'
'Are . . . (nice people) . . .'
'Going . . . (to the circus) . . .'
'Away . . . (for a holiday) . . .'
'To . . . (the country) . . .'
'Explore . . . (the Amazon) . . .'
'A . . . (cave) . . .'
'Giant!'

Once you say whatever comes to mind, then it's as if the story is being told by some outside force. I wouldn't be surprised to find that there are cultures which use the method as a form of divination. The group learn that this method of storytelling won't work unless they relax, stop worrying about being 'obvious' and remain attentive. I have played it in darkened rooms with the group lying on their backs with their heads at the centre of a circle. I remember at RADA we once pulled curtains over ourselves and lay there like a huge pudding. After the group has played the game with their eyes shut, get them to walk about and observe any perceptual changes. (Colours become brighter, people and spaces seem of a different size, focus is sharper.) Our normal thinking dulls perception, but the word-at-a-time game can shut some of the normal screening off. (It's not a good game for German speakers because of the rules about verbs coming at the end!)

I divide students into groups of four and get them to compose 'letters' a word at a time. They all relax and one of the players writes the letter down. I was describing this technique to an Eng. Lit. graduate.

'I don't think I could ever learn such a game,' she said
'Try it,' I said, and wrote '89' at the top of a sheet of paper.
'What's that?' she asked.

'The beginning of the address.'

'I don't know what to put.'

This intelligent girl was suffering. She was claiming to be 'un-creative' but was really just terrified she'd give something away.

'You know how addresses start on letters.'

'Well . . . all right. "The".'

'Elms', I wrote.

'89 The Elms can't be an address.'

'It'll do.'

'I can't think of anything else. I've got a block.'

I wrote 'block' down. Then I wrote 'Jan'.

'March' she said, looking helpful.

I put an oblique stroke between 'Jan' and 'March'. She looked as if she was under great stress. She wanted to fail but didn't know how to. She was afraid that the game might make her reveal secret things about herself.

'Dear', I wrote.

'Henry', she said after a long pause.

'I.'

'Hope.'

'Mrs.'

'I don't know who to put.'

'Any name. There isn't any way to choose a name that's wrong.'

'Exeter', she said, and seemed suddenly to realise that the game could be fun. The completed 'letter' read like this:

89 The Elms Block
Jan/March

Dear Henry,

I hope Mrs Exeter has been behaving well. Mum hopes that you will take off your bra. You will not proceed to any other perversions. The Vicar says Mrs White is a cow. Do you allow Mrs White to help you go to the bathroom?

Yours sincerely,
Arthur

PS I hate you.

Not an inspired letter, but once she got over her initial resistance she became fascinated by the game, and played it many times.

Word-at-a-time letters usually go through four stages: (1) the letters are usually cautious or nonsensical and full of concealed sexual references; (2) the letters are obscene and psychotic; (3) they are full of religious feeling; (4) finally, they express vulnerability and loneliness.

Improvisations go through similar stages if you don't censor them, and if you work with the same group day after day. Here is a sequence of 'letters' which were written late one night, by three drama students (two boys and a girl). They said it took them a couple of hours, what with talking, and opening more beers, and so on. I'd told them that the stories changed if they persisted in writing them, but I hadn't told them what to expect. They stopped when they were too scared to write any more. You can see the 'armour' peeling off letter by letter. Some of the paragraphs have titles, which I think were arrived at by spelling them out a letter at a time.

1. 'How did he walk on the water when it was raining? I don't think that God exists (in garbage cans). Polacks began to fix their dynamite to the end of their tools which shuddered and vibrated radically. "John is a prick," said Mary, "why can't he fuck my arse, the bastard!" Jeremy and Fiona lay in a compromising position with green and yellow forceps plucking their pubic hair which rustled like reeds in a storm which was raging then. Tomorrow we must go with Jane to old mansions and buy all the paraphernalia required for our happy transactions in the nuptial bed. Why did Mary pull Jeremy's trousers off his legs and burn with green fingers? She stroked his beard and began fondling his nosebag. It began to get warm in the greenhouse, plants wilted and detumesced. If the rain couldn't get into the trough all the plants would die. How will Mother walk when it begins raining?'

2. 'Because Mary felt ill, she went to the doctors. Did he feel reluctant to examine her? She couldn't pass water and fart when asked. "You may leave the basin on the table if water is spilling down your legs." I thought that we can perhaps catch ourselves in bed. Basins frighten ghosts and mice, but spiders walk around chairs and breathe softly. Can I hear myself breathe? Only God can produce Christ's image on church walls without seeming to characterise. If water falls gently on to the spider it will die. Tomorrow is Christ's birthday and we must celebrate with balloons and razors. Should we allow Christ to die? Perhaps he can save us, perhaps he can obliterate us. Fear is always present with me. God is dead. Big tits can make me feel happy, and saved. Mary and I are not related and can only marry if God permits. Why can't we live by ourselves?'

3. '*Purgation.* Lightning strikes trees but only when it rains hard. Water runs along green branches carrying specks of bird-shit. Clouds follow the sun which shines only on holidays. Thunder is loud but

soft in rain. Why can trees blow their leaves towards the houses? Why does rain trickle down my trees? I like rain when it splatters against my house and face. Should ghosts haunt my house? I would like it if God left me alone. Ghosts like butter, mice like ghosts, butter likes me. Poetry destroys all images and reincarnation. Why, why can't I live without people and Jesus and poetry? If it destroys me it destroys everything. Bombs destroy people, God and me. Are bombs created by God or are poets Gods, or is love a bomb which destroys rain?'

4. 'Autumn. He walked through the trees carrying a body which bumped gently against the ground, which was hard and frozen. She held his hand, softly whispering "Dead!" Can't leaves drift under the bodies without breaking? Is Mother dying or has she died without screaming "Dead!" whispered Mary. He shook the leaves off Mother and began sprinkling dirt over her grave. After death will God see her face? Will Mother laugh at God or cry "Dead!"? Should we mourn her parting? Leaves tremble and fall swiftly. Time carries her scythe tenderly without cutting her throat. Leaves cut my heart, but Jesus cuts my mother. Between them their relationship seems brittle and lifeless like dead leaves.'

5. 'Love lost. Sunshine brightens my life. Yesterday, today, tomorrow; all my loves have flown towards oblivion. Death approaches from lost loves. Is death the answer? Can Christ save lost lovers or do angels meet flying shadows under sunlit gardens? Black night frightens angels. Dark alleys frighten lovers. Only lovers know love and see nothing but sunshine. Perhaps death hides people from the heaven-sent sunshine, or love hides from death. When you travel through darkness, hold love tightly, for you will need all the strength of your love to be unafraid of death. Why should we not love again, though we may lose our lives from lost loves? Death cannot change us, or destroy us, while God loves lovers.'

6. 'Shipwrecks are dangerous to people on ships. Waves cause shipwrecks and are beautiful. How can beautiful waves destroy people without turning ugly? Jesus walks: untroubled footsteps sound across vast oceans of beautiful waves. Shipwrecks begin when love disappears. Jesus hears no footsteps, only the screams of the dying waves which patter his feet. Why do mermaids not hear God? Is death inevitable? Do shipwrecks begin when ears are hearing nothing but footsteps? Can I hear waves beating on nothing? Only if I make footsteps heard. Christmas comes when God is deaf to our screams, and waves become destructive and silent like Jesus's feet.'

7. 'Sabbat. Seven dwarfs stood silently watching. Six leprechauns,

being present at the funeral, began dancing. Five Jews scrabbled in mud for money which the angels took. Three dwarfs raped two leprechauns, who said that one was enough.'

8. '*Hells I view.* Black shines brightly under white silk curtains, light filters through black windows but fades colours anyway. Windows shine at people from afar. Darkness surrounds me as I gaze at people in the street. Is my body there or am I looking at it through dark windows?'

9. '*Seagulls.* Look at the seagulls circling above this place, like shadows falling at noon. Wings are made for flying higher and higher and swifter and stronger than anything crawling below. How do birds know what it is like to be earthbound? Perhaps they envy creatures who crawl and swim. If I could fly, like them, at the end of autumn where leaves lie brown and decaying, then I would know that God is a being who flies.'

10. 'Snow is gentle and cold. It falls from above us. Death is only snow. It falls to cover our lives. But we cannot melt away death like sunshine melts snow. Coldness comes, only once the snow has fallen. *If I can melt my snow will also melt,* but because I am never fully warm I cannot live. Terror is cold. Fear is cold and only I can depend on heat. Love is warm. Ah! If only we had love always, we could conquer, and live forever. The people who love themselves cannot melt their snow. Only you can melt my snow, for our love can never fail, for however cold it becomes, we shall love each other and therefore melt each other's snows and live forever.'

11. 'Happiness is always transient. Perhaps we should try to be happier and better with our friends. Friendship is transient but transcience meets often with lasting friendship. Why can't we meet other people and make friendships last? Am I ever going to meet my friends in honest friendship? Or will we ever see our own friendships die through lack of love? Which is the better? I don't like to leave friends behind but friendship will come again. Love is permanent only when friendship and trust exists. If friendship is transient, trust must be the permanent basis of love.'

12. 'Strings vibrate when they feel varying pressures upon them. Sounds echo through empty buildings. Light shines brightly, but only enters through open spaces in walls. My room vibrates silently and darkly. No light enters my room. It feels no emotion, like a static building where strings never vibrate. I cannot live alone, listening to silence and seeing nothing but walls and darkness. Why does light not enter my room? Must I feel deaf to vibrating strings and see nothing?

Where am I, where are you? Where are the people who play music and vibrate strings? When will I hear and see music? I can't tell. Only you can help me see and hear. I only live, hoping that you love me. Give me your hand, and take away my darkness and silence.'

13. 'Summer roses die when winter strangles the ground. Weeds flourish when roses die. I lived in a thorn bush until roses began to die, then I left my thorn bush and ran towards the sun. I felt it warm my body as I had no clothes on. Approaching dusk saw me shiver, but I still ran towards the sun, and finally dropped towards the end of life. Roses covered my body. Dawn came and warmed the roses and me. Then at noon I burned. My body could not feel pain. I stood among the flourishing roses. They did not burn. Midnight came. I tried to return to my thorn bush but I was cold. If I cannot grow into a rose, I must die, and become a weed.'

14. 'Walls encircle me. My heart has walls which surround my blood, beating steadily and relentlessly it pushes through my veins because I am so alive. Talk to me please. The walls are thin and crumbling. Life is being drained from within my body. Stop the current. I must break through the walls which hold my body. Death will soon release the aching heart, but I am not afraid. Here is my heart, now take a piece and smash down my walls.'

If you play this game with children, then it's important not to insist on *leading*. Here's a 'story' I improvised with a 'disturbed' nine-year-old boy. His words are in italics, and you can see how little I contributed.

'A *year* ago *strangely* enough *dead* people *strangled* my *mother*. How *did* they *do* this? "*Help!*" cried *Thing-a-me-boober*, "*I went* over *Heaven* and *Hell*, where *did* you *stop*?" Hell *is* the *ugliest* place *I* have *ever* seen. *Devil* George *swims* through *waves* of *flame* to *strengthen* his *bones*. Mother *screamed* when *she* saw *George* holding *a* stick *called* a *pitchfork*. She *fainted* when *my* friend *hit* her *over* the *head* with *a* bucket *of* molten *metal*. Meanwhile, *back* in *my* own *Casbah* I *got* very *drunk*.'

A game can stare you in the face for years before you 'see' it. It wasn't until I'd left the studio that I thought of asking students to act the stories out as they told them.

I get the actors to work in pairs, with their arms round each other, to say 'We' instead of 'I', and to use the present tense. I discourage them from putting in adjectives, or saying 'But'. It's normal for them to encounter something unpleasant, and to hold it off with adjectives by saying 'We ... met ... a ... big ... huge ... terrifying

... angry ... black ... monster ... *but* ... we ... escaped.' Once they've mastered the basic technique of the game (which is very easy) then I forbid them to escape from the monsters. 'Kill it or be killed,' I say, 'or make friends with it, outwit it.' I remind them that there isn't really a monster, so what does it matter if they allow themselves to be torn apart? If they get eaten or killed I say 'Go on, don't stop the game.' Then they can fight their way out of the monster, or continue in heaven, or whatever. They can mime sitting astride enormous turds and paddle through the intestines. If they get to heaven they can find God is missing and take over the place, or arm-wrestle him, or anything.

The audience can hardly believe that it's possible to improvise scenes in this way, and they're delighted to see actors working in such sympathy. I used to ask the audience for titles first, and I usually combined two titles to make one; the actors would then improvise *Dracula and the Bald Lighthouse Keeper*, or *Rin-Tin-Tin and the Fall of the Roman Empire*.

Some people avoid getting involved in action. All they'll produce is stories like '*We-are-going-to-the-market-where-we-buy-bread-and-now-we-walk-to-the-beach-where-we-watch-the-seagulls* . . .' It's a good idea to start such people off inside a womb, or on another planet, or being hunted for murder, or some other dramatic situation.

The game can be intensified by having one partner close his eyes, while the other partner stops him from bumping into the furniture. In another version both partners close their eyes, while the group stand round them and protect them. If the group is in a good state, that is to say warm and friendly, then they'll begin to add things to the story. If a wind is mentioned the group will spontaneously make wind noises, or perhaps flap coats around them to make a draught. If the storytellers are in the forest, then bird sounds will be made, or rustlings. Soon the group begin to dictate parts of the action, providing encounters with animals or monsters. An extraordinary energy is released, an almost sinister excitement sweeps over the group, and all sorts of sensitivity exercises are discovered. The group will 'fly' the story tellers, and bury them in heaps of bodies or be 'spiders' crawling all over their skins.

It's amazing to be one of the 'storytellers' because everything becomes so real for you. Once your eyes are shut, and you're involved in the story, and people begin to supply even very approximate effects, the brain suddenly links it all up, and fills in the gaps. If someone touches your face with a wet leaf you hallucinate a whole forest, you know what kind of trees are there, the type of animals, and so on.

One extraordinary way to play word-at-a-time games is to ask a whole group to tell the story, all speaking together. I don't know how to convince you that this is possible, but most groups can succeed at it, if you approach them at the right moment. Start with everyone pressed together, and say 'Start with "We" and all speak at the same time.' I suppose it works because many people say the same words, and the minority who go 'wrong' are swamped out by the majority.

4
'Playwriting'

An improviser can study status transactions, and advancing, and 'reincorporating', and can learn to free-associate, and to generate narrative spontaneously, and yet still find it difficult to compose stories. This is really for aesthetic reasons, or conceptual reasons. He shouldn't really think of making up stories, but of *interrupting routines*.

If I say 'Make up a story', then most people are paralysed. If I say 'describe a routine and then interrupt it', people see no problem. A film like *The Last Detail* is based on the routine of two sailors travelling across America with a prisoner whom they have to deliver to a prison. The routine is interrupted by their decision to give him a good time. The story I fantasised earlier about the bear who chased me was presumably an interruption of the routine 'Walking through the forest'. Red Riding Hood presents an interruption of the routine 'Taking a basket of goodies to Grandma'.

Many people think of finding more *interesting* routines, which doesn't solve the problem. It may be interesting to have a vet rectally examining an elephant, or to show brain surgeons doing a particularly delicate operation, but these activities remain routines. If two lavatory attendants break a routine by starting a brain operation, or if a window cleaner begins to examine the elephant, then this is likely to generate a narrative. Conversely, two brain surgeons working as lavatory cleaners immediately sounds like part of a story. If I describe mountaineers climbing a mountain, then the routine says that they first climb it, and then they climb down, which isn't much of a story. A film of a mountain climb isn't necessarily anything more than a documentary. If we interrupt the routine of mountain-climbing by having them discover a crashed plane, or if we snow them up and have them start eating each other, or whatever, then we begin story-telling. As a story progresses it begins to establish other routines and these in their turn have to be broken. In the story about the bear I escaped to an island and began making love to a beautiful girl. This can also be considered as a routine that it's necessary to interrupt. I interrupted it with the bear, but I could have chosen one of an infinity of other ways. I could have found that she was wearing a wig to hide her complete baldness, or that I was impotent, or that my penis was growing so long that it had made its way to the shore of the lake where it was being attacked by the bear. I could have discovered that she was my sister—Maupassant set such a story in a brothel.

It doesn't matter how stupidly you interrupt a routine, you will be automatically creating a narrative, and people will listen. The scene in *The Tempest* where Caliban hears the clown coming works marvel-lously, but it's ludicrous. The first routine suggests that Caliban will defend himself, or leave. He crawls under a sheet. When the clown enters he sees this monster hiding under the sheet. If we treat this as a routine, then it's obvious that the clown runs away. What he does is incredible—the very last thing anyone would do is to crawl under the sheet beside the monster. It's actually the *best* thing to do, since it spectacularly breaks the routine.

We could introduce this concept by getting each actor in a scene to prearrange something that'll surprise his partner. In a scene where a couple are about to go to bed, maybe the husband suddenly turns into a boot fetishist, or maybe the wife will suddenly start to laugh hysterically, or find she's growing feathers. If you set out to do some-thing in a scene that your partner can't anticipate, you automatically generate a narrative.

Sometimes stories themselves become so predictable that they be-come routines. Nowadays if your princess kisses the frog, it's probably better if she becomes a frog herself, or if the frog she kissed just be-comes six feet higher. It's no good the knight killing the dragon and deflowering the virgin any more. Killing the virgin and deflowering the dragon is more likely to hold the audience's attention.

One way that storytellers wreck their talent is by *cancelling*. A student of mine wrote a scene in which a girl friend messed up her ex-boy friend's apartment in an act of revenge. He arrived and they had a row. Once the row was over and she had left, the playwright had a sensation of 'failure', or having done *nothing*—which was true. When I told the writer to consider the row as a routine which needed to be broken, she wrote a scene in which at the height of the row the girl suddenly injected the ex-boy friend with a syringe, and locked herself in the bathroom. One moment there was a row going on, and the next the man was suddenly terrified of what she might have done to him.

Many students dry up at the moment they realise that the routine they're describing is nearing its completion. They absolutely understand that a routine *needs* to be broken, or they wouldn't feel so unimaginative. Their problem is that they haven't realised what's wrong *consciously*. Once they understand the concept of 'interrupting routines', then they aren't stuck for ideas any more.

Another way that improvisers screw themselves up is by moving the action elsewhere. An improvisation starts with a girl asking a boy for the time. He says it's four o'clock. She says that the others are late, and they begin talking about these imaginary others, and what happened last time, and the scene fizzles out. I tell them that they got diverted into a discussion of events that happened another time, and that there was nothing for the audience to see. I start them again with the opening dialogue. She asks what time it is. He says, 'Four o'clock.' I shout out: 'Say it's time to begin.' 'It's time to begin,' he says. 'Must we?' she asks. He says, 'Well you know how strict he is', and again they begin talking about something outside the scene. I tell them I don't care what they do so long as the action remains onstage. 'Get a bucket,' I say, and the actor mimes carrying on a bucket. 'Is it really necessary?' implores the actress. 'Yes,' he replies, 'open your mouth, I'll put the funnel in.' 'I've put on twenty pounds in the last week,' she complains. 'He likes them fat,' he says, pouring the 'contents' of the 'bucket' into the 'funnel' while she pretends to be swelling up. The scene now seems inspired, and the audience are fascinated. (Speke found this scene in reality: a tribe where the king's wives were forcibly fed, and sprawled about like great seals.)

One of the first games I used at the studio involved getting Actor A to order Actor B about: 'Sit down. Stand up. Go to the wall. Yawn. Say "I'm tired." Look around. Walk to the door . . .' and so on. We weren't trying to create narratives; we only wanted the actors to get used to obeying each other, and to ordering each other around. This game (if you can call it a game) exposed them to an 'audience' without their having to think about success or failure.

Now that I'm teaching 'playwriting' in a Canadian university, I've adapted this early game into a way of teaching narrative skills. Two students obey a third who tells them what to say and do. The third student, the 'playwright', will be under a certain amount of stress, but if he blocks I tell him to say 'prompt', and then someone tells him what to say next. We don't play the game in order to get 'good stories', although 'good stories' may emerge; the important thing is to investigate exactly why the playwright 'blocks'.

A playwright who gets his two students to wash up soon stops and says 'I can't think of anything.' If I say 'Break the routine' he has one student break a plate on purpose. He now has a quarrel which he can develop for a while, but which is also a routine. They decide to put the plate together, and find a piece is missing. They investigate and find a hole in the floor. They peer through the hole and start talking about what they see underneath. The playwright then gets stuck again. What he's done is to move the action offstage, so I tell him he's been *deflected*, and that he's to get the action onstage again. He tells them to tear up the floorboards, and the 'block' dissolves.

An audience will remain interested if the story is advancing in some sort of organised manner, but they want to see *routines* interrupted, and the action continuing *between* the actors. When a Greek messenger comes in with some ghastly story about events that have happened somewhere else, the important thing is the effect the revelation produces on the other characters. Otherwise it stops being theatre, and becomes 'literature'.

A 'playwright' begins a story by saying: 'Dennis, sit on the chair, and look ill. Betty, say "Are you feeling well?". Dennis, say "No, could you get me a glass of water." Betty, get Dennis a glass of water. Drink it, Dennis. Betty, say "How do you feel?". Dennis, say "Much better now" . . .'

At this point the 'playwright' becomes confused, so I stop him and explain that he's *cancelled* everything out. He introduces the idea of sickness, and then he removes it. I take the story back to when Dennis drinks the glass of water. 'Dennis, find that the water goes right through you, and is splashing on the floor under the chair. Betty, get him another glass of water. Dennis, examine yourself to try to work out what happened. Betty, give him the water, and put the glass under the chair to catch it when it runs through again. Dennis, say "Can you help me?". Betty, say "You'll have to take your clothes off, then." Dennis, mime undressing . . .' And so on. The level of invention is no higher, but the story is no longer being *cancelled*, and it holds the attention.

There's nothing very profound about such stories, and they don't require much imagination, but people are very happy to watch them. The rules are: (1) interrupt a routine; (2) keep the action *onstage*—

don't get *diverted* on to an action that has happened elsewhere, or at some other time; (3) don't *cancel* the story.

5

I began this essay by saying that an improviser shouldn't be concerned with content, because the content arrives automatically. This is true, and also not true. The best improvisers do, at some level, know what their work is about. They may have trouble expressing it to you, but they do understand the implications of what they are doing; and so do the audience.

I think of an improvisation we did years ago: Anthony Trent played being a prisoner in a cell. Lucy Fleming arrived, I don't remember how, and he endowed her with invisibility. At first he was terrified, but she calmed him down, and said she had come to rescue him. She led him out of the prison and as he stepped free he fell dead. It had the same kind of effect as Ambrose Bierce's story *Incident at Owl Creek Bridge*.

I remember Richardson Morgan playing a scene in which I said he was to be fired, and in which he said he was failing at his work because he had cancer. I think Ben Benison was the boss and he treated Ric with amazing harshness. It was about the cruellest scene I've ever seen and the audience were hysterical with laughter. I've never heard people laugh more. The actors seemed to be dragging all the audience's greatest fears into the open, laying out all their insecurities, and the anxiety was releasing itself in waves of roaring, tearing laughter, and the actors absolutely knew what they were doing, and just how slowly to turn the screw.

You have to trick students into believing that content isn't important and that it looks after itself, or they never get anywhere. It's the same kind of trick you use when you tell them that they are *not* their imaginations, that their imaginations have nothing to do with them, and that they're in no way responsible for what their 'mind' gives them. In the end they learn how to abandon control while at the same time they exercise control. They begin to understand that everything is just a shell. You have to misdirect people to absolve them of responsibility. Then, much later, they become strong enough to resume the responsibility themselves. By that time they have a more truthful concept of what they are.

Masks and Trance

I

George Devine

George Devine gave a Mask class to the Royal Court writers' group in 1958. He arrived with a box full of dusty Masks that had last been used some years before at the Old Vic Theatre School. I didn't like the look of them: they reminded me of surgical prostheses, and I didn't like what he was saying either. Already I was feeling threatened. George talked to us for about forty minutes, and then gave us a demonstration. He retired to the far end of the long, shadowy room, put a Mask on, looked in a mirror, and turned to face us—or rather 'it', 'the Mask', turned to face us. We saw a 'toad-god' who laughed and laughed as if we were funny and despicable. I don't know how long the 'scene' lasted, it was timeless. Then George removed the Mask and suggested that we try.

Next day he was despondent. He thought the class had been a failure and that this had been his fault. He said that none of the Masks had been 'inhabited', by which he meant that none of us had been *possessed* by the Masks. I tried to explain how amazed we'd been, but he insisted that the class had been a poor one, and that I was wrong to be so enthusiastic.

William Gaskill borrowed the Masks, and began to give Mask classes along the lines laid down by George. He collected some old clothes, and some props, and developed the theory that the actor should shock himself with the Mask's reflection. The time at the mirror was to be kept short, and the student was to be pushed into acting on whatever impulse came to him. George's ideas related to Oriental theatre (Noguchi had designed his King Lear) but we had seen the toad-god, and thought more in terms of voodoo than the Noh Theatre. Gaskill persuaded me to give Mask classes as well: 'It shouldn't all be left to me,' he said, and we both gave classes to groups who visited the theatre.

It's true that an actor can wear a Mask casually, and just pretend to be another person, but Gaskill and myself were absolutely clear that we were trying to induce *trance* states. The reason why one automatically talks and writes of Masks with a capital 'M' is that one really feels that the genuine Mask actor is inhabited by a spirit. Nonsense perhaps, but that's what the experience is like, and has always been like. To understand the Mask it's also necessary to understand the nature of trance itself.

One day Devine invited me to lunch, which he never did unless he wanted to discuss something. He was embarrassed (he was actually a shy man), and finally when we were almost through coffee and the restaurant was practically empty, he said that he thought Bill and I had misunderstood the nature of the Mask. At this time George was giving comedy classes at the Studio, so I suggested a swop: I would give his comedy classes, and he would give my Mask classes.

George allowed his students to work in a very casual way. Bill and I had tried to condition a response to the wearing of a Mask by insisting that whenever one was on the face, the actor should attempt to enter the 'Mask state'. This led to Masks being handled as if sacred. George shocked me by allowing actors to talk as themselves while actually wearing the Masks. They'd choose clothes or wander about with the Masks on without any attempt to be in character. I think George was overreacting to the way we'd been teaching, because even in performance these Masks often spoke with the wearer's voice, although George had explained that they'd need speech lessons before they could speak 'as the Masks'. Eventually, George said that the students who had worked first with William Gaskill and myself were usually the better ones, so that our method must have something to recommend it. I think this was because we used to hurl the students into the work, whereas George was much gentler. He was very good at explaining exactly when a Mask was 'inhabited', but it was really up to the actors. Many of his students played safe, and kept to their preferred areas acting with Masks on, rather than being possessed. George's attitude was really very different from mine, and possibly Gaskill's; George was primarily interested in developing characters that could be used *without the Mask* when the actor was cast in plays. I saw the Masks as astounding performers, as offering a new form of theatre, and I didn't care what Mask creatures arrived, so long as they were possessed. The Masks we were using covered the top half of the face, leaving the mouth and lower half of the cheeks exposed. George had learnt the technique from Michel Saint-Denis in the 1930s, and Michel had been taught by Jacques Copeau (his uncle). These half masks are usually called 'comic masks' but George called them 'Character Masks'. He thought it important to hand on the tradition unchanged, and he was shocked when he found that I was mixing Character Masks with Tragic Masks (Tragic Masks work by a quite different technique—see page 184). My students showed him one of the mixed scenes they had prepared with me, and they reported him as saying that it did work, but that he still didn't like it! When I visited him during his last illness, almost the last thing he said to me was 'I still don't think that Mask work was right.'

George cited Chaplin's Tramp as a Mask, since the character had come from the clothes and the make-up. Here's Chaplin's own account (from his autobiography).

'On the way to the wardrobe I thought I would dress in baggy pants, big shoes, and a cane and a derby hat. I wanted everything to be a contradiction; the pants baggy, the coat tight, the hat small and the shoes large. I was undecided whether to look young or old, but remembering Sennett had expected me to be a much older man, I added a small moustache which, I reasoned, would add age without hiding my expression . . . .

'. . . I had no idea of the character. But the moment I was dressed, the clothes and make-up made me feel the kind of person he was. I began to know him, and by the time I walked on the stage he was fully born. When I confronted Sennett I assumed the character and strutted about, swinging my cane and parading before him. Gags and comedy ideas went racing through my mind . . . .

'. . . My character was different and unfamiliar to the Americans. But with the clothes on I felt he was a reality, a living person. In fact he ignited all sorts of crazy ideas that I would never have dreamt of until I was dressed and made-up as the Tramp.'

Elsewhere Chaplin has said, 'I realised I would have to spend the rest of my life finding out about the creature. For me he was fixed, complete, the moment I looked in the mirror and saw him for the first time, yet even now I don't know all the things that are to be known about him.'[1] (Isabel Quigly, *Charlie Chaplin—Early Comedies*, Studio Vista, 1968.)

2

Russians

At first I thought that Mask work was completely unlike Stanislavsky's concept of actor training, but this isn't true. Here's Stanislavsky describing the Mask state in *Building a Character*. Kostya, a drama student, has been told to put on a character make-up, but nothing satisfies him. He creams his face to remove the grease-paint and then, unexpectedly . . .

'All the other colours blurred. . . . It was difficult to distinguish where my nose was, or my eyes, or my lips. I smeared some of the same cream on my beard and moustache and then finally all over my wig. Some of the hair clotted into lumps . . . . and then, almost as if I were in some delirium, I trembled, my heart pounded, I did away with my eyebrows, powdered myself at random, smeared the back of my hands with a greenish colour and the palms with light pink. I did all this with a quick, sure touch, for this time I knew who I was representing, and what kind of fellow he was!'

He then paced the room feeling 'how all the parts of my body, features, facial lines, fell into their proper places and established themselves. . . . I glanced in the mirror and did not recognise myself. Since I had looked into it the last time a fresh transformation had taken place in me. "It is he, it is he!" I exclaimed. . . .'

He presents himself to the director (Tortsov), introducing himself as 'the critic'. He's surprised to find his body doing things by itself, things he hadn't intended.

'Quite unexpectedly my twisted leg came out in advance of me and threw my body more to the right. I removed my top hat with careful exaggeration and executed a polite bow. . . .'

He then played a scene with the director, having no difficulty in sustaining this weird character he had become, and knowing always exactly what to say. Later Kostya reflects: 'Can I really say that this creature is not part of me? I derived him from my own nature. I divided myself, as it were, into two personalities. One continued as an actor, the other as an observer.'

At the time when Copeau was working with Masks in France, Stanislavsky's favourite pupil Vakhtangov was working with them in Russia. Nikolai Gorchakov has left an account of those rehearsals. Vakhtangov set up a circus in which the Masks were to be auditioned as clowns. They were to do things that would make the spectators '. . . applaud wildly, rush on the stage and hug and kiss you! Or at least roll on the floor with laughter. Go ahead, start! . . .'

Vakhtangov threw an incredible number of instructions to the Masks until they were lost and confused. Someone played circus music and they had no choice but to perform. They tried imaginary gymnastics, and ice-skated, and pretended to juggle, and finally succeeded in getting warm applause from the onlookers. 'Do you really think you've hit on the "grain" of the Masks merely by doing a few exercises in front of the audience?' said Vakhtangov. 'You haven't even started to act as Masks! . . . You must vie with one another in captivating the audience by every possible means—talk, act, dance, sing, do acrobatics, do anything. Understand?'

Things got worse until finally Vakhtangov left, the Masks continuing without him. Suddenly two of them became genuine Masks in the characters of Tartaglia and Pantalone. Tartaglia was eating a cake, and Pantalone was starving. Tartaglia spoke with a stutter (which was unexpected) and said that Pantalone would have to earn it, but he 'graciously allowed Pantalone to eat the crumbs remaining on his palm each time he swallowed a bit. This made Pantalone very happy, and it was fun watching him pick up these crumbs while Tartaglia lectured him on the necessity of work. . . .

'The episode was fairly long, but we were so enchanted we did not notice it. We were not much interested in their chatter, but were fascinated by their naive seriousness, the kind one sees only in two children when one is sucking a toffee and the other cannot tear his eyes away from this sweet process, looking enviously at the happy owner. . . .

'Tartaglia was so carried away that he began to tease Pantalone, passing the cake under his nose every time he nipped a bit off. Suddenly, Pantalone opened wide his mouth and snapped up about three-quarters of what remained. Tartaglia burst into tears while Pantalone, his mouth full, gestured that it served him right—he should not have teased him.'

Vakhtangov had been watching from a doorway. He immediately set up another scene with the same characters. Pantalone was to be a dentist, and Tartaglia his patient. Tartaglia panicked, stepped out of character and said he didn't want to do it.

' "And what do the dentists say to that?" Vakhtangov turned gravely to his partners.

' "There have been many cases in history of medicine of patients refusing to be treated," Kudryavtsev replies seriously, without forgetting that he was Pantalone, the learned secretary of King Altoum's court. "Such refusal is a sure sign of illness. In this particular case I presume we'll have to extract the aching teeth not only through the mouth, but also through other apertures, ears and nostrils included. . . ." '

Afterwards Vakhtangov commented that they had at first tried to 'think up' what to do. 'I don't deny the importance of thinking, inventing or planning, but if you have to improvise on the spot (and that's exactly what we have to do), you must act and not think. It's action we must have—wise, foolish or naive, simple or complicated, but *action.*' (Nikolai Gorchakov, *The Vakhtangov School of Stage Art,* Foreign Languages Publishing House, Moscow.)

Vakhtangov forced his students to act *spontaneously.* This produces a light trance state in which the actors feel as if something else is controlling them. They 'know' what to do, whereas normally they 'choose' what to do. The state is regressive, but they experience no self-consciousness.

3 Destroying the Mask

Masks seem exotic when you first learn about them, but to my mind Mask acting is no stranger than any other kind: no more weird than the fact that an actor can blush when his character is embarrassed, or turn white with fear, or that a cold will stop for the duration of the performance, and then start streaming again as soon as the curtain falls. 'What's Hecuba to him?' asks Hamlet, and the mystery remains. Actors can be possessed by the character they play just as they can be possessed by Masks. Many actors have been unable to really 'find' a character until they put on the make-up, or until they try on the wig, or the costume. We find the Mask strange because we don't understand how irrational our responses to the face are anyway, and we don't realise that much of our lives is spent in some form of trance, i.e. absorbed. What we assume to be 'normal consciousness' is comparatively rare, it's like the light in the refrigerator: when you look in, there you are ON but what's happening when you don't look in?

It's difficult to understand the power of the Mask if you've only seen it in illustrations, or in museums. The Mask in the showcase may have been intended as an ornament on the top of a vibrating, swishing haystack. Exhibited without its costume, and without a film, or even photograph, of the Mask in use, we respond to it only as an aesthetic object. Many Masks are beautiful or striking, but that's not the point. A Mask is a device for driving the personality out of the body and allowing a spirit to take possession of it. A very beautiful Mask may be completely dead, while a piece of old sacking with a mouth and eye-holes torn in it may have tremendous vitality.

In its original culture nothing had more power than the Mask. It was used as an oracle, a judge, an arbitrator. Some were so sacred that any outsider who caught a glimpse of them was executed. They cured diseases, they made women sterile. Some tribes were so scared of their power that they carved the eye-holes so that the wearers could see only the ground. Some Masks were led on chains to keep them from attacking the onlookers. One African Mask had a staff, the touch of which was believed to cause leprosy. In some cultures dead people are reincarnated as Masks—the back of the skull is sliced off, a stick rammed in from ear to ear, and someone dances, gripping the stick with his teeth. It's difficult to imagine the intensity of that experience.

Masks are surrounded by rituals that reinforce their power. A Tibetan Mask was taken out of its shrine once a year and set up overnight in a locked chapel. Two novice monks sat all night chanting prayers to prevent the spirit of the Mask from breaking loose. For miles around the villagers barred their doors at sunset and no one ventured out. Next day the Mask was lowered over the head of the dancer who was to incarnate the spirit at the centre of a great ceremony. What must it feel like to be that dancer, when the terrifying face becomes his own?

We don't know much about Masks in this culture, partly because the church sees the Mask as pagan, and tries to suppress it wherever it has the power (the Vatican has a museum full of Masks confiscated from the 'natives'), but also because this culture is usually hostile to trance states. We distrust spontaneity, and try to replace it by *reason*: the Mask was driven out of theatre in the same way that improvisation was driven out of music. Shakers have stopped shaking. Quakers don't quake any more. Hypnotised people used to stagger about, and tremble. Victorian mediums used to rampage about the room. Education itself might be seen as primarily an anti-trance activity.[2]

The church struggled against the Mask for centuries, but what can't be done by force is eventually done by the all-pervading influence of Western education. The US Army burned the voodoo temples in Haiti and the priests were sentenced to hard labour with little effect, but voodoo is now being suppressed in a more subtle way. The ceremonies are faked for tourists. The genuine ceremonies now last for a much shorter time.

I see the Mask as something that is continually flaring up in this culture, only to be almost immediately snuffed out. No sooner have I established a tradition of Mask work somewhere than the students start getting taught the 'correct' movements, just as they learn a phoney 'Commedia dell' Arte' technique. The manipulated Mask is hardly worth having, and is easy to drive out of the theatre. The Mask begins as a sacred object, and then becomes secular and is used in festivals and in the theatre. Finally it is remembered only in the feeble imitations of Masks sold in the tourist shops. The Mask dies when it is entirely subjected to the will of the performer.

4

Faces

We have instinctive responses to faces. Parental feelings seem to be triggered by flat faces and big foreheads. We try and be rational and assert that 'people can't help their appearance', yet we feel we know all about Snow White and the Witch, or Laurel and Hardy, just by the look of them. The truth is that we learn to hold characteristic expressions as a way of maintaining our personalities, and we're far more influenced by faces than we realise. When I was a child there were faces in books that were so terrible that I had to jam the books tight into the bookcase for fear they would somehow leak out into the house. Adults lose this vision in which the face *is* the person, but after their first Mask class students are amazed by passers-by in the street—suddenly they see 'evil' people, and 'innocent' people, and people holding their faces in Masks of pain, or grief, or pride, or whatever. Our faces get 'fixed' with age as the muscles shorten, but even in very young people you can see that a decision has been taken to appear tough, or stupid, or defiant. (Why should anyone wish to look stupid? Because then your teachers expect less of you.) Sometimes in acting class a student will break out of his habitual facial expression and you won't know who he is until you look at his clothes. I've seen this transformation several times, and each time the student is flooded with great joy and exhilaration.[3]

Even if you just alter the face with make-up, astounding effects can be produced. A journalist called Bill Richardson told me that he'd been asked to take part in a circus matinee as one of the clowns. It was when he was a cub reporter, and his editor had thought it might make an interesting story. Once the make-up was on he became 'possessed' and found himself able to tumble about, catch his feet in buckets, and so on, as if he'd been a clown in another incarnation. He stayed with the circus for some weeks, but he never got the same feeling without the make-up.

Another journalist, John Howard Griffin, disguised himself as a black man. He wrote:

'The transformation was total and shocking. I had expected to see myself disguised, but this was something else. I was imprisoned in the flesh of an utter stranger, an unsympathetic one with whom I felt no kinship. All traces of the John Griffin I had been were wiped from existence. I looked in the mirror and saw reflected nothing of the

white John Griffin's past. No, the reflections led back to Africa, back
to the shanty and the ghetto, back to the fruitless struggles against the
mark of blackness. Suddenly, almost with no mental preparation, no
advance hint, it became clear and it permeated my whole being. My
inclination was to fight against it. I had gone too far. . . . The completeness of the transformation appalled me. It was unlike anything
I had imagined. I became two men, the observing one and the one
who panicked, who felt negroid even into the depths of his entrails.'
(John Howard Griffin, *Black Like Me,* Panther, 1969.)

It's not surprising then to find that Masks produce changes in the
personality, or that the first sight of oneself wearing a Mask and
reflected in a mirror should be so disturbing. A bad Mask will produce
little effect, but a good Mask will give you the feeling that you know
all about the creature in the mirror. You feel that the Mask is about
to take over. It is at this moment of crisis that the Mask teacher will
urge you to continue. In most social situations you are expected to
maintain a consistent personality. In a Mask class you are encouraged
to 'let go', and allow yourself to become possessed.

5

Trance

Many actors report 'split' states of consciousness, or
amnesias; they speak of their body acting automatically, or as being
inhabited by the character they are playing.

Fanny Kemble: 'The curious part of acting, to me, is the sort of
double process which the mind carries on at once, the combined
operation of one's faculties, so to speak, in diametrically opposite
directions; for instance, in that very last scene of Mrs Beverley, while
I was half dead with crying in the midst of *real* grief, created by an
entirely *unreal* cause, I perceived that my tears were falling like rain
all over my silk dress, and spoiling it; and I calculated and measured
most accurately the space that my father would require to fall in, and
moved myself and my train accordingly in the midst of the anguish I
was to feign, and absolutely did endure.' (William Archer, *Masks and
Faces*, 1888.)

Sybil Thorndike: 'When you're an actor you cease to be male and
female, you're a person, and you're a person with all the other persons
inside you.' (*Great Acting*, BBC Publications, 1967.)

Edith Evans: '. . . I seem to have an awful lot of people inside me.
Do you know what I mean? If I understand them I feel terribly like

them when I'm doing them. . . . by thinking you turn into the person, if you think strongly enough. It's quite odd sometimes, you know. You are it, for quite a bit, and then you're not. . . .' (*Great Acting*.)

In another kind of culture I think it's clear that such actors could easily talk of being 'possessed' by the character. It's true that some actors will maintain that they always remain 'themselves' when they're acting, but how do they know? Improvisers who maintain that they're in a normal state of consciousness when they improvise often have unsuspected gaps in their memories which only emerge when you question them closely.

It's the same with Mask actors. I remember Roddy Maude-Roxby in a Mask that got angry during a show at Expo 67. He, or 'it', started throwing chairs about, so I walked on stage to stop the scene. 'S' goin' to be all right', said the Mask, waving me aside. Afterwards Roddy remembered the chairs, but not that I'd entered the scene and tried to stop him. If he'd been in a deeper trance he'd have forgotten everything. The same kind of amnesias can be detected in any spontaneous work. An improviser writes: '. . . If a scene goes badly I remember it. If it goes well I forget very quickly.' Orgasms are the same.

Normally we only know of our trance states by the time jumps. When an improviser feels that two hours have passed in twenty minutes, we're entitled to ask where was he for the missing hour and forty minutes.

Many people think that to be awake is the same as to be conscious, but they can be deeply hypnotised while believing that they are in 'everyday consciousness'. A student assured me that he'd spent two hours on stage fooling a hypnotist, which is unlikely. Then he said that funnily enough he'd been singled out to tell the audience that he'd really just been pretending, and that he hadn't minded when they laughed, because it did—by coincidence—happen to be true!

I knew a hypnotist's assistant who used to be left in store windows as an advert for the show.

'Of course he doesn't really hypnotise me,' he said.

'No?'

'No, he used to push needles through me and it hurt, so finally I told him and now he doesn't push them through me any more.'

'But why do you agree to sit motionless in shop windows all day?'

'Well, I like him.'

I can't imagine anyone in a normal state of consciousness sitting motionless in shop windows day after day *and* doing the evening show. How much then are we to trust what anyone tells us about their state of mind?

We don't think of ourselves as moving in and out of trance because we're trained not to. It's impossible to be 'in control' all the time, but we convince ourselves that we are. Other people help to stop us drifting. They will laugh if we don't seem immediately in possession of ourselves, and we'll laugh too in acknowledgement of our inappropriate behaviour.

In 'normal consciousness' I am aware of myself as 'thinking verbally'. In sports which leave no time for verbalisation, trance states are common. If you think: 'The ball's coming at that angle but it's spinning so that I'll anticipate the direction of the bounce by . . .' you miss! You don't know you're in a trance state because whenever you check up, there you are, playing table tennis, but you may have been in just as deep a trance as the bobsleigh rider who didn't know he'd lost a thumb until he shook hands.

Most people only recognise 'trance' when the subject looks confused—out of touch with the reality around him. We even think of hypnosis as 'sleep'. In many trance states people are *more* in touch, more observant. I remember an experiment in which deep trance subjects were first asked how many objects there had been in the waiting-room. When they were put into trance and asked again, it was found that they had actually observed more than ten times the number of objects than they consciously remembered. Zen Masters, and sorcerers, are notoriously difficult to creep up on (Castaneda's Don Juan, for example). In Mask work people report that perceptions are more intense, and that although they see differently, they see and sense *more*.

I see the 'personality' as a public-relations department for the real mind, which remains unknown. My personality always seems to be functioning, at some level, in terms of what other people think. If I am alone in a room and someone knocks on the door, then I 'come back to myself'. I do this in order to check up that my social image is presentable: are my flies done up? Is my social face properly assembled? If someone enters, and I decide that I don't have to guard myself, then I can get 'lost in the conversation'. Normal consciousness is related to transactions, real or imagined, with other people. That's how I experience it, and I note widespread reports of people in isolation, or totally rejected by other people, who experience 'personality disintegration'.

When you're worried about what other people might think, the personality is always present. In life-or-death situations something else takes over. A friend scalded himself and his mind split immediately into two parts, one of which was a child screaming with pain, while the other was cold and detached and told him exactly what to do (he was alone at the time). If a cobra dropped out of the air vent into the middle of an acting class, the students might find themselves on the piano, or outside the door, with no memory of how they got there. In extremity the body takes over for us, pushing the personality aside as an unnecessary encumbrance.

6

Induction

How do we enter trance states? I would prefer to ask 'How do we stay out of them?' In the middle of a dark night I wake up, how do I know I'm awake? I test for consciousness by moving a muscle. If I block this impulse to move I feel a tremendous anxiety. The control I exercise over the musculature reassures me that 'I'm me'. By tensing muscles, by shifting position, by scratching, sighing, yawning, blinking, and so on, we maintain 'normal consciousness'. Entranced subjects will sit quite motionless for hours. An audience 'held' by a theatrical performance suddenly find a need to move, to shift position, to cough, as the spell breaks.

If you lie down and make your body relax, going through it from feet to head, and loosening any points of tension that you find, then you easily float away into fantasy. The substance and shape of your body seem to change. You feel as if the air is breathing you, rather than you breathing the air, and the rhythm is slow and smooth like a great tide. It's very easy to lose yourself, but if you feel the presence of a hostile person in the room you break this trance, seizing hold of the musculature, and becoming 'yourself' once more.

Meditators use stillness as a means of inducing trance. So do present-day hypnotists. The subject doesn't have to be told to be still, he knows intuitively not to assert control of his body by picking his nose or tapping his feet.

When you are 'absorbed' you no longer control the musculature. You can drive for miles, or play a movement from a sonata while your personality pays no attention at all. Nor is your performance necessarily worse. When a hypnotist takes over the function normally exercised by the personality, there's no need to leave the trance. Mask teachers, priests in possession cults, and hypnotists all play high status in voice and movement. A high-status person whom you accept as dominant can easily propel you into unusual states of being. You're likely to respond to his suggestions, and see, like Polonius, the cloud looking like a whale. If the Queen knocked unexpectedly on your door and said 'I wonder if I might use your lavatory?' then you'd probably be in a very odd state indeed.

Eysenck tells the seemingly improbable story of a hypnotist who worked for a total of three hundred hours on one subject with no apparent result. When the frustrated hypnotist finally snarled, 'Go to sleep, you *****!' the subject went straight into deep trance. I would interpret such an incident as the subject yielding to the status attack of the hypnotist.

I once asked a girl to close her eyes while I put a coin under one of three cups. Secretly I put a coin under each cup. When I asked her to guess which cup the coin was under, she was, of course, correct. After she'd made a correct choice about six times, she was convinced I was somehow controlling her thoughts, and moved into a rather dis-associated state, so I explained, and she 'snapped out of it'. I would suggest this as a possible means of inducing hypnosis. Alan Mitchell describes a technique of 'confusion' used by the American hypnotist, Erickson. He writes:

'Erickson made a number of conflicting suggestions to a patient: "Lift your left arm, now your right. Up with the left, down with the right. Swing the left arm out and the left arm follows." Eventually the subject became so confused by these directions, which were woolly and conflicting, that he was glad to clutch at any straw, so long as it was given to him firmly enough and in a loud voice. Then, while he was so confused, if he were told: "Go to sleep", apparently he would drop off immediately into a deep sleep.' (*Harley Street Hypnotist*, Harrap, 1959.)

Again we see that the subject is made to feel that his body is out of control, and becomes subject to a high-status person. Some hypnotists sit you down, ask you to stare upwards into their eyes and suggest that your eyelids are wanting to close—which works because looking upwards is tiring, and because staring up into a high-status person's eyes makes you feel inferior. Another method involves getting you to hold your arm out sideways while suggesting that it's getting heavier. If you think the hypnotist is responsible for the heaviness rather than gravity, then you are likely to accept his control. Hypnotists don't, as sometimes claimed, ask you to put your hands together and then tell you that you can't part them, but they do ask you to link them in such a way that it's awkward to part them. If you believe the hypnotist responsible for such awkwardness, then you may abandon the attempt to separate them. If you squeeze your index finger hard, and then wait, you'll feel it starting to swell—I imagine this is an illusion caused by the weakening of the muscles of the compressing hand. This too can be a way of inducing trance so long as the subject doesn't realise that the 'swelling' would be experienced anyway, even without the hypnotist's suggestion.[4]

Once you understand that you're no longer held responsible for your actions, then there's no need to maintain a 'personality'. Student improvisers asked to *pretend* to be hypnotised, show a sudden improvement. Students asked to pretend to be *hypnotists* show no such improvement.

Many ways of entering trance involve interfering with verbalisation. Repetitive singing or chanting are effective, or holding the mind on to single words; such techniques are often thought of as 'Oriental', but they're universal.[5]

One dramatic way of entering trance is by 'trumping'. This was used in a West Indian play at the Royal Court, with the unwanted result that actors kept going into real trance, and not just acting it. It works partly by the 'crowd effect', everyone repeating the same action and sound, but also by over-oxygenating the blood. It looks like a 'forward-moving two-step stomp'.

'With the step forward the body is bent forwards from the waist so sharply as to seem propelled by force. At the same time the breath exhaled, or inhaled, with great effort and sound. The forcefulness of the action gives justification to the term "labouring" ... When the spirit possession does take place ... an individual's legs may seem riveted to the ground ... or he may be thrown to the ground.' (S. E. Simpson, *Religious Cults of Caribbean: Trinidad, Jamaica and Haiti*, Institute of Caribbean Studies, University of Puerto Rico, 1970.)

Crowds are trance-inducing because the anonymity imposed by the crowd absolves you of the need to maintain your identity.

7

Possession

The type of trance I am concerned with in this essay is the 'controlled trance', in which permission to remain 'entranced' is given by other people, either by an individual or a group. Such trances may be rare, or may pass unrecognised in this culture, but we should consider them as a normal part of human behaviour. Researchers who have studied possession cults report that it is the better adjusted citizens who are most likely to become possessed. Many people regard 'trance' as a sign of madness, just as they presume that 'madmen' must be easy to hypnotise. The truth is that if madmen were capable of being under 'social control' they would never have revealed the behaviour that categorised them as insane. It's a tautology to say that normal people are the most suggestible, since it's because they're the most suggestible that they're the most normal!

If we compare Mask work with 'possession cults', then we can see many similarities. It's true that the possessed person is often supposed to remember nothing that happens during the trance—but this is also observed sometimes in Mask work, even though it's not demanded. And two types of possession are often described: an amnesiac and a lucid state. Possessed people don't seem to need speech lessons (which Masks do, as described later), but there are many descriptions of inarticulate sounds *preceding* speech. And sometimes a deeply possessed Mask will speak from the first moment.

Every Mask teacher will recognise this situation, reported by Simpson of a Shango cult: 'One person said, "The drummers are not beating well tonight." A drummer called out that "It is no use to drum if you get no response." Later a woman stood up and shouted: "You are not singing at all tonight." The leader appeared and denounced the group for its lack of enthusiasm.'

Like Mask teachers, the 'priests' in possession cults are high status, but 'indulgent' to the possessed trancers. Maya Deren describes an incident in Haiti when someone possessed by the God Ghede* arrived at the wrong time. The Houngan (priest) objected.

' "Oh I just dropped in", he (Ghede) said, making a self-effacing gesture, "to look around a bit. I'll just stroll around and look things over." ' (Ghede then asked for nine cassavas—flat breads.) 'Ghede stood eating two of them at once as if he was part of the audience, and watched the great loa (spirit) Ogoun and Damballa. Then the audience was distracted by the problem of a man who had climbed up a tree under possession of Damballa. As the possession seemed about to leave him the Houngan was begging Damballa to bring the man to earth before leaving (else the man might fall and kill himself).' Ghede then missed some of his cassavas. 'Suddenly Ghede threw a great tantrum about the thieves who had stolen his remaining cassavas.

* Also spelt Ghédé, Gheda, (Papa), Gueda, etc. by different writers.

He caught hold of the Houngan and shrieked and stamped his feet, meanwhile Damballa and Ogoun were being ignored. There was no choice but to buy Ghede more cassavas and some biscuits to placate him.

'Now as the loa turned to walk off with the new food, the Houngan, smiling, said to him, "Are you sure it wasn't a man in a little multi-coloured cap who stole those cassavas?"

'Ghede wheeled with enormous eyes of innocence. "A little cap? What man in a little cap?" ... Someone called out: "Are you sure you don't know who stole your cassavas?" Whereupon, looking at us out of the corner of his eye with a delightful and endearing expression, Ghede winked once, slowly, and walked away.' (*The Divine Horsemen*, Thames and Hudson, London, 1953; Delta Books, New York, 1970.)

Ghede, God of death, and of sexuality, is consumed by raging hungers, but note the paradox that the supernatural creature who we would expect to be 'super-adult' is very childlike—exactly as the Masks are. Ghede, in Deren's description, sounds exactly like a Mask.

'We asked him why he liked to wear smoked glasses. "Well," he explained, "I spend so much time in the dark underworld that it makes my eyes sensitive to the sun." "Why", we asked then, "do you remove the right lens so often?" "Well, my dear," he answered, "it's this way: with my left eye, I watch over the whole universe. As for the right, I keep that eye on my food, so that no thief will get it." '

The character of a Mask will *not* be like the wearer's character. Simpson, writing of the Shango cults, says: 'My informants denied that there is a close correspondence between the personality character-istics of a power and his followers. Sometimes a power manifests itself on a "child" ("horse") whose personality is the exact opposite of the god's. A devotee may be possessed by a violent power at one time and by a quiet power on another occasion according to the work to be done.... One informant said: "What a person is afraid to do, he does when possessed." '

My suspicion is that the number of 'personality types' that emerge in Mask work is pretty limited. To be sure, we would have to compare films from different cultures, and analyse the movements and sounds of the 'spirits'. This research hasn't been carried out, but just as myths from all over the world show similar structures, so I believe that wherever there is a 'Pantalone-type' Mask there will be Pantalones. The same characters persisted in the Commedia dell' Arte not because the tradition was sterile, but because the Masks themselves imposed certain ways of behaving. Chaplin's Tramp has always existed. Harpo, and Stan Laurel, and Pappa Gueda, and Ranga the Witch, and the Braggard Soldier, are just there, wherever there is a human brain.

I consider the possessed trance as a particular form of the hypnotic trance. Some people have denied this, but all the phenomena typical of possession can be induced by hypnosis. It's true that clinical hypnosis looks very different, but that is because the hypnotist isn't arranging a performance before an approving audience.[6] As there is hardly any literature on Mask possession, I'll quote some examples of spirit possession. Anyone teaching the Mask is likely at some time to encounter deep trance states, so it's useful to understand their nature.

Here's Lucian's description of a priestess being possessed at Delphi: 'She went blundering frantically about the shrine, with the god mounted on the nape of her neck, knocking over the tripods that stood in her path. The hair rose on her scalp, and when she tossed her head the wreaths went flying over the bare floor . . . her mouth foamed frenziedly; she groaned, gasped, uttered weird sounds, and made the huge cave re-echo with her dismal shrieks. In the end Apollo forced her to intelligible speech. . . . Before her spirit could be restored to the light of common day, a spell of unconsciousness intervened. Apollo was washing her mind with Lethe water, to make her forget the fateful secrets she had learned during his effulgent visitation. The spirit of divine truth departed and returned to whence it came; Phemonoe collapsed on the floor, and was revived with difficulty.' (Translated by Robert Graves, *Pharsalia*, Penguin, 1956.)

The fear, and the feeling of the god mounting on to the neck, or head, is typical of possession as encountered in the New World cults.[7] But compare Lucan's description above with one by David G. Mandelbaum writing of possession in a village in South India.

'A spasm of shivering works through the diviner, then another, and his head begins to shake from side to side. The head movements continue with increasing velocity until it seems as if no human vertebrae could stand the strain. The diviner may fall to his knees and beat his palms against the earth with a furious tattoo, but the deity does not speak through him until his hair is loosened. The long Kota locks are tied up with a cord which has ritual significance, and this cord must be dislodged by the force of the head motion. When the diviner's hair does fall free about his oscillating head, a strangled sob bursts forth from him—the first articulation of the god speaking through his chosen medium. With jerky, strangled utterance, the diviner's voice serves as the mouthpiece of the deity.' (*Anthropology of Folk Religion*, Charles Leslie, 1960.)

William Sargant has compared the possessed trance to the Pavlovian state of 'transmarginal inhibition'. When a brain is subjected to great stress a protective breakdown occurs: first the brain begins to give the same response to strong as to weak signals (the grading goes), next the brain responds *more* strongly to *weak* signals, and then conditioned responses reverse—he cites the case of Maya Deren as an example of 'transmarginal inhibition'. During her study of the voodoo cults in Haiti, she became possessed herself on several occasions. Once she arrived to film a ceremony, but 'blanked out' when the drums started, and recovered consciousness to find that not only was the ceremony over, but that she had conducted it herself. She says:

'The possessed benefits least of all men from his own possession. He may suffer for it in material loss, in the sometimes painful, always exhausted aftermath. And to the degree that his consciousness persists into its first moments or becomes aware of it at the very end, he experiences an overwhelming fear. Never have I seen the face of such anguish, ordeal and blind terror as at moments when the loa comes.'

One would imagine that people would struggle to avoid this terrifying experience, but it's obvious that many people desire it. It's part of the voodoo mythology that the god should possess you 'against your will'. I would think that Maya Deren was subject to a high level of conflict, but it's significant that she was possessed by the beautiful, sexy goddess Erzulie, and she did get an amazing chapter of her book.

I. M. Lewis says: 'The possessed person who in the seance is the centre of attention says in effect, "Look at me, I am dancing". . . . Haitian voodoo ceremonies are quite clearly theatres, in which problems and conflicts relating to the life situations of the participants are dramatically enacted with great symbolic force. . . . Everything takes on the tone and character of modern psychodrama or group therapy. Abreaction is the order of the day. Repressed urges and desires, the idiosyncratic as well as the socially conditioned, are given full public rein.' (*Ecstatic Religion,* Penguin, 1971.)

Maya Deren's first possession occurred when she was a guest of honour at a voodoo ceremony. She was absorbed in talking to the Houngan and wasn't attending to the drums or the singing. This would tend to make her *more* vulnerable. Then she was called to take part in the ceremony for a moment, and 'forgot' what she had to do, even though she had done it often at previous ceremonies. What she did 'happened' to be right and she returned to her chair, to find that the drums and singing were louder and 'sharper'.

I would say that she was now already in light trance. She was then caught up in the singing until she found herself 'standing bolt upright, singing or perhaps even screaming the song'. She felt 'winded' and took no part in the dancing.

She describes a strong feeling of being at one with the group: 'I have but to rise, to step forward, to become a part of this glorious movement, flowing with it, its motion becoming mine, as the roll of the sea might become the inundation of my own body. At such moments one does not move *to* the sound, one *is* the movement of the sound, created and borne by it; hence nothing is difficult.'

She then crosses to her servant, only to find that her leg 'roots to the ground'. She experiences an 'unpleasant lightness in the head', and repeats the words 'hold together' to herself. She goes outside and smokes a cigarette and feels her head 'tightening, integrating, becoming solid once more'.

When she hears the salute to the god Odin, she 'has' to return in order not to give offence. Had she *really* wanted to escape she could of course have 'become ill'. She touches the hand of a possessed person and feels a momentary shock like 'electricity', and other people indicate to her that she is likely to become possessed. She is troubled by her 'persistent vulnerability' and all round her people are falling into trance. She decides to continue: 'To run away would be cowardice. I could resist, but I must not escape. And I can resist best, I think to myself, if I put aside the fears and nervousness; if, instead of suspecting my vulnerability, I set myself in brazen competition with all this which would compel me to its authority.'

At some level she clearly wants to enter trance, but she believes she is being forced into it *against her will*. The spirits are to be fully responsible for casting aside her personality. She's had all the warning signals, and now she joins in the singing and the dancing and feels no fear. She feels incredibly tired but she doesn't stop until suddenly it becomes *easier,* although she doesn't notice the exact moment at which 'the pace which seemed unbearably demanding had slipped down a notch into a slow motion'.

It's clear that her time sense is distorting, and that she's already in a very odd state of consciousness. Her leg 'roots' to the ground again. The 'slower' drums will actually be speeding up as the drummers try to push her into deep trance. She sees everything as very beautiful and she turns to a neighbour to say, 'See how lovely that is' when she finds herself isolated, alone in a circle.

'I realise like a shaft of terror struck through me, that it is no longer myself whom I watch. Yet it *is* myself, for as that terror strikes, we two are made one again, joined by and upon the point of the left leg. The white darkness starts to shoot up; I wrench my foot free but the effort catapults me over what seems a vast, vast distance, and I come to rest on a firmness of arms and bodies which would hold me up. But these have voices—great insistent, singing voices—whose sound would smother me. With every muscle I pull loose and again plunge across a vast space. . . . My skull is a drum; each great beat drives that leg, like the point of a stake, into the ground. The singing is at my very ear, inside my head. This sound will drown me! "Why don't they stop! Why don't they stop!" I cannot wrench the leg free. I am caught in this cylinder, this well of sound. There is nothing anywhere except this. There is no way out. The white darkness moves up the veins of my leg like a swift tide rising, rising; it is a great force which I cannot sustain or contain, which surely will burst my skin. "Mercy" I scream within me. I hear it echoed by the voices, shrill and unearthly: "Erzulie!" The bright darkness floods up through my body, reaches my head, engulfs me. I am sucked down and exploded at once. That is all.'

This sounds more like the priestess at Delphi than hypnosis, but isn't just a spectacular induction technique. Alfred Metraux observes that 'People who are used to possession pass quickly through the whole range of nervous symptoms, and then, suddenly, there they are: in full trance. Even as much preamble as this may be dispensed with when a ceremony is in full swing and demands instantaneous entry on the part of the gods.' (*Voodoo in Haiti,* translated by H. Charteris, André Deutsch, 1972.) He also points out that the intensity of the attack depends on the nature of the god being incarnated. I see Sargent's 'transmarginal inhibition' as being just *another* way of entering trance.

As for the terror that she insists on, there are many accounts of 'calm' possession, so I don't think terror is 'built-in' to the process, or rather that it's the mythology that produces the terror. Interestingly Maya Deren said elsewhere, and before ever she went to Haiti: 'Total amnesia, although less spectacular than many other forms of mental disorder, has always seemed to me the most terrifying.' ('An Anagram of Ideas on Art', *Form and Film,* 1946.)

In possession cults the worshippers incarnate the gods, and their posture, movements, and voices change as does the facial expression. Oesterreich says: 'Transformation of the physiognomy appears in all descriptions.' (Oesterreich also mentions an eleven-year-old girl who began speaking in a 'deep bass voice'.) The spirits that arrive are almost always well known to the congregation, and the priest will have the requisite costumes or props ready for them. Extended improvisations then take place which are very theatrical. Here's Jane Belo describing an Indonesian possession ceremony:

'The crowd that gathered was alert and attentive, the whole spirit like that of a game in which everyone would take part. Everyone would join in the singing which directed the trancer's performance. People would call out jibes to the performers, urging them on, taunting them with phrases known to infuriate them. The crowd enjoyed this very much indeed. When the time came to bring the act to an end, a whole group would fall on the trancer, who struggled fiercely in convulsions precipitated by the attack. Amid great excitement, everyone would fall over everyone else in a headlong rough-and-tumble. They would then set themselves to nursing the trancer back to normal consciousness. All would then be just as intent on caring for the man who was coming back to himself as they had been a few minutes before in taunting and exciting the creature he had "become".' (*Trance in Bali*, Columbia University Press, New York, 1960.)

Voodoo trancers may be possessed by several different gods one after another, and the same god may inhabit several people at the same time—in Haiti there was once a mass demonstration in which several hundred people all possessed by Papa Gheda, marched on the presidential palace. It's reported that voodoo trancers remember nothing about their possessions, but Jane Belo, writing of trance in Indonesia, describes two types of possession: one in which a 'power is present that is different from his "I", and makes two simultaneous integrations, and that in which there is a temporary but total change of the personality in which the person is "transformed" into another being or object.' (*Trance in Bali*.)

Here's an example of voodoo gods improvising together described by Metraux: 'These impromptus, which vary in style, are much appreciated by the audience, who yell with laughter, join in the dialogue, and noisily show their pleasure or discontent. Take an example: someone possessed by Zaka appears under the peristyle in the get-up of a peasant. By canny movements he mimes the anxiety of a countryman come to town, and who fears to be robbed. Now another possessed person joins him, one might almost say 'comes on'. It is Guede-nibo of the Guede family, which watches over the dead. Zaka is clearly terrified by the presence of his gloomy colleague and tries to propitiate him, inviting him to have something to eat and to drink some rum. Guede, who is making a show as a townsman, exchanges courtesies with him, trying to tease him. He asks him: "What have you got in your bag?" He searches it and examines the contents. Alarmed, Zaka cries "Stop, stop!" The bag is returned to him only to be surreptitiously lifted off him while he is examining one of the sick. Zaka, in despair, calls for cards and shells in order to discover the thief by means of divination. The audience chants "Play, Zaka, play".' (And so on.) (*Voodoo in Haiti*.)

Any Mask teacher will recognise the scenes reported to occur during 'possession' as typical of the Mask. One would expect the gods to be presented as supermen, but in all 'trance' cultures we find a mythology which describes the gods as acting in a childlike way. As Melville says, 'The gods are like children and must be told what to do.'

8

Teaching Mask Work

For an introductory Mask class I will set up a table with a variety of props on it. They'll be on a table because the act of bending down may turn a new Mask off. I avoid any props that would present 'difficulties'. An umbrella might encourage a Mask to think how to open it. An alarm clock might suggest winding it up. Anything that would require a Mask to have a mental age of more than two and a half I would remove. The objects on the table are the sort that would interest young children. I choose things that give a variety of tactile experiences: a scarf, a carrot, bells, silver foil, a jar, a balloon, a piece of fur, a doll, a toy animal, a stick, rubber tubing, flowers, sweets. Children's books are all right if they're small, and it helps if they're in a foreign language. (My wife, Ingrid, wraps up little presents for the Masks in the classes she gives; each tiny packet has a sweet, or a little toy in it, which is something the Masks like.)

I put some furniture on the stage, and set up a screen to one side. Behind the screen are hats, and coats, and pyjamas, boiler suits, and a few dresses. If the clothes are a little out of fashion, so much the better. Real clothes are generally better than stage costumes, though. Sheets of coloured material are good. I used to have some big felt 'shoes' that some Masks liked—I think they were made to fit inside gumboots in cold weather.

Once the students are ready I change my status, and play 'high'. I don't bounce around and wave my arms like I would for a comedy class. I become stiller, 'serious' and more 'adult'. The change in me produces a change of feeling in the students which I exploit by assuring them that the Masks are *not* dangerous, that whatever happens I can handle it, and that all that matters is that they must take off the Mask when I ask them to. The more I reassure them the more jumpy they get, and by the time they come to take a Mask many of them will be trembling. The skill lies in creating the correct balance between interest and anxiety.

I also have to establish that they will not be held responsible for their actions while in the Mask. I illustrate this with stories.

We had a Mask that had a thick droopy nose and angry eyebrows. It was a deep, congested red in colour, and it liked to pick up sticks and hit people. It was quite safe so long as the teacher knew this and said 'Take the Mask off!' sharply at the critical moment. Someone borrowed it once—Pauline Melville, who had taken over my classes at Morley College. Next day she returned the Masks and said that someone had been hit on the arm. I had to explain that it was my fault for not warning her. (And I pointed to the Mask that hit people.) I once saw three similar droopy-nosed Masks—they were Kabuki Masks, and they were on the *hanamichi* (the platform that runs through the audience) and yes, they had sticks and were threatening people.

Another Mask was called Mr Parks. This one used to laugh, and stare into the air, and sit on the extreme edge of chairs and fall off sideways. Shay Gorman created the character. I took the Mask along to a course I gave in Hampshire. The students were entering from behind a screen and suddenly I heard Mr Parks's laughter. It entered with the same posture Shay Gorman had adopted, and looked up as if something was very amusing about the ceiling, and then it kept sitting on the extreme edge of a chair as if it wanted to fall off. Fortunately it didn't, because the wearer wasn't very athletic. It really makes no sense that a Mask should be able to transmit that sort of information to its wearer.

Once students begin to observe for themselves the way that Masks compel certain sorts of behaviour, then they really begin to feel the presence of 'spirits'. I remember a Mask I'd just made. A student tried it out and turned into a hunched, twisted, gurgling creature. Then a latecomer arrived, picked up the same Mask, and the identical creature appeared. I tell students to take any Mask as long as it's comfortable. Probably they'll be manoeuvring to pick one that they think they can do well, but this doesn't really matter because it'll look quite different when they see it reflected in the mirror. Once the student has found a comfortable Mask, one that doesn't dig into his eyes, I arrange his hair so that it covers the elastic and the top of the forehead of the Mask.

I then say: 'Relax. Don't think of anything. When I show you the mirror, *make your mouth fit the Mask, and hold it so that the mouth and the Mask make one face*. You'll know all about the creature in the mirror, so you don't have to think about it. Become the thing you see, turn away from the mirror, and go to the table. There'll be something that it wants. Let it find it. Disobey anything I'm saying if it wants to, but if I say "Take the Mask off", then you must take it off.'

I present the mirror very smoothly, slicing it upwards into the space between me and the actor. The shock of seeing the reflection is to be as strong as possible. After two seconds I begin to step aside, swinging the mirror with me, so that the actor will automatically take a step, and will be facing the table with the props as the mirror leaves him. If the actor seems to be resisting the change I might say 'You're changing now', or 'Make the face fit the Mask.' I use a head-sized mirror because the information they need comes from the face. If the mirror is bigger, then they see their whole body and are likely to start posturing. I don't want them to *think* about being another creature, I want them to experience being another creature.[8]

Some students will compulsively touch their Mask as soon as they see their reflection. This is a defence: they want to reassure themselves that it's 'only a mask'. If students seem seriously afraid then I tell them to cross their fingers or something. Once they accept such a method of keeping themselves 'safe' they've already entered a 'magical universe'. When they agree to uncross their fingers or whatever, the effects of the Mask will be even stronger. In possession cults you can protect yourself by clinging to the beams or 'tying knots in your underwear'. Some students go rigid, and then remove the Mask, visibly shaken, and say 'Nothing happened.' Other students 'think out' what to do, and then hop around pretending to be boxers, or posture like Harlequins or whatever. 'Don't have any words in your head', I say.

When a student tries on a Mask for the second time I may say 'When you look in the mirror let the Mask make a sound, and keep the sound going all through the scene.' This is a meditation technique very effective in blocking verbalisation (like Tibetan monks chanting 'Oooooommmmm'). I often say things like 'Yes, that's excellent', or 'Who is it?' or 'Amazing' even before students have looked in the mirror, so that the feeling of being different, and hidden, is reinforced. The Masks begin to pant, and wheeze, and howl, which freaks out the people watching even more, and 'pumps the atmosphere up'. In voodoo cults the drums throb for hours to call the gods across the ocean from Africa.

Once one person is possessed, others usually follow almost immediately. In a beginners' Mask class there is usually a 'dead' twenty minutes before the first Mask appears—if you're lucky. My method is to 'seed' the class with a fully developed Mask. The presence of a 'possessed' Mask allows students to 'let go', and alarms and reassures at the same time. The same phenomenon is reported in possession cults; and it's easier to hypnotise someone who has just seen it done to someone else.

I encourage students to throw themselves in, and to stop being 'critical', by saying: 'Make mistakes! These Masks are more extreme, more powerful than ordinary faces! Don't be timid. Make big mistakes. Don't worry about being wrong! Rely on me to stop you!' Sometimes I say: 'What you saw in the mirror was *right*! But you only showed me a shadow of it. Try the Mask again. You'll never get anywhere if you aren't brave.' Sometimes I see that a person is transformed for just a moment as they look in a mirror, but then take hold of themselves to cancel it out. I stop them, make them remove the Mask and then start again immediately.

A girl puts on a Mask and is transformed. She seems to illuminate the room, but instantly she removes it.

'Be gentle with the Mask,' I say. When people feel that the Mask has made them betray themselves they'll throw it down. I've seen one hurled from centre stage to the back of the stalls. In the present case my warning reinforces the feeling that unexpected and violent things may happen.

'I couldn't do it,' she says.

'But it was marvellous.'

'It felt wrong.'

'You mean you didn't like the thing you had turned into.'

'That's right.'

'That means you can do it, the experience was *real*.'

I reassure her, and let her watch and see that no one is coming to harm.

The problem is not one of getting the students to experience the 'presence' of another personality—almost everyone gets a strong kick from their reflection—the difficulty lies in stopping the student from making the change 'himself'. There's no reason for the student to start 'thinking' when he already 'knows' intuitively exactly what sort of creature he is. Getting him to hold his mouth in a fixed position, and having him make sounds helps to block verbalisation, and 'finding a prop' helps to tear the Mask away from the mirror. Unfortunately, even the effort of walking may throw the actor into normal consciousness. That's why I hold the mirror near the table (less than eight feet), and in extreme cases I start the Mask at the table, or sitting in a chair.

A new Mask is like a baby that knows nothing about the world. Everything looks astounding to it, and it has little access to its wearer's skills. Very often a Mask will have to learn how to sit, or bend down, or how to hold things. It's as if you build up another personality from scratch; it's as if a part of the mind gets separated, and then develops on its own. There are exceptions, but in most cases the very best Masks start off knowing the least. They don't know how to take the lids off jars; they don't understand the idea of wrapping things (given a present they just admire the paper). When objects fall to the floor it's as if they've ceased to exist. One student always left the room before wearing a particularly regressive Mask. I asked her why, and she said, 'It's silly, but I'm afraid I might wet myself, so I always go to the toilet.'

Normal Masks go through a period of learning, so that after a dozen or so classes they have a limited vocabulary, a number of 'props' that they regularly handle, and some sort of history based on interactions with other Masks. A Mask that grabs everything will have learned that the other Masks will punish it, and so on. Actors who 'can't do' Mask work are never able to let the Mask be truly stupid and ignorant. They try to transfer their own skills directly. Instead of allowing a Mask to explore a closed umbrella they'll 'take over' and open it. Instead of letting the Mask suffer because it hasn't learned to sit in a chair they'll 'make' it sit. By their impatience, and desire to exert control, they bypass a necessary process. The Mask feeling leaks away and we are left with the actor pretending to be another person, instead of *being* another person.

Some Masks are 'muscle-bound', and act like 'monsters'. I don't encourage these unless they're all an actor can produce. The most important thing is that an actor should dredge up some sort of 'spirit', but I prefer Masks that release the actor physically and vocally. I encourage Masks that are 'human', like big extrovert children, or expressive of very intense feelings: greed, lust, or tenderness, for example. As soon as a Mask arrives that seems useful I get the actor to repeat it. I say, 'Tell yourself you're looking in the mirror for the first time, the Mask will do the rest.' This stops the actor from trying to remember what the Mask did 'last time'.

Soon there are a number of recognisable 'personalities' that I can put together in scenes. I usually tell each Mask that it owns all the props, and that it's going to meet some nice people. At first Masks are often rather grotesque, very depressed or manic—and sometimes frightening. Interacting socialises them. They make friends and enemies. We now have a community of Masks, each with its own costume, props, and personal history.

They probably still don't *speak*—and the inability to speak is almost a sign of good Mask work. Actors are amazed to find that it's necessary to give the Masks 'speech lessons'. Masks usually understand words said to them, but they have the comprehension of a young child. Long words are ignored, or produce bewilderment.

I set up a scene in which the Mask is to meet a 'very nice voice teacher'. I collect the props that I think will interest the Mask, and I get someone to stay close to it with a mirror.

'Come in', I say. 'Sit?'

It looks baffled.

'Sit,' I say, and I sit on a chair. If it 'catches on' it'll imitate me and probably make some sort of sound. 'Stand,' I say, and we play 'sitting and standing' like two idiots. Then I give the Mask a present, perhaps a balloon. 'Balloon,' I say, and if it doesn't want it, or won't say the word, I don't pressure it. If it likes the balloon, I say 'Yellow balloon' or whatever. Whenever the Mask begins to turn off, it gets a recharge from the mirror, and I keep well back, and hand it things at arm's length. If I get too close to it I'll probably turn it off. I have to be careful not to invade the Mask's 'space', although proximity between Masks will deepen their trance.

When other people act as voice teachers they usually want to bully the Masks. I suppose this comes from the way we treat young children. They touch the Masks; they try to blackmail them into speaking, refusing to give them presents until they obey. If a word is said, the 'teachers' try frantically to get the pronunciation exactly right. Then the Mask suffers and won't co-operate.

By far the best way is to have one Mask that already speaks work as teacher. Such Masks often express annoyance at their pupils' 'stupidity', but there's something very magical in removing the human being from the process so that the Masks hand on their own traditions. Masks can even hold the mirrors.

I'm happy if I get three sounds which resemble words in a five-minute session. Many words can't be said at the beginning because of the way the mouth is being held. Three words is a great achievement. Once the Mask has learned a dozen or so words it begins to transfer words from its wearer's vocabulary, or to pick them up from other Masks.

Speech lessons sound silly, but remember Chaplin, who never really found the right voice for his Tramp. He made many experiments and finally made him sing in gibberish (*Modern Times*). 'Charlie' always sounds like Chaplin when he talks, and I think Chaplin knew this, and this is probably why he abandoned the character. If he'd been able to work in a Mask class he'd almost certainly have been able to find a voice.

An actor may develop several Masks, each with its own characteristics and vocabulary. If I use an unfamiliar word to a Mask it'll ask me what it means, and it'll *always* remember that word. What is freaky is that each Mask remembers what it knows, and also what it doesn't know. An actor left the Studio just when his Mask was learning to speak. After two years he returned, and started another speech lesson, and he was using exactly the vocabulary he had learned at the previous class. Hypnotic subjects are reported to be in rapport with all the other occasions when they were in trance, and the same is true of Mask characters.

I speed up the learning of words by getting the Masks to count up to ten, or to say the alphabet. Nursery rhymes are useful. I get Masks to recite little poems to the audience who applaud wildly. One nursery rhyme can teach so many words that the Mask goes straight into simple speech.

Here are some notes by Mask students on what the Mask state feels like.

'I found that the inability to speak was the freakiest feeling, combined with a feeling of being on an energetic high, and having a total disregard for the audience. Colours seemed to deepen in intensity, and objects became possessions. The terrible feeling of having to succeed in front of people faded into the background, and body movements lost their stiffness and inhibitions. Sounds came unplanned to my throat.

'Once out of the Mask I find I am exhausted emotionally and physically, and cannot resume the Mask for a while without a rest. As an improviser I am nervous about appearing 'right', but once in a Mask, there's no such feeling and the Mask can improvise indefinitely (if happy).'

This student was an experienced amateur actress, and had learned an untruthful but effective way of presenting herself, based on strong 'demonstrations of feeling'. She was very 'armoured' against the audience, but in Mask work she was 'released', and seemed wonderfully gifted. My suspicion is that her extreme exhaustion may have been linked to residual anxieties about 'letting go'. I worked with her for a year, mostly on improvisation, and she was just beginning to transfer her Mask skills into her acting skills. With luck she should be out of the cul-de-sac.

Another student writes:

'I always come away from a Mask class with a feeling of *renewed* freshness, a light feeling.

'I like the Mask state very much—I guess you could say it acts on me the way some drugs would affect other people—an escape perhaps?

'My sense of touch and sound are increased, I want to touch and feel everything, loud sounds don't bother me. Colours are much brighter and more meaningful—I am more aware of them.

'Something happens to my eyes.

'A childlike sense of discovery.

'As a Mask there are a lot of things that can do a lot of harm—being hit—seeing someone else take their Mask off . . . a sense of failure during a Mask class. Maybe when I say harm I don't mean physically —but mentally it boggles the mind a lot—because you are literally a young child *open* to all the world will offer and the first experience is usually the lasting one.

'I feel much happier with myself as an actor now—because I have had some Mask training—can I tell why I feel better? I don't know. I just have a lot more confidence. I feel 'right' in the Mask state, whatever I do is fine, no emotional hangups.

'It's hard for me to take a Mask off that has worked for a long period of time successfully—once when I did take it off, I felt my face was being ripped off with it.'

A third student writes:

'When I had my first successful speech lesson, I felt that I knew how to say the words but the Mask didn't. A part of me knew how, and a part of me did not. The latter part was much the stronger of the two and maintained control without a struggle. . . .

'Masks do not like to pretend. In order to do the scene where the Mask enters from outdoors, I had to go out to the hall door and then come in. On the other hand it was easy for her (the Mask) to pretend that Ingrid's purse was a tea-cosy because she had no idea what a tea-cosy was.'

I remember some rather staid Swedish schoolteachers being let loose in a garden wearing Masks that they had developed indoors.

They shrieked with delight, raced over the flower beds and started tearing up the flowers. I stopped the scene, and found some of them very upset, since they'd never have imagined themselves behaving in such a way.

Students are likely to have vivid dreams when they begin Mask work. One very gifted student found himself sleepwalking for the first time in years. A Canadian student was trying a Mask on at home and went out into his garden wearing it when the temperature was minus twenty Centigrade. He was astounded to find that he was standing in the snow in his bare feet. Masks are very strange and should be approached with caution, not because they're really dangerous, but because a bad experience may put a teacher or student off for good.

At the moments when a Mask 'works' the student feel a decision-lessness, and an inevitability. The teacher sees a sudden 'naturalness', and that the student is no longer 'acting'. At first the Mask may flash on for just a couple of seconds. I have to see and explain exactly when the change occurs. The two states are actually very different, but most students are insensitive to changes in consciousness. Some students hold rigidly to 'normal consciousness', but most keep switching from their control to the Mask's control and back again. It becomes possible to say 'The mask switched off when you touched the table', or 'It flashed on for a second when you saw the other Mask.' Once a student understands the immense difference between controlling a Mask and being controlled by a Mask, then he can be taught. It doesn't matter if he loses the Mask state a couple of seconds after leaving the mirror, because once he understands the point at which the change occurs, the trance state can be extended. The essential thing is to identify the two sensations: (1) the student working the Mask, which we don't want; (2) the Mask working the student, a state which the student learns to sustain.

When the actors have developed one or two characters, and have learned to sustain them, I push them into playing more complex situations. There's a sort of 'hump' you have to get them over. I invent the sort of situations that a three-year-old would respond to: playing 'shop', stealing, being shouted at by angry grown-ups, and so on. I also set up 'marathon' scenes in which the Masks interrelate for a long time—up to an hour. If someone turns off they can get a 're-charge' from the mirror, or they can rejoin the audience. More Masks arrive as other Masks leave. Once this stage is reached, then the Masks function as *entertainers*. You put Masks together and enjoy the scenes that emerge. They have their own 'world', and it's fascinating to watch them exploring it.

In normal life the personality conceals or checks impulses. Mask characters work on the opposite principle: they are childlike, impulsive, open; their machinations are completely transparent to the audience, although not necessarily to each other. If you look at, say, the adults on a bus, you can see that they work to express a 'deadness'.

If Masks were subjected to the same pressures as our children are, then they also would become dull and inexpressive. We adults have learned to be opaque. We live among hard surfaces that reflect sound back to us, so we're constantly telling our children to be quiet. Our lives are surrounded with precious objects—glass, china, televisions, stereos—so that movement has to be restrained. Any adult who acted like a three-year-old would be intolerable to us.

John Holt made this point when discussing the 'wooden' look of retarded children (in *How Children Fail*.) A fourteen-year-old with a mental age of six doesn't 'act six' because we won't let him, but he can't 'act fourteen' either, so he looks stupid as a defence. A child of one and a half can look bright and alert, but an adult with a mental age of ten has to look like a moron because this is the most acceptable persona he's able to assemble. When Veronica Sherbourne allows retarded children to behave spontaneously, we see at once that the deadness was only a cloak, a crippling disguise, yet we 'normal' people are wooden and inexpressive compared to the Masks.

This is why Mask teachers or the priests at possession ceremonies are so indulgent. When Masks are set free among a crowd they are permitted all sorts of behaviour which would be instantly forbidden to normal people.[9]

One famous French teacher of the Mask—who won't approve of this essay—divides students immediately into those who can work Masks and those who can't. I think this is damaging. One of my best improvisers (Anthony Trent) spent eight weeks working very hard until a Mask possessed him. Whether a student can succeed or not depends partly on the skill of the teacher, and the incentive of the student. When I began teaching I thought that only about one in ten of my students could really 'become the Mask'. Recently I created a Mask play with a company of actors, and because they *had* to succeed, everyone did—to some extent. Where possession is the norm (at least in the West Indies and Indonesia), there are always some people who don't become possessed. Maybe these just don't have sufficient incentive.

The great improvement in my Mask teaching came when I thought of having people standing by to present mirrors *during* the scenes. The moment the Mask actor 'comes to himself' he snaps a finger and maybe two or three mirrors are rushed at him. This makes the learning process much easier. Masks can also have little mirrors in their pockets to turn themselves back on.

Mask work is particularly suitable for 'tough' adolescents who may normally think of drama as sissy. It appeals to them because it feels dangerous. I've seen excellent, and very sensitive Mask work by rather violent teenagers. Personally I think Mask work is something almost anyone can learn to enjoy. It's very refreshing to be able to shed the personality thrust on you by other people.

9

The Waif

I'll consider one particular Mask in more detail. This is 'the Waif' and it was made almost as a joke. I had smeared plasticine over a wig stand to serve as a base for further modelling. Then I stuck on three bits of plasticine, two circles and a lump, so that it had a nose and eyes. The result looked very 'alive'. I decided that this 'joke' was worth making into a Mask—a decision which the people around me objected to, so I knew there must be something rather disturbing about this particular face. When the layers of paper were dry I painted it bluish grey, with a white nose and white protruding eyes.

My wife Ingrid tried out the Mask and created a 'lost child' character, very nervous and wondering. Everyone became very fond of it. We turned it on in a garden once and it said everything seemed to be 'burning'. It seemed to see the world in a visionary manner. Ingrid and I both kept notes on it. Here are some of mine.

'When first created it looked at everything as if amazed. It made "cor!" and "ooooooooorh" noises. It covers Ingrid's top lip, which makes Ingrid's mouth form a strange shape, as if her own top lip were fixed to the Mask.

'I gave the Waif an ice cream on a stick. She tried to eat the paper. I took the paper off and showed her how to hold it. She held it by the chocolate coating. I explained again and she held the stick. She didn't wipe or lick the chocolate from her hand, she didn't seem to know there was a sticky mess on it.

'The Waif has a strong rapport with me, so I play scenes with her.

I am sweeping when she enters the acting area. She asks what I am doing. I say "sweeping", and offer her the broom. She takes the broom and holds it as if it was a baby. She hugs it as if it were alive, and nothing to do with sweeping. When she leaves she takes it with her and says "sweep" as if that were the broom's name.

'I have used the Waif to civilise the violent Mask. This is an incredibly violent old man who picks up sticks and threatens to hit people. The Waif seems to be about four years old, so I set up a scene in which she was to arrive as his granddaughter. Everything the Waif touches she treats as someone else's, so I told the 'grandfather' that he was to tell her not to touch anything, and then leave. There was a teddy bear on the table. The Waif entered nervously holding a little suitcase, and was fascinated by the teddy bear. Granddad was gruff with her, and left. She picked up the teddy bear, and Granddad came back enraged and hit her (not hard). The Waif was appalled. Since this time the two Masks have almost become inseparable, and Granddad is now very protective, and interacts well with other Masks.'

Here are some notes on the Waif by Ingrid:

'I get very high on Mask work—it's like stepping out of my skin and experiencing something much more fluid and dynamic—sometimes when the Mask is turned on there is a part of me sitting in a distant corner of my mind that watches and notices changed body sensations, emotions, etc. But it's very passive, this watcher—does nothing that criticises or interferes—and sometimes it's not there at all. Then it's like the "I" blanks out and "something else" steps in and experiences. When Ingrid switches back she can't always remember what that something else did or experienced. But while I am the Mask I experience it, or rather the Mask experiences itself like I do myself . . . only the way the Mask experiences itself is more intense. Things are more alive. The universe becomes magical—the body full of sensations. I suppose this is where the "high" comes from. . . .

'It's like you get the freedom to explore all the personalities that any human being may develop into—all the shapes and feelings that could have been Ingrid but aren't. Some Masks don't trigger any response . . . maybe these are spirits outside Ingrid's repertoire, that is any one person may have a *limited* number of possibilities when he develops his personality. Most of the time it's like becoming a child again, but some Masks feel very adult even though their knowledge is limited. With the Waif I feel a distinct maturing process . . . she now feels like a thirteen-to-fourteen-year-old; at first she felt six or seven years old.'

Ingrid found that the Mask work helped her development as an improviser. At first, she says, she was 'extremely cautious and afraid of appearing in front of the class, and I couldn't bear being out in situations that made me appear vulnerable. The Waif had none of these qualities. She wasn't afraid to *feel* the emotions that came. She didn't really care about or notice the audience; also she is much freer in her relations with other Masks than Ingrid is with other people. I suppose for these reasons it was very nice for me to slip into this other creature and experience things I normally avoided or hadn't experienced since childhood. It was a tremendous release—like a marvellous kind of therapy, because the feeling of release would still be with me after I'd taken off the Mask. However, I could still never have done all those things without the Mask on.'

If we wanted to be analytical we could say that the flatness of the Mask, and its high forehead, are likely to trigger parental feelings. The eyes are very wide apart as if looking into the distance, and helping to give it its wondering look. Where the bottom of the Mask covers the wearer's top lip, a faint orange lip is painted onto the Mask. Everyone who has created a 'Waif' character with the Mask has lined their lip up with the Mask's, and then held it frozen. I wrote my play *The Last Bird* for this Mask, and the Danish actress Karen-lis Ahrenkiel played the role in the Aarhus production. It was only when she froze her top lip in this way that she suddenly found the character. The eyes of the Mask aren't level, which gives a lopsided feeling, and is probably the cause of the characteristic twisting movements that the Waif always has.

10

Executioners, 'Noses' and 'Men'

Another type of character Mask is the Executioner. This is a figure I resurrected from my childhood for a children's play, *The Defeat of Giant Big-Nose*. The actors wear dark clothes and soft black leather helmets which mould to the head and expose only the mouth and chin. Black tapes are sewn on so that they can be tied—which they never are, but the tapes help the brutal feeling and draw attention to the chin. Each actor cuts his own eye-holes, making them as small as possible. Only a glint of an eye is occasionally visible. If necessary pinpricks can be made around the hole, but the constriction of vision helps the actor to feel 'different'.

To work this Mask you face another Executioner, and hold a grimace that shows both sets of teeth. You must never entirely lose this grimace. With it you can speak 'in character'—the voice has a threatening roughness—and it releases very brutal feelings in the body. You feel aggressive, powerful and wide. If you expose both sets of teeth you're bound to sense yourself differently. Try it now: grimace and look round the room, move about and try and sense the differences. Some people who find it impossible to work the half masks break through after working Executioner Masks. Women never look 'right' as Executioners, but the grimace also releases strong feelings in them.

'Noses' may be a 'way in' for some students. You need a long, pointed red nose held on by elastic, and a fluffy wig or soft hat. You then climb into a large sack or wrap a sheet round you—white seems to be preferred—and make yourself into a sort of tube that takes little steps and skips about. You place all your attention on the nose and hold it there, and then you face another 'Nose' and you both jabber in high-pitched gibberish, holding wide grins. 'Noses' are maniacally happy, move very quickly, and never do what they are told. They can be controlled by telling them to do the opposite of what you want them to do. They prefer to work in pairs, often turning each other on again by 'mirroring' each other for a moment. Very soon the high-pitched gibberish begins to throw up words, but they always jabber a lot. When they're really turned on they're amazing. The red noses seem to be pulling them around.

Executioners and 'Noses' are likely to be hindered if they use mirrors. It's much better, in the early stages, if they just use each other. Later on, mirrors can be useful.

'Men' are plastic commercial masks which are just round eyes, round noses and little moustaches—you see through the pupils of the 'eyes'. The actors wear overalls and soft hats. They use each other as mirrors and raise their hats to each other—straight up and down. They grin all the time, keep their elbows in to their sides as much as possible, and take short steps. They speak in gibberish, which soon gives way to language. With luck very real characters will suddenly emerge, and the actors will suddenly 'know' what to do, instead of 'deciding'.

II

Pre-Mask Exercises

Most of my 'acting theory' comes from my study of the Mask, and there are many acting exercises that can be used as pre-Mask exercises. Here are some of them.

Face Masks

Face Masks probably go back at least to Copeau. I sit four actors on a bench, show them a mirror and say 'Make a face, nothing like your face, hold it, don't lose the expression.' The audience laugh at the transformation, but the actors don't feel that 'they' are being laughed at. 'Get up,' I say, 'shake hands with each other, say something.' Most actors find that their bodies move in a quite different way, but some hold on to themselves and 'insert a barrier' in the neck, so that the changes in the face can't effect the posture of the body. It's easy to draw gentle attention to this, and to encourage the actors to let their bodies 'do what they want to do'. The actors then play scenes while holding faces that express some sort of emotion. The greater the emotion expressed on the face the greater the change in behaviour and the easier it is to improvise. I use the Face Mask as a rehearsal technique. Actors pick faces at random and then play the text. They often get insights into the nature of the scene in this way, and they lose their fear of overacting, which makes many actors appear inhibited.

If all the actors hold an identical face, then they accept each other's ideas more readily.

Some students 'can't' make a face. They'll change expression just a little, desperately clinging on to their self-image. You can overcome this by asking them to make an emotional sound, and then hold the face that accompanies it. If you snarl, the face automatically becomes savage.

It's a simple step from the Face Mask to Executioner Masks or 'Noses' even for very uptight people.

Placing the Mind

The placing of the personality in a particular part of the body is cultural. Most Europeans place themselves in the head, because they have been taught that they *are* the brain. In reality of course the brain can't feel the concave of the skull, and if we believed with Lucretius that the brain was an organ for cooling the blood, we would place ourselves somewhere else. The Greeks and Romans were in the chest, the Japanese a hand's breath below the navel, Witla Indians in the whole body, and even outside it. We only imagine ourselves as 'somewhere'.

Meditation teachers in the East have asked their students to practise placing the mind in different parts of the body, or in the

Universe, as a means of inducing trance. The author of *The Cloud of Unknowing* writes 'Where do I want you to be? Nowhere!'[10] Michael Chekhov, a distinguished acting teacher (and friend of Vakhtangov) suggested that students should practise moving the mind around as an aid to character work. He suggested that they should invent 'imaginary bodies' and operate them from 'imaginary centres'. He writes:

'You are going to imagine that in the same space you occupy with your own, real body there exists another body—the imaginary body of your character . . . you clothe yourself, as it were, with this body; you put it on like a garment. What will be the result of this "masquerade"? After a while (or perhaps in a flash!) you will begin to feel and think of yourself as *another person*. . . .

'Your *whole being, psychologically and physically,* will be changed— I would not hesitate to say even *possessed*—by the character . . . your reasoning mind, however skilful it may be, is apt to leave you cold and passive, whereas the imaginary body has the power to appeal directly to your will and feelings.' (*To the Actor,* Harper and Row, 1953.)

I suggest that you try out Chekov's suggestion. The effects are very strong, and students are amazed at the feelings created in them. Chekov says:

'So long as the centre remains in the middle of your chest (pretend it's a few inches deep), you will feel that you are still yourself and in full command, only more energetically and harmoniously so, with your body approaching an "ideal type". But as soon as you try to shift the centre to some other place within or outside your body, you will feel that your whole psychological and physical attitude will change, just as it changes when you step into an imaginary body. You will notice that the centre is able to draw and concentrate your whole being into one spot from which your activity emanates and radiates.

'Try a few experiments for a while. Put a soft, warm, not too small centre in the region of your abdomen and you may experience a psychology that is self-satisfied, earthy, a bit heavy and even humorous. Place a tiny, hard centre on the tip of your nose and you will become curious, inquisitive, prying and even meddlesome. Move the centre to one of your eyes and notice how quickly it seems that you have become sly, cunning and perhaps hypocritical. Imagine a big, heavy, dull and sloppy centre placed outside the seat of your pants and you have a cowardly, not too honest, droll character. A centre located a few feet outside your eyes or forehead may invoke the sensation of a sharp, penetrating and even a sagacious mind. A warm, hot and even fiery centre situated without your heart may awaken in you heroic, loving and courageous feelings.

'You can also imagine a movable centre. Let it sway slowly before your forehead and circle your head from time to time, and you will sense the psychology of a bewildered person; or let it circle irregularly around your whole body, in varying tempos, now going up and now sinking down, and the effect will no doubt be one of intoxication.'

I find it sad that Chekov's work is not continued by more teachers. Few actors have really tried it out. In rehearsal it's sometimes been perfect for helping an actor to find a 'character'. And its relation to Mask work is obvious.

Costume

I ask the actors to dress up as characters. Most put on too many clothes. It's quite normal for a student to wear three hats at once, believing himself 'original'. I encourage them to take fewer articles.

A girl puts on a pink tutu. She wears a bus conductor's hat, the peak low over her eyes, and one shoe. As soon as she moves she assumes an aggressive posture, like an angry child. She stops instantly and starts to remove the costume. I say, 'You felt something!' She replies, 'It was too childish.' I tell her to stop criticising, and to keep any costume that makes her feel different. She improvises a scene with the costume on and she's very confident, most unlike her usual timid self.

Someone wears a boiler suit stuffed with balloons to make him 'huge'. He still looks 'himself'. I say, 'Move and imagine that the costume is your body surface', and suddenly he becomes a 'fat man'.

Pretending that the costume is the actual body surface has a powerful transforming effect on most people. We all of us have a 'body image' which may not be at all the same as our actual body. Some people imagine themselves as a blob with bits sticking out, and others have a finely articulated body image. Sometimes a person who has slimmed will still have, visibly, a 'fat' body image.

Once students have found transforming costumes I set them to play scenes in gibberish, and later in speech.

Animals

If the class act as animals, playing together or clawing at each other, or 'mating', very regressed states occur. Playing different animals develops movement and voice skills, but it may also unlock other personalities. I gradually turn the animals into 'people'. I got this idea from Vernon Hickling, one of my first teaching colleagues in Battersea, but the idea is ancient.

Toddlers

I read that small children don't punch each other, but 'pat', and that the child with the hand nearest the head loses the confrontations. I taught this at first as a status exercise. But sometimes the result was that the whole class were romping about like big children.

Being Handled

Trance states are likely whenever you abandon control of the musculature. Many people can get an incredible 'high' from being moved about while they remain relaxed. Pass them round a circle, lift them, and (especially) roll them about on a soft surface. For some people it's very liberating, but the movers have to be skilled.

12

Text

Scholars have advanced many reasons for the use of Masks by the players of the Commedia dell' Arte, but they miss the obvious one—that Masks improvise for *hours*, in an effortless way. It's difficult to 'act' a Commedia scenario at any high level of achievement. Masks take to it like ducks to water.

Masks don't fit so well into 'normal' theatre, unless the director understands their problems. The technique of 'blocking' the moves has to be abandoned, since at first the Masks move where they want to, and it's no use getting the designer to work out which Masks are to represent which characters.

The biggest problem is that the Masks refuse to repeat scenes. Even when you tell them they are going to take part in a play, they insist on being spontaneous. If you force them to act in plays, then they switch off, and you are left with the actors pretending to be Masks.

I now rehearse the Masks away from the text, letting them play scenes together, and trying to find a Mask that will more or less fit the dialogue. At the same time I rehearse the actor on the text, but I don't set the moves, and I'm mainly concerned that he should understand it, and learn it.

When I decide it's time to put the Masks on to the text, I choose a scene, and I tell the Masks they're going to act in a play. I stand by the mirror and feed the first line to the Mask as it sees its reflection. It then turns away from the mirror, says its line, and maybe proceeds to the next line. I keep showing it the mirror as I feed it lines, and after about half a page we stop and rest. For the actor it will probably have been an amazing experience. Everything suddenly becomes 'real' and the Mask has quite different reactions from those he'd intended.

When they come to repeat the scene it's very important to say, '*Tell yourself that this has never happened to you before.*' Everything is then OK. Until I learned this last trick the whole business of getting fully possessed Masks to function on text seemed insoluble.

With this technique you can use Masks almost like actors. It's a little different, because of course the Masks only know what they have 'learned' or managed to 'transfer' from the skills of the wearer. If a stranger enters the rehearsal room all work will stop while the Masks turn to look at him. If a staircase is suddenly introduced the Masks may stop in amazement and you realise that they've never met the concept of another level before. My play *The Last Bird* was written for a mixture of Masks and people. In one rehearsal of the Copenhagen production, the Mask actors suddenly removed the Masks and rolled on the floor in hysterical laughter. The script said the Masks were to make bird noises, and their lips had absolutely refused to 'whistle'. I had to give a 'bird noise' lesson; even so, they never became very good at it.

If you are not happy with the Masks—that is if they seem miscast— you can change everything by running the scene with other Masks. Everything will now alter, and the 'truths' of the scene will be different. In the case of *The Last Bird*, which was written for two Masks already created (Grandfather and the Waif), the original Grandfather mask never worked. Finally we used a commercial plastic 'old man' mask.

Masks aren't 'pretending', they actually undergo the experiences. I remember an actress whom I asked to approach a man lying in a 'wood' to ask him the way. The class were impressed and said her performance was very truthful. Then I asked her to repeat the exercise as a Mask, and everything was transformed. The Mask was afraid of being in the 'wood'. It thought the man must be dead and was terrified to go near him.

In *The Last Bird*, Death was to reap the Grandfather. It was a 'good' scene, and the actors were working well. But when we tried the scene with the Mask, Grandfather stopped doing anything one could recognise as 'acting' and stared transfixed at the point of the scythe. It was just cardboard with aluminium foil covering it, but suddenly it seemed the most terrible instrument in the universe. Dick Kajsør, who was playing Death, backed off. 'I can't kill him,' he said, very upset, as we all were. It took about an hour before we could try the scene again.

When I directed the second production of the play (at Aarhus) everything was fine until we added the Masks. Then the actors were appalled. It seemed impossible that they were to present this play night after night when it disturbed them so much. The play is about a colonial war, and what had been a game became a monstrous reality. Tragedy is horrible when you really experience it. Olivier has been reported as saying he doesn't want to do any more of the great tragic roles because it's too painful—he'd rather play comedy.

In the first production Birthe Neumann 'found' the Waif almost immediately. In the Aarhus production Karen-lis Ahrenkiel could turn the Waif on, but the thing wouldn't speak. It seemed desperately unhappy, and thrashed its arms around and howled, and didn't want anything to do with the text. It was eerie. It was as if it had a determination not to do the play because it knew the terrible things that were to happen to it—Grandfather dies, the Waif is raped by the Executioners, the wings are sawn off the Angel, Jesus sinks when he tries to walk on the water, and so on. When we had finally coaxed and lured the Waif into performing the part (and at one time I thought I'd have to cast someone else), it was a very emotional time. Tears and mucus would pour out of the nose holes. Even in performance you would hear it howling as it groped off stage during the blackouts. Directed with actors, the play would have lost some of this raw emotion. With Masks it seemed almost cruel to show it to an audience who might be expecting museum theatre.

One of the strangest paradoxes about the Mask is that the actor who is magnificent wearing it may be colourless and unconvincing when he isn't. This is something obvious to everyone, including the actor himself. In the Mask events really happen. The wearers experience everything with great vividness. Without the Mask they perpetually judge themselves. In time the Mask abilities spill over into the acting, but it's a very gradual process.

My methods make it relatively easy to put character Masks into plays, but you won't see good Mask work in the theatre very often. Usually the Masks arrive with the costumes—just in time for the dress rehearsal, and the actor is expected to wear the Mask designed for him irrespective of whether it turns him on or not. In my Mask productions I begin rehearsing with fifty or sixty Masks and let the actors discover which ones fit the roles in the play. My designers work with the actors and assemble the costumes to the Mask's tastes. I've even taken the Masks out shopping to choose their costumes in department stores—which creates some odd scenes. I don't cast an actor to play a Masked role until I know he has the ability to become 'possessed'. If necessary I rewrite scenes to fit in with the Mask's requirements. The depth of possession during performance depends on the freedom with which mirrors are used. In my productions there are usually mirrors on stage, and people standing by to present a mirror if a Mask snaps its fingers. Some Masks have little mirrors on their person. The style of the production has to allow for these eccentricities. When the Mask is used, theatre has to be theatrical, not just a 'slice of life'.

Once the Masks have learned their roles, and have mastered the 'This-is-for-the-first-time' trick, then they'll do more or less the same thing each performance. It's silly to preset exactly how they should move, but similar patterns will always appear. If a moth flies in, maybe they'll be momentarily distracted and start chasing it, or snapping at it as it flies past, but the actors then assert their control, call in a mirror, and set the Mask back on its track again.

13

Tragic Masks

George Devine gave a second Mask class to the writers' group, this time showing us the full, or 'Tragic' Mask. These Masks cover the whole face and make the wearer feel *safe* (if he doesn't feel claustrophobic) because there's no way his expression can betray him. He can't look confused, or embarrassed, or scared, so he isn't. Some students find a physical release for the first time when they perform with their face covered, and it's usual to improvise with more emotion. Thespis was said to have invented tragedy in this way, using canvas cloths to cover the actors' faces. I once asked Michel Saint-Denis how Copeau, his uncle, came to be interested in Mask work.[11] He said one of Copeau's students had been wooden and totally lacking in absorption; all she worried about was whether the audience was admiring her. In desperation Copeau made her repeat the scene with a handkerchief in front of her face, and she relaxed, became expressive, and was very moving.

If one of the greatest half Masks of the cinema is Chaplin, then one of the greatest full Masks is Garbo. Critics raved about her face: '. . . Her face, early called the face of the century, had an extraordinary plasticity, a mirrorlike quality; people could see in it their own conflicts and desires.' (Norman Zierold, *Garbo*, W. H. Allen, London, 1970.) People who worked with her noticed that her face didn't change. Robert Taylor said: 'The muscles in her face would not move, and yet her eyes would express exactly what she needed.' Clarence Brown said: 'I have seen her change from love to hate and never alter her facial expression. I would be somewhat unhappy and take the scene again. The expression still would not change. Still unhappy, I would go ahead and say "Print it." And when I looked at the print, there it was. The eyes told it all. Her face wouldn't change but on the screen would be that transition from love to hate.' (Kevin Brownlow, *The Parade's Gone By*, Sphere, 1973.)

Garbo had a stand-in who was identical to her, and who was said to have 'everything that Garbo has except whatever it is Garbo has'. What Garbo had was a body that transmitted and received. It was her spine that should have been raved about: every vertebra alive and separated so that feelings flowed in and out from the centre. She responded spontaneously with emotion and warmth, and what she felt, the audience felt, yet the information transmitted by the body was perceived as emanating from the face. You can watch a marvellous actor from the back of a big theatre, his face just a microdot on the retina, and have the illusion you've seen every tiny expression. Such an actor can make a wooden Mask smile, its carved lips tremble, its painted brows narrow.

The reason usually given for the changes of expression that occur in Mask work is that the Masks are asymmetrical, and that as they move about we see different angles. This may be true in a few cases, but if you hold a Mask and move it about it won't smile knowingly, or seem about to weep, or become filled with terror. It's only when a Mask is being worn by a skilled performer that the expression changes. If you buy a magazine with full-sized head and shoulders on the cover and hold it in front of your face, very few Mask effects occur. If you tear the cover off and strap it on your face the magic still won't work. Only when you cut the neck and shoulders away, so that the angle between this mask and the wearer's body can change with every head movement, does it become a 'face'. We 'read' the body, and especially the head–neck relationship, but we experience ourselves as reading the Mask. If you look at the head–neck relationship in great paintings you'll see amazing distortions which increase the emotional effect. The angle between head and neck, and neck and body is crucial to us. There are reports of crowds panicking with horror when they witness public executions; they don't panic when the head is severed, but they do when the executioner holds it up and turns it to face the crowd.

To some extent we can say that the half, or comic, Masks are low status, and the full Tragic Masks are high status. If there are two different types of Mask experience, then we should expect to find the same phenomena in possession cults—and we do. Jane Belo writes:

'When the manifestations are abandoned and violent, they are related to the exhibitions of riotous behaviour which break out at cremations and in great crowds, when the habitual decorum is cast aside. Other individuals who go into trance may seek a more quiescent change, sitting immobile during a ritual sequence until the spirit of the god "comes into" them, when they behave as an altered personality, demanding and imperious.' (*Trance in Bali.*)

The first exercise George set involved an actor sitting in a chair, putting on a full Mask with head lowered, and then raising the head as if looking into the distance. It was interesting to see how much more we did than was asked of us, either because we felt the need to 'act', i.e. to add something extra, or because we weren't used to doing anything so simple; hands fumbled unnecessarily, the head wasn't brought up smoothly, and it trembled. With the face covered every movement of the body was emphasised.

When a full Mask is absolutely still the spectator stares at the face like a person entranced. The art of the full Mask lies in moving the Mask in such a way that the attention is never distracted away from the face, by the body. This implies a method of acting, a style, that all great tragedians master, whether they're wearing a Mask or not— Duse for example, and almost certainly Rachel. When the student first wears a full Mask his body betrays him, his posture isn't good enough, he's hesitant, his 'space' is restricted. When the Mask is still, or when it moves smoothly and decisively, or in slow motion, then the room seems to fill with power. Invisible ice forms on the walls. When the Mask does anything trivial, or moves in a trivial way, the power gutters out.

Many students believe that the full Mask can only do a limited number of things without turning off, but this is because of the limitations in the performer's technique. A great Mask actor can do anything, and still keep the Mask expressive and 'alive'. In Kurosawa's *Seven Samurai,* when the peasants lose heart and start to scatter, the leader of the Samurai—that great actor—runs to block their retreat. Running at full speed with drawn sword, his technique is still that of the full Mask.

George said that learning the full Mask was as difficult as learning to sing; that while a half Mask could spring into existence at the first moment, the full Mask required a long training. The posture had to be right, and the body had to be fully expressive.

I don't think George ever wrote about his Mask work, and I'm embarrassed to be explaining his ideas for him, but I have found an account by Jean Dorcy of Mask work at Copeau's school (Ecole de Vieux-Colombier) in 1922 (*The Mime,* Robert Speller, New York, 1961). He writes:

'What happens to the actor who puts on a mask? He is cut off from the outer world. The night he deliberately enters allows him first to reject everything that hampered him. Then, by an effort of concentration, to reach a void, a state of un-being. From this moment forwards, he will be able to come back to life and to behave in a new and truly dramatic way.'

The Masks that Dorcy used were 'neutral'—'mime' Masks. I don't know at what point the Tragic Mask was introduced, but the technique was clearly based on the neutral Mask work. Here's Dorcy explaining how he 'shoed' the Mask, i.e. put it on.

'Here are the rites I followed . . .

'A. Well seated in the middle of the chair, not leaning against the back of the seat. Legs spaced to ensure perfect balance. Feet flat on the ground.

'B. Stretch the right arm horizontally forward, shoulder high; it holds the mask, hanging by its elastic. The left hand, also stretched out, helps to shoe the mask, thumb holding the chin, index and second finger seizing the opening of the mouth.

'C. Simultaneously, inhale, close the eyes and shoe the mask.

'In all this only the arms and hands are active. They carry out the small movements necessary to fasten the mask on the face, arrange the hair, verify the proper adjustment of the elastic so that the mask will cling well and hold without slackness.

'D. Simultaneously, breathe and place forearms and hands on the thighs. The arms, as well as the elbows, touch the torso, fingers not quite reaching the knees.

'E. Open the eyes, inhale then, simultaneously, close the eyes, exhale and bend the head forward. While bending the head, the back becomes slightly rounded. In this phase, arms, hands, torso, and head are completely relaxed.

'F. It is here in this position that the clearing of the mind occurs. Repeat mentally or utter, if this helps, during the necessary time (2,

5, 10, 25 seconds): "I am not thinking of anything, I am not thinking of anything. . . ."

'If, through nervousness, or because the heart was beating too strongly, the "I am not thinking of anything" was ineffective, concentrate on the blackish, grey, steel, saffron, blue, or other shade found inside the eye, and extend it indefinitely in thought: almost always, this shade blots out conscious thought.

'G. Simultaneously, inhale and sit upright, then exhale and open your eyes.

'Now the mask actor, sufficiently recollected, can be inhabited by characters, objects, thoughts; he is ready to perform dramatically.

'This was my method. One of us (Yvonne Galli) achieved this clearing of the mind, this preliminary state better and more rapidly. Had she another Sesame? I have never asked for her technique.

'When the actor is not seated but standing, nothing changes; however (see 'E'), the back should not be rounded, for the weight of the head would draw the torso forward.

'All these phases are for beginners. Later the technique will be altered . . . .'

Closing your eyes and 'looking' into the darkness of the eyelids is a common trance-inducing technique. I used it when I wanted to study my hypnagogic imagery. Notice that Dorcy leaves his body alone except for those parts which he must move in order to put the Mask on.

George set simple scenarios for his actors, and insisted that they find a simple, direct way of moving, and that the Mask should be *presented* to the audience. It wasn't good to turn away or to hold the Mask at too sharp an angle. Once the technical aspects of a scene had been mastered, he asked the actor to invent a tragic background for it. A man lifting his head to look at the far horizon might imagine himself looking over a battlefield of corpses, or the sea that had drowned his sons. George didn't invent the 'given circumstances' and he didn't ask what they were. It was a private matter. If the actor was brave enough, then he would choose something that was profoundly upsetting for him. If so then the Mask would transmit his grief to the audience, and would seem to shine with magical intensity.

I've sometimes checked up on the lighting after a scene, because I couldn't believe that a spotlight wasn't focused exactly where the Mask was standing, or a chance beam of sunlight wasn't leaking through the blinds. This was the quality that George looked for in the full-Mask work, a sort of ethereal radiance—actually I think a

'Gestalt' separation of figure from ground. An actor would remove a Mask, very shaken, and George would say 'Ah! You felt something', with approval. Such Masks he referred to as 'inhabited'—possessed by the tragic spirit.

He set exercises involving more than one actor, but the technique was always the same. Here are five exercises that he gave out on duplicated sheets to a class at the Studio.

A. A statue—a mourner comes with flowers—on leaving kisses the statue's hand—it comes to life—gets down from its pedestal—crushes the mourner as if still of stone.

B. Two very old people dream of themselves as young—he as a bird, she as a cat—they play—the cat finally kills the bird.

C. Two young people in love—in the sunshine—a storm rises—she runs away in fright—he makes to go but she returns with a very old face on her still young body.

D. A guilty person is sleepwalking—is visited by a ghost of his or her victim—the ghost pursues, sending the victim mad.

E. A young girl takes poison to avoid a mismarriage—she dies on the bed—her mother or nurse comes in and finds her dead.

George's Masks were stylised faces with an air of sadness about them. They were beautiful objects to look at and handle. I used them for several years myself until the Theatre asked for them back. Eventually someone stole them.

I saw a film called *David* some years ago. It was made in 1951, and was a Welsh contribution to the Festival of Britain—a documentary about the life of a miner, a man called Griffiths, who had always longed for education, and who had been injured in the mine and was now working as a school caretaker. The part was played by the man himself, and at a point when it seemed as if the dreams of the father are about to be achieved by the student son, a telegram arrives. We see the caretaker scrubbing out the school hall; about one-third of it is done. The telegraph boy crosses the hall, gives him the telegraph and waits for an answer. The caretaker reads the telegram, which tells him of the death of his son; he expresses nothing, or rather does nothing in *order* to express anything. He's changed, but it's impossible to say how the change has been achieved. Probably his timing alters. The boy leaves, and the caretaker returns to his job of scrubbing the other two-thirds of the hall.

If an actor had played the scene he would almost certainly have tried to display his grief. The caretaker, acting out his own story, underwent the experience again, and it's not anything I'll ever forget.

It's difficult to be sure of anything that one saw only once, many years ago, but my memory is that it was like a Tragic Mask exercise, and I use it as that. A Mask starts some action, the messenger interrupts. The Mask reads the message and waves the messenger away, and then continues the action. What the message says is for the actor to decide, but it has to be something shattering to him.

Something happens to people in moments of great seriousness. When Annigoni was painting the Queen she told him that usually she feels like an ordinary woman, but that when she wears the robes of state she 'becomes the Queen'. We all know how a wreath should be placed on a memorial during a great ceremony: we may have to be told where to stand, and when to move forward, but the way we move and hold our bodies is instinctive. We know we mustn't do anything trivial or repetitive. Our movements will be as simple as possible. Our bodies will be straight. We won't hurry. There will be a smoothness about us. The people you see standing around after mine disasters, or similar tragedies, have a stillness and simplicity of movement. They rise in status. They are straighter, they don't make little nervous movements—not when the shock is on them—and I would guess that they hold eye contacts for longer than normal.

It is this high-status seriousness which is typical of the full Mask. I teach people to be *still*—if they can!—and I explain the type of movements that diminish the power of the Mask, but I also have to awaken feelings of grieving and seriousness. In moments of awe, or of grief, something takes over the body and tells it what to do, how to behave. The personality stops doing all the trivial things that help to maintain 'normal consciousness'. Jean Dorcy's technique is clearly intended to produce this sort of serious trance state; so was Michel Saint-Denis's, and so was George's. A different kind of spirit is involved from that which inhabits the half Mask.

I now have a number of full Masks which I occasionally use, but at the moment I prefer 'photo' Masks. These are photographs of faces that I cut out of magazines, and stick on to plastic backing so that the sweat doesn't ruin them. In some ways these are the most amazing Masks I've ever seen, and as they're easy to make you could experiment yourself. Modern photography is of such high quality that you can hardly believe that it's not a face you're watching. Also each Mask has its own built-in lighting. People gasp when they see them, and get frightened. Sometimes I've had to stop a class because we've all felt sick. This happens if you work for a long time, say an hour, during which the tensions can become unbearable.

The students wearing the Masks feel completely safe, since they are light, and don't even make the face feel confined. The gasps from the onlookers add to the wearer's pleasure. Normally we keep altering our faces to reassure other people. The effect is subliminal, but when it's missing we can't understand the anxiety created in us. We continually reassure people by making unnecessary movements, we twitch, we 'get comfortable', we move the head about, and so on. When all such reassurances are removed we experience the Mask as supernatural.

I start the actors against the wall which they lean on for support. This means that they don't wobble, or shake. It's amazing how few people can stand really still; yet nothing is more powerful than absolute stillness on a stage. The first Masks I let them try won't have eye-holes. Being blind makes the actor feel even safer, on the 'head-in-the-sand' principle. I say things like 'Slide along the wall until you find the actor playing the scene with you. Freeze. In your own time, make a gesture and hold it. Slide down the wall. Huddle together and be afraid of us. Always keep the Mask held like a shield between your face and us. Laugh at us. Stand up. Get angry. Come towards us. Point at someone who has mistreated you. . . .' and so on.

As the Masks approach the class it's normal to see people scrambling out of their chairs to get away. They laugh nervously, but they *move*. If I want to increase the power then I set a scene in which the actors work out some fantasy that upsets them. Then they look at the Mask, not thinking about it, but remembering the image. If they perform with the image of the Mask in the forefront of their minds, then suddenly the Mask blazes with power. In the old days actors in the Noh Theatre might look at the Mask for an *hour*.

When actors insist on 'thinking' about the Mask, I tell them to 'attend' to it instead. I say, 'Imagine you're in a great forest and you hear a sound you can't identify quite close to you. Is it a bear? Is it dangerous? The mind goes empty as you stay motionless waiting for the sound to be repeated. This mindless listening is like attending to a Mask.' This usually works. If you attend to a Mask you'll see it start to change—probably because your eyes are getting tired. Don't stop these changes. The edges crawl about, it may suddenly seem like a real face in your hands. Fine, don't lose the sensation, put the Mask on gently and hold the image in your mind. If you lose it, take the Mask off.

A student at RADA worked out an elegant way of using the photo Mask. He had the actors stand in a line facing the audience, and act out a play in which a landlord raped a woman who wouldn't pay the rent. Each Mask acted in its 'own space'. One Mask knocked at a 'door' and another Mask answered a second 'door'. We saw *two* mimed 'doors', but we put them together in the brain. The rape was weird: the landlord tore at the air in front of him, while the girl Mask two places away from him defended herself from the imaginary attack. As he sank to his knees, she sank back, so that the rape was enacted by each person separately. Another class heard about this scene and wanted to try it. Their play went wrong, the woman didn't react at all. Then we saw that her Mask was disintegrating. It only had a cardboard backing, and her tears were dissolving it.

Four more actors tried the scene, but they chose a child Mask for the woman, and then the actress knelt down, reducing her height, so they decided to make it the rape of a child. The four characters were the landlord, child, father, and social worker. They went through the scene stage by stage in hideous detail, the landlord finding that Mum and Dad were out, getting himself admitted, and so on. The actors couldn't see each other, and the timing was often wrong, so that we were having to correct the lack of synchronisation as well as the lack of space: the landlord was making feeble copulatory movements while the child was still being forced to the ground. When the landlord panicked he ran on the spot, and then froze. When the father found his daughter, the landlord's still figure was unbearable, even though he was no longer 'in the scene'. My impression is that everyone was weeping, but we couldn't really get the emotion out of us. We couldn't really speak, or work. It was as if we had seen the actual event.

The actors could never have gone so 'deep' and been so serious if it wasn't for the protection and anonymity of the Masks. Everyone looked white. We agreed to end the class; there really wasn't any way to continue.

You'll understand that these are students I knew very well. At first no one will choose really terrible scenes, because secretly they don't want to get upset—there's a point beyond which they aren't prepared to suffer. As the group becomes more trusting and affectionate, they will eventually follow wherever the Tragic Masks lead them.

14

Dangers

Many people express alarm about the 'dangers of Mask work'. I think this is an expression of the general hostility to trance and is unfounded. The 'magical' thinking that underlies the fear can be shown by the fact that the presence of a doctor is thought to make things OK. One of my first students was a brain surgeon, and this made everyone very happy, although he knew no more about Mask work than anyone else did.

People seem to be afraid of three things: (1) that the students will be violent; (2) that the students will go 'mad'; (3) that the students will refuse to remove the Mask when instructed (a combination of the first two).

It's true that there are many reports of violent and frightening 'possessions'. Steward Wavell describes a ceremony in which Malayan men were riding hobby-horses and becoming possessed by the spirits of horses.

'One centaur had leapt towards a group of women gnashing his teeth, pawing at the ground, kicking, snapping and biting, rushing backwards and then leaping again. Men rushed forwards to drag the centaur back, but his strength was phenomenal. Three times he was grabbed and restrained but managed to break himself free. Two of the women had fainted. One had been badly bitten. . . . Finally, the old *pawang,* pressing forefinger and thumb on the centaur's temples, gave a sharp jerk to the man's head which must have given a severe shock to his spinal cord. The man recovered, looked dazed for a while, and the dancing continued as if nothing had happened.

'The headman took the incident as a matter of course. Such outbursts sometimes occurred, he said. It was the bitten girl's fault: she should not have been wearing a flower in her hair. A flower on a girl was bound to excite any *hantu* (horse-god).' (Wavell, Butt and Epton, *Trances,* Dutton, 1966.)

Jane Belo describes 'violence' occurring during Balinese ceremonies. A man entered trance while dressed in a 'pig' costume of sugar-cane fibre; while incarnating a pig-god he was insulted by someone who cried out 'To the market!' The 'pig' attacked, and scattered the crowd.

'Then the pig turned and leaped down again on to the ground, from a height of at least five feet, landed on all fours with as much ease as if he'd been all his life a four-footed creature.

'Still angry, he attacked the overturned stone trough, butting it and pushing it along the ground with his head. Men, seeing that he was getting out of control, hurried to restrain him. Others brought great jars of water which they poured in the centre of the court, making a wet and muddy place, sloshy as a pigsty. . . . By this time most of the fibre covering had come off him, only the head and snout remaining. Someone got close enough to him to tear this off, as they called out, "Wallow, wallow!" '

The 'pig' went into the mud and rolled about in ecstasy, and then a crowd of men grabbed him, 'precipitating a fit of powerful convulsions'. They poured water over him, and as he grew quiet they massaged him. Then they carried him to the 'sleeping platform' and he 'woke up'.

Another example of a 'pig-god' going out of control also resulted from an insult. Jane Belo writes:

'He [the pig] was rubbing himself along the wall of a building on which dozens of people were standing. Suddenly he fell over and began to cry dreadfully, beating the ground with his legs and arms. Five or six men jumped up and tried to hold him. He was defending himself fiercely. They put him on the mat and began to massage him, but he cried and shouted and had dreadful convulsions.

'It seemed that one of the children standing on the pavilion had spat at him. . . . At last he became calmer and fell asleep for a long time. There was no feed brought for him and no mud bath, as we saw before, I suppose because of this accident. The crowd was very annoyed by the sudden end of it, and all went home.

'G.N. noted that many people had called out: "Who was that who was so very insulting? . . . It's not right for him to come out of trance yet, he hasn't had enough of playing. When he's had enough, as soon as he's caught, he'll come out of trance." '

Such scenes do not take place in Mask classes because we don't require them. Notice that in the above examples the 'pigs' remain pigs, and the 'horses' are still horses. The violence is completely in character, and is *approved* and expected. The rules are broken, the violence occurs, and the group agrees that it's justified. If the violence wasn't 'in character' then the performer would be removed. In the West Indies people who are *really* violent, that is, who don't get possessed *properly*, are told to see psychiatrists, just as they would be if they acted 'crazily' in any other situation. The 'violence' is part of the game.

Masks can be terrifying but the ability to inspire terror doesn't mean they're actually *dangerous*, not even the cannibal Masks of Vancouver Island. Here's Ruth Benedict:

'That which distinguished the Cannibal was his passion for human flesh. His dance was that of a frenzied addict enamoured of the "food" that was held before him, a prepared corpse carried on the outstretched arms of a woman. On great occasions the Cannibal ate the bodies of slaves who had been killed for the purpose.'

This 'Cannibal' used to bit chunks out of the spectators—an

interesting example of audience participation: 'Count was kept of the mouthfuls of skin the Cannibal had taken from the arms of the on-lookers, and he took emetics until he had voided them. He often did not swallow them at all.' (*Patterns of Culture*, Mentor 1946.)

Obviously this wasn't something the actor went into casually, but the cannibalism was *planned*. It's alarming to hear of people going berserk and biting chunks out of people, but such behaviour had complete approval, and there's nothing to suggest that the Cannibal was out of control.

Phillip Druckner, in *Indians of the Northwest Coast* (American Museum Science Books, 1963), surmises that the 'corpse' that was eaten may have been faked (a bear carcase with a carved head). As to the biting of spectators he says: 'This was not a trick, although it is said that the dancer actually cut off the skin with a sharp knife con-cealed in his hand. The persons to whom this was done were not selected at random—it was arranged beforehand that they were to allow themselves to be bitten, and they were subsequently rewarded with special gifts.'

It would be easier to argue that it's the Masks who are in danger, not the onlookers. Ingrid once put on a Mask and a fur coat at a party and someone came up and hit her. Wild Pehrt, an Austrian 'Demon' Mask, sometimes got torn to pieces by the onlookers. (There are several stone crosses around Salzburg where Wild Pehrts are said to be buried.)

The violence that occurs is the violence permitted by custom (in a way this is true of all violence). Suppose I were to introduce 'handlers' whose job was to control anyone who went berserk. Violence would then be part of the game, and permitted. Mask teachers get the kind of behaviour that they prepare for.

I was told a horrifying story (in Alberta) of a schoolteacher who got her class to make Masks. They put them on, and picked up a boy and tried to throw him out of a window: 'Only the timely arrival of a more experienced teacher prevented a tragedy.' No doubt by now the story has grown to include the mass suicide of the class after raping the teacher, but in fact nothing violent seems to have happened at all.

'Was anyone actually hurt?' I asked.

'No, thank heavens.'

'Why did they pick on the boy?'

'That's the strange thing, he was the most popular boy in the class.'

'What exactly did the teacher say to them?'

'She said they were to do exactly what the Masks made them feel like doing—ah, and that they were to hate someone.'

'Did they get the boy out of the window?'

'Fortunately, the other teacher came in in time.'

The real story was obviously one of an inexperienced teacher panicking. In fact they must have been a nice group of children, since they chose to 'hate' the most *popular* boy. In my schooldays I remember boys being hung out of high windows by their ankles. These boys didn't even get anyone *through* the window. No one was trying to murder anyone. They had just been given permission to misbehave, and that's what they were doing. My advice is that if you understand the nature of the transaction between you and the class, and if you go into the work gently, Mask work is much less dangerous than, say, gymnastics.

I did once have a Mask hold up a chair as if it was going to attack me. I walked towards it, said 'Take the Mask off', and held the chair while the actor took off the Mask. My confidence stemmed from the fact that there was no reason why the actor *should* attack me. He relied on my authority to be in a trance in the first place.

A teacher who is secretly frightened of the Masks will teach himself, and his students, to avoid Mask work. I know several teachers who say that they'll 'never touch Mask work again', but they won't tell me what happened! If anyone had got their arm broken, or had been rushed off to a mental hospital, then they'd tell me. What must have happened is that the teacher's status suffered. He got himself into a situation he couldn't understand or control, and it deeply disturbed and embarrassed him.

I once saw a Mask cut its hand slightly because a mirror it was tapping at suddenly smashed. That was *my* fault for not anticipating the danger. I saw a girl hit hard on the bottom by another girl who disliked her, and who obviously used the Mask as an excuse—similar exploitations of trance states are reported from Haiti. The only serious injury I've heard of in a drama class occurred during a 'method' improvisation (Margaretta D'Arcy broke her arm). I've never known physical or mental injury to result from a *Mask* class.

Masks may cause physical harm when the teacher is believed to be in control, but in fact has been distracted. The Mask may be depending on the teacher to say 'Take the Mask off.' When the instruction doesn't come, as a rule the Mask turns itself off, but it might, I suppose, make an error, and hit harder than it 'intends'. We have the paradox that the Masks are safest when the teacher is absent, since the actors then operate their own controls.

As for the fear of madness, I would answer that the ability to become possessed is a sign of correct social adjustment, and that really disturbed people censor themselves out. Either they *can't* do it, or they're too afraid to even try. People who feel themselves at risk avoid situations where they feel likely to 'go to pieces'. Compared to marriage, appearing on a TV show, family quarrels, playing rugby, being fired from one's job or other stressful social experiences, the Mask is very gentle and makes few demands. Ordinary people can face the death of people they love, or their house burning down, without having their sanity threatened. The fear that the Mask will somehow drive people out of their minds stems from the taboo against trance states.

In a paper on 'The Failure to Eliminate Hypothesis' P. C. Wason described an experiment in which students were asked to guess the rule that had been used to generate a given series of numbers. One student offered no hypothesis at all, but instead developed 'psychotic symptoms . . . and had to be removed by ambulance'. No one would suggest that Wason shouldn't have continued his experiment, but I'm sure that after a similar incident Mask work would have been stopped immediately. When a student cracked up during a summer school at which I was teaching, everyone went around saying 'What a good job she didn't take part in the Mask work'!

The truth is that in acting class, improvisation class, and Mask class we meet opposition from people who believe, in the teeth of all the evidence, that emotional abreaction is 'wrong'. Many other cultures have encouraged the 'loose upper lip', but we even try to suppress grieving. England is full of bereaved people who have never discharged their grief and who sit around like stones. We are even encouraged to *hit* people when they get hysterical!

As for actors refusing to remove the Mask, it's never happened to me in the way people mean, although I imagine it could happen. There are reports of people in clinical hypnosis who have 'stayed asleep' (though not for long!) but we have to ask what people would gain from such behaviour. If someone refused to come out of trance during a public hypnosis show, then he'd be put in a dressing-room to sleep it off, and would miss all the fun. In clinical hypnosis, the only purpose of such an action would lie in the opportunity to embarrass and confuse the hypnotist. If the hypnotist remained calm, then there'd be no pay-off. In case of any trouble with people refusing to remove the Mask, all you'd have to do would be to say 'OK, fine, good,' and keep your status. Then the refusal would be pointless. Always remember that unless the subject is crazy, or freaked out on drugs, then his trance has a purpose, and exists because of the support of the teacher and the rest of the class. Go close to the Mask, put your arm around its shoulders. Your physical proximity to an entranced person usually switches Masks off.

Sometimes a student will be very upset, and will keep the Mask on to hide tears. Put your arm round such people, lead them to the side and let them sit down. I remember a man in his fifties who turned into a 'monster' and obviously felt extremely violent. He lifted a chair in slow motion as if to smash it to the floor. I walked in towards him, saying 'It's all right, take the Mask off', and he put the chair down and leaned on it for support. I put my arm around him and said 'It's all right, it's all right.' He was shaking. (When someone is very upset it usually helps to hold them rather firmly—the message you give is that you're willing to be close to them and to support them. Patting people who are upset isn't really much use. It's more like trying to push them away.)

Gradually this student relaxed, and then took his Mask off. He explained that he'd always felt that he was a gentle person, and that all his life he'd been unable to understand how people could do violent things; I explained that this Mask always made people feel like that, but he was insistent that the feelings were 'his'. I pointed out that he couldn't be *more* violent than the rest of us were, and that we all had great extremes of emotion locked away inside us. I added, privately, that he should remember the experience, and that maybe he ought to change his view of himself a little. Surely it was less lonely to know that he was actually just like the rest of us.

During a weekend course a student went into a very deep trance, and became a little old man consumed by paroxysms of lust. He seemed to blaze with an inner light. One of the old gods had returned to earth. The student was shaken, but quite calm until the other students talked to him during lunch and made him appreciate how odd it had been. I had to reassure him that he wasn't going crazy and that the Mask had been very successful.

Good drama teaching, of any kind, threatens to alter the personality. The better the teacher the more powerful the effects. In any actor training we work in the voice and the body, and feelings of 'disintegration' are likely to occur. I remember asking an actress to mime an animal with her eyes shut, and to let her hands just move 'by themselves'. Suddenly she hallucinated a real animal! It's more difficult to handle this sort of situation. I told her that it did sometimes happen to people, and that it meant she had become very absorbed. At least in

Mask work you can pass the responsibility over to the Mask. The problem is not that one's students really do go crazy, but that they may withdraw from work they regard as dangerous. They judge the 'danger' by the calmness, or jumpiness of the teacher. In reality the work is very therapeutic, but in this culture any irrational experience gets defined as 'mad'.

The Mask teacher has to develop a coolness, a therapeutic blandness. There is nothing his students can do that will surprise or disconcert him. Like a meditation teacher, he conveys the feeling that nothing really alarming is happening. If he doesn't project stability and confidence, then his students will be frightened away. Here's the Zen Master Yasutani talking with a distressed student.

Student: (*Crying*) Just about five minutes ago I had a frightful experience. Suddenly I felt as though the whole universe had crashed into my stomach, and I burst out crying. I can't stop crying even now.

Yasutani: Many strange experiences take place when you do zazen, some of them agreeable, some of them, like your present one, fearful. But they have no particular significance. If you become elated by a pleasant occurrence and frightened by a dreadful one, such experiences may hinder you. But if you don't cling to them such experiences will naturally pass away.

Again, with another student:

Yasutani: If I were to cut off my hand or my leg, the real I would not be decreased one whit. Strictly speaking, this body and mind are also you but only a fraction. The essence of your true nature is no different from that of this stick in front of me or this table or this clock—in fact every single object in this universe. When you directly experience the truth of this, it will be so convincing that you will exclaim 'How true!' because not only your brain but all your being will participate in this knowledge.

Student: (*Suddenly crying*) But I am afraid! I don't know what of, but I am afraid!

Yasutani: There is nothing to fear. Just deepen and deepen the questioning until all your preconceived notions of who and what you are vanish, and all at once you will realise that the entire universe is no different

> from yourself. You are at a crucial stage. Don't
> retreat—march on! (Kapleau, *The Three Pillars of
> Zen*, Beacon, 1967.)

If you were to use Mask work literally as 'therapy', and to try and psychoanalyse the content of scenes, then I've no doubt you could produce some amazing conflicts, and really screw everyone up. Mask work, or any spontaneous acting, can be therapeutic because of the intense abreactions involved; but the teacher's job is to keep the student *safe*, and to protect him so that he can regress.[12] This is the opposite of the Freudian view that people regress in search of greater security. In acting class, students only regress when they feel protected by a high-status teacher.

When the students begin Mask work, and 'characters' inhabit them for the first time, it's normal for everything to be extremely grotesque. The spirits often seem straight out of the paintings of Hieronymus Bosch (Bosch himself acted in plays in which Masks were used). Grotesque and frightening things are released as soon as people begin to work with spontaneity. Even if a class works on improvisation every day for only a week or so, then they start producing very 'sick' scenes: they become cannibals pretending to eat each other, and so on. But when you give the student permission to explore this material he very soon uncovers layers of unsuspected gentleness and tenderness. It is no longer sexual feelings and violence that are deeply repressed in this culture now, whatever it may have been like in *fin-de-siècle* Vienna. We repress our benevolence and tenderness.

NOTES

1. There are other accounts of Chaplin's discovery of Charlie, and I've seen an early film in which Chaplin plays 'Charlie' without the moustache, but there's no doubt that Chaplin experienced the character as stemming from the change in his appearance, rather than from a more intellectual process.
2. Nina Epton met a Balinese who told her that before he left to be educated in Europe he could 'leap into the other world' of trance in twenty seconds, but that even if he can succeed these days it takes at least half an hour. (Wavell, Butt and Epton, *Trances*, Allen and Unwin, 1967.)
3. The psychologist Wilhelm Reich developed the idea of 'character armour', which he said was 'A protection of the ego against external and internal dangers. As a protective mechanism which has become chronic it can rightly be called *armour* . . . in unpleasurable situations the armouring increases, in pleasurable situations it decreases. The degree of character mobility, the ability to open up to a situation or to close up against it,

constitutes the difference between the healthy and the neurotic character structure.' (*Character Analysis*, translated by V. R. Carfagno, Vision Press, 1973.)

He might have been talking about good and bad acting. Drama students who are 'tight' and 'inflexible' and 'alone' are able to receive and transmit only a very narrow range of feeling. They experience muscle tension as 'acting'. In *The Function of the Orgasm* (translated by T. P. Wolfe, Panther, 1968), Reich says:

'The facial expression *as a whole*—independent of the individual parts—has to be observed carefully. We know the depressed face of the melancholic patient. It is peculiar how the expression of flaccidity can be associated with a severe chronic tension of the musculature. There are people with an always artificially beaming face; there are "stiff" and "sagging" cheeks. Usually, the patients are able to find the corresponding expression themselves, if the attitude is repeatedly pointed out and described to them, or shown to them by imitating it. One patient with "stiff" cheeks said: "My cheeks are as if heavy with tears." Suppressed crying easily leads to a masklike stiffness of the facial musculature. At an early age, children develop a fear of "faces" which they used to delight in making; they are afraid because they are told that if they make a face it'll stay that way, and because the very impulses they express in their grimaces are impulses for which they are likely to be reprimanded or punished. Thus they check these impulses and hold their faces "rigidly under control".'

I remember my own friends 'changing' during their adolescence. One grew an RAF moustache and spoke with a phoney officer-type voice—in adult life he actually became an Air Force officer and got a medal in the Suez fiasco. Other friends modelled themselves on sportsmen, or film stars, or adults they admired. Props like a walking-stick, a pipe, or an individual choice of clothing help to support an identity. If you shave off a beard you 'feel' different. A bride in her regalia is supposed to 'become a bride'. Oscar Wilde dressed as a convict on Clapham Junction was defenceless in a way that he would never have been in his *own* clothes. The appearance, and especially the face fixes the personality. This is why plastic surgery has been suggested as a way of reforming criminals—the opposite approach to outdated nose-slicing. In Vietnam, terrible burns to the body are reported to produce relatively little change in the personality. Relatively minor facial burns have severe consequences.

4. Here is a description by Melvin Powers of how he introduces the 'eye test'. It shows the nature of the transaction very clearly.

'It is suggested to the subject that at the count of three he will be unable to open his eyes. Let's say that you had done this, and that the subject, in spite of this suggestion, has opened his eyes. What is to be done? . . . He may feel that he is not a good subject, or worse still, that you are not a good hypnotist, since he had so easily opened his eyes, when he had been challenged to do so. It is at this point . . . that so many hypnotists lose their subjects. . . . To avoid this: after the subject has closed his eyes, continue to give him suggestions that he is in a deep state of relaxation, and that as you (the hypnotist) complete a count of three, he, the subject, will move deeper and deeper into the ease of the hypnotic state. Begin your procedure. Take a great deal of time before you finally use the "eye test". . . . At this point, give the subject the following suggestions: "When I complete the count of three you will open your eyes, and look at the crystal ball. Then after I give you the suggestion and when I complete the count of three again, you will fall into a very deep, sound hypnotic sleep." '

If this doesn't work Powers says: 'Should the test fail the first time, or even the second, be certain not to show the least sign of annoyance. After a pause proceed again in a matter-of-fact and businesslike manner so as to ensure the fullest co-operation on the part of the subject. It is very important that the subject be made to understand that the failure to close the eyes was not an actual test but merely a part of the induction procedure. . . . The subject feels that the difficulty lies in the fact that he has not as yet been adequately conditioned. This conviction is a much healthier one than the recognition that the hypnosis has been a failure, since he isn't aware that he has been exposed to hypnosis at all. . . . Tell him that at the next attempt he will be more responsive.' (*Advanced Self-Hypnosis*, Thorsons, 1962.)

5. Here's a fourteenth-century English meditation teacher describing the 'one word' technique. He says: 'A naked intention directed to God, and himself alone, is wholly sufficient. . . . The shorter the word the better, being more like the working of the Spirit. A word like "God" or "Love". Choose which you like, or perhaps some other, so long as it is of one syllable. And fix this word fast to your heart, so that it is always there come what may. It will be your shield and spear in peace and war alike. With this word you will hammer the cloud and the darkness about you. With this word you will suppress all thought under the cloud of forgetting. So much so that if ever you are tempted to think of what it is you are seeking, this one word will be sufficient answer. And if you would go on to think learnedly about the significance and analysis of that same word, tell yourself that you would have it whole, and not in bits and pieces.' (*The Cloud of Unknowing*, translated by Clifton Wolters, Penguin, 1961.)

Naming everything that you are doing also interferes with the 'voice in the head': 'I am breathing. I am thinking about breathing. I am noticing a bird. I am feeling the weight of my arm on the chair. . . .' This doesn't suppress verbalisation, but it diverts it.

Dancing to repetitive rythms is trance-inducing. People report that the body seems to be moving by itself as they move into the trance state. Drummers at possession cults drum louder and with more syncopation in order to 'throw people over the edge'.

Other methods involve weakening the ego by drugs, by increasing the excitement so that the subject is emotionally exhausted, by spinning the person round and round and inducing giddiness. One method reported from the West Indies involves smashing people on the head with a sacred brick. When Professor Eysenck says that only such-and-such a percentage of the population can enter trance, one wonders if he has really tried all the methods.

6. In clinical hypnosis a reluctance to perform has been observed, but

this is surely because there's no pay-off. The hypnotist isn't suggesting dramatic scenes to play, and there's no audience to reward them. Hilgard writes:

'I asked a young woman subject who was practising appearing awake while hypnotised to examine some interesting objects in a box on a table at the far end of the room and to comment to me on them as if she were not hypnotised. She was quite reluctant to make this effort, eventually starting to do it with a final plea: "Do you really want me to do this? I'll do it if you say so." '

Another subject of Hilgard said: 'Once I was going to swallow, but I decided it wasn't worth the effort. At one point I was trying to decide if my legs were crossed, but I couldn't tell, and I didn't quite have the initiative to find out.' Another subject said: 'I panic in an open-ended situation where I am not given *specific* directions. I like very *definite suggestions* from the hypnotist.' Hilgard comments: 'Thus the planning function, while not entirely lost, is turned over very largely to the hypnotist, willingly and comfortably, with some annoyance being shown when the subject is asked to take responsibility for what he has to do.' (Ernest R. Hilgard, *The Experience of Hypnosis*, Harcourt Brace, 1968.)

7. There's something very odd about the idea that spirits enter at the neck. This belief crops up all over the place. For example, here's Ena Twigg, a medium, describing how she enters trance.

'I get a sensation at the back of my neck, right at the top of the spine. It's as if there was a blockage. I may be sitting, giving clairaudience or clairvoyance, and I feel myself gradually subdued.'

8. Morton Sobell found that the size of a mirror was very important during his years of imprisonment on Alcatraz.

'On the Rock we had only small five-by-seven-inch shaving-mirrors; there were no others. Somehow the size of the mirror seemed to be critical in self-recognition, probably because the larger mirror allowed me to see my face as a part of my head and my whole body. Ordinarily we correlate all these images, because they are all available to us. On the Rock this was not true.' (*On Doing Time*, Charles Scribner, 1974.)

9. Here are some of Goethe's observations (from his *Travels in Italy*) on the astonishing way Mask behaviour can be reinforced by the crowd.

'The masks begin to multiply. Young men dressed in the holiday attire of the women of the lowest class, exposing an open breast and displaying an impudent self-complacency, are mostly the first to be seen. They caress the men they meet, allow themselves all familiarities with the women they encounter, as being persons the same as themselves, and for the rest do whatever humour, wit or wantonness suggests. . . .

'With rapid steps, declaiming as before a court of justice, an advocate pushes through the crowd. He bawls up at the windows, lays hold of passers-by masked or unmasked, threatens every person with a process, impeaches this man in a long narration with ridiculous crimes and specifies to another the list of his debts. He rates the women for their coquetries, the girls for the number of their lovers. He appeals by way of proof to a book he carries about with him, producing documents as well, and setting everything forth with a shrill voice and fluent tongue. When you fancy he is at an end he is only beginning, when you think he is leaving he turns back. He flies at one without addressing him, he seizes hold of another who is already past. Should he come across a brother of his profession, the folly rises to its height. . . .

'The quakers show themselves in the character of tasteless dandies. They hop about on their toes with great agility, and carry about large black rings without glass to serve them in the way of opera-glasses, with which they peer into every carriage, and gaze up at all windows. Usually they make a stiff bow, and, especially on meeting each other, express their job by hopping several times straight up into the air, uttering at the same time a shrill, piercing, inarticulate cry, in which the consonants "brr" prevail. . . .

'When four or five girls have once caught a man on whom they have designs, there is no deliverance for him. The throng prevents his escape, and let him turn how he will, the besom is under his nose. To defend himself in earnest against such provocations would be a very dangerous experiment, seeing the masks are inviolate and under the special protection of the watch. . . .

'No coach passes with impunity, without suffering at the hands of some maskers or other. No foot passenger is secure from them. An abbot in black dress becomes a target for missiles on all hands; and seeing that gypsum and chalk always leave their mark wherever they alight, the abbot soon gets spotted all over with white and grey.' (Translated by A. J. W. Morrison and Charles Nesbit, G. Bell and Sons.)

10. 'What I will say is this: See that in no sense you withdraw into yourself. And, briefly, I do not want you to be outside or above, behind or beside yourself either.

' "Well," you will say, "where am I to be? Nowhere according to you!" And you will be quite right! "Nowhere" is where I want you! Why, when you are "nowhere" physically, you are "everywhere" spiritually.' (*The Cloud of Unknowing*—see note 5.)

11. George had an extract from Saint-Denis's book *Theatre: The Rediscovery of Style* (Theatre Art Books, New York, 1960) handed out to his students at the studio. Here it is: 'This silent improvisation culminated in the use of masks, full-face masks of normal human size, simple and harmonious masks representing the four ages of man: the adolescent, the adult, mature middle age and old age. In getting the students to wear masks, we were not aiming at aesthetic results nor was it our intention to revive the art of mime. To us, a mask was a temporary instrument which we offered to the curiosity of the young actor, in the hope that it might help his concentration, strengthen his inner feelings, diminish his self-consciousness, and lead him to develop his powers of outward expression.

'A mask is a concrete object. When you put it on your face you receive from it a strong impulse which you have got to obey. But the mask is also an inanimate object which the personality of the actor will bring to life. As his inner feelings accumulate behind the mask, so the actor's face relaxes. His body, which is made more expressive by the very immobility of the mask, will be brought to action by the strength of inner feeling.

'Once the actor has acquired the elementary technique that is demanded by wearing a mask, he will begin to realise that masks dislike agitation, that they can only be animated by controlled, strong, and utterly simple actions which depend upon the richness of the inner life within the calm and balanced body of the performer. The mask absorbs the actor's personality from which it feeds. It warms his feelings and cools his head. It enables the actor to experience, in its most virulent form, the chemistry of acting: at the very moment when the actor's feelings are at their height, beneath the mask, the urgent necessity of controlling his physical actions compels him to detachment and lucidity.

'Submission to the lesson of the mask enables an actor of talent to discover a broad, inspired and objective style of acting. It is a good preparatory school for tragedy and drama in its greatest styles. Scenarios using up to three actors were drawn from striking dramatic moments in classical tragedies and dramas. Further than this silent improvisation cannot go.'

12. I had to comfort someone who was a student of a student of mine—neither of whom had been trained; the first had only been in a play I directed. She writes: 'My Mask was white and immediately grabbed my interest. As I stared I felt my face changing into his, a mildly smiling, very open face.'

She then played a scene together with another, rather frightening Mask.

'I walked into the closet and shut the door. Immediately my fear changed to terror—I was trapped. I knelt down holding the door shut tightly, but I knew his form would soon fill the window. I couldn't stand that, so just as his coat came into view in a corner of the window I pulled my head down. I was screaming. I did so for a long time till finally I felt that surely by now my director would have stopped G [the other Mask]. As I stepped out I was grabbed by that horrible-faced creature, it was still there till finally I ripped my Mask off and screamed, "I'm taking the Mask off." I was very happy with my Mask, how simple it was to get into (the easiest it's ever been) but very annoyed otherwise. I was annoyed by not having someone there who knew enough to save me, my Mask, from the fear, from not having someone say "Stop! Take the Mask off. . . ."' The Mask was very open, and would be anxious to take whatever was prepared for it. It was vulnerable. The other Mask fed on its fear. The condition was like being hypnotised yet not unaware of surroundings or real things but still in the hypnotic state—doing very different things, moving, making sounds, freedom to do things in another . . . what? Face? State? Can't find the word.'

She was as upset as if the event had been real. I would agree with her that she should have been protected. It's the first time she had worn the Mask. If she had been through other emotional scenes, then it might have been OK to let her go through it. She would have been upset, but she wouldn't have felt hostile. The effect of allowing her to experience the 'terror' is likely to make her more inhibited, not less. All Mask work should be *graded*.

Appendix

The Waif

Here are some earlier notes also by Ingrid:

'I'm writing this about two weeks after my first experience with the Waif; it seems like I've known her much longer. We've fantasised about her past history and believe that she's spent most of her life in an orphanage, until one night she played with matches and burned the whole place down. Since then she's spent her time rather aimlessly collecting things like used contraceptives and old bottle-tops which she found in the park. I suppose that the making of relationships with other people is going to be one of the turning-points of her life.

'The first thing she became attached to was a blue balloon which she clutches firmly in her sticky fingers. At first she was very shy of the other Masks and didn't really know how to make friends.

'One day she was sent to visit Grandfather, who at that time was just known as "the angry man that hit people". When she arrived she found a small brown teddy bear lying on the table, which she immediately became attached to and claimed for herself. At that point Grandfather, who had been growling in the background like an old rheumatic dog, leaped on the Waif from behind and snatched the bear away. This produced loud wailing noises and tears.

'For the Waif the teddy was perfect—soft, fluffy, something to clutch and fumble. Contact with objects made her more secure. Having the teddy snatched away was the most violently upsetting thing that had happened to her up to that point.

'I remember Ingrid coming back into focus and feeling real tears and terror and thinking "Christ, this is ridiculous—when I take the Mask off everyone will see that I've been crying, that I really am upset", but I couldn't stop the feelings. It was as if the Waif's experience had triggered off a deep emotional response in myself, as if a part of me was watching the trauma but could do nothing to stop it. It's very difficult to say whether it was "me" that was in a bad state towards the end, but I'm certain that if I hadn't been wearing the Mask, i.e. playing a small girl who had her teddy taken away, I would have "felt" nothing, only acted being upset. The Waif could never "act" her responses because her emotional life is so real and alive. After this

Mask session I realised to what extent I'd learned to repress my feelings, especially when things make me unhappy.

'Soon after this Keith arranged a "nice" scene where Grandfather returned the teddy. Her happiness at getting it back was equally intense. And Grandfather became a very important person for her.

'Loves sweets. Was given a grape and it kept falling out of her mouth. She doesn't seem to have any teeth—can only suck, smacking tongue and palate together.

'It was a long time before she realised she was being watched. She didn't seem to mind the audience providing they didn't get too close. Keith is a good friend—always seems to recognise his presence and to direct some of the things she says to him. I don't get this with other Masks.

'Speech: the "smacking" or "sucking" of her top teeth over bottom lip was the first noise she made—as she became more confident her favourite noise was "cor". When she was happy she also made a short, hard "ha" and "hee" sound. Learning short words like "sit" "stand" and "sweet" wasn't difficult, and she was eager to learn. It wasn't long before she was able to learn "Mary had a little lamb" but she always made up the end to suit herself. She was puzzled by words like "fleece" and "bound" and didn't seem able to accept them— probably why she made up half the rhyme.

> Mary had a little lamb
> It was white as snow
> And everywhere that Mary went
> She had a little lamb.

'This was one of her versions, although I'd have to do it with the Mask to make sure. She learned to count up to ten before learning the rhyme. Her motive I think was because there was an audience, and as she is a bit of an exhibitionist, it was nice to do. Being rewarded with sweets was also good.'

Three Dreams

Some dreams announce themselves as *messages*. There's nothing casual about them. You wake up and they're completely vivid in your mind, and you keep thinking about them. Here are three such dreams.

My family are eating rubber eggs and they call me over to eat mine. The surface is cracked, and I can see deep into the disgusting interior. I put my egg on a high shelf and leave it there; but my family are eating theirs, a little slowly but with a pretence of enjoying them.

A treasure is assembled for me by my teachers. The diamonds are glass and the pearls plastic and the gold is tarnished. I stand guard over the treasure, until I realise it's junk and go far away.

There is a box that we are forbidden to open. It contains a great serpent and once opened this monster will stream out forever. I lift the lid, and for a moment it seems as if the serpent will destroy us; but then it dissipates into thin air, and there, at the bottom of the box, is the real treasure.